D0611044

PORTUGUESE

Phrase Book
&Dictionary

Philippa Goodrich
Language consultant: Cristina Mendes-Llewellyn

Portuguese Phrase Book & Dictionary

Published by BBC Active, an imprint of Educational Publishers LLP, part of the Pearson Education Group, Edinburgh Gate, Harlow, Essex CM20 2JE.

Published 2005
Ninth impression 2011

ISBN: 978-0-563-51923-2

Managing Editor: Joanna Kirby
Project Editor: Josie Frame
Index Editor: Paula Peebles
Designer: Elizabeth Burns
Concept design: Pentacor Book Design
Cover design: Two Associates
Cover photo copyright © Bo Zaunders/CORBIS
Senior Production Controller: Man Fai Lau

Printed and bound in China. CTPSC/09

a (unstressed)	a in 'about'	ah	dia	*deeah*
e (stressed)	e in 'bell'	e	hotel	*otel*
	e in 'grey'	êh	dizer	*deezêhr*
e (unstressed)	u in 'umbrella'	u	ameri-cano	*ahmuricahno*
e (unstressed, at the end of a word)	hardly pronounced		come	*kom*
i	ee in 'feet'	ee	vinte	*veent*
o (stressed)	o in 'not'	o	nós	*nosh*
	au in 'autumn'	oh	outro	*ohtroo*
o (unstressed)	oo in 'look'	oo	poder	*poodêhr*
o (unstressed, at the end of a word)	hardly pronounced	–	passado	*pahssad*
u	oo in 'look'	oo	tudo	*tood*

✳ nasal sounds

Nasal sounds are pronounced through the mouth and nose at the same time and always have a til (˜) over the vowel: são, põe, mãe. Nasal sounds also appear before or after an m or n: bom, viagens. A nasal sound is represented in this book by a til (˜) over the vowel or over the m or the n:

mãe, *mãhee*

viagens, *veeajeeñsh*

bom, *bohm̃*

✳ consonants

Most Portuguese consonants are similar to their English equivalents.

Exceptions:

PORTUGUESE CONSONANTS	APPROX ENGLISH EQUIVALENT	SHOWN IN BOOK AS	EXAMPLE	
c (+ e or i)	s in 'see'	s	cem	**seh**m̃
c (+ all other vowels)	k in 'kite'	k	casa	**ka**zah
ç	s in 'see'	s	açúcar	ahsoo**kahr**
ch	sh in 'shop'	sh	chá	**sha**
g (+ e or i)	s in 'usual'	j	gelado	ju**la**doo
g (+ all other vowels)	g in 'go'	g	gato	**ga**too
j	s in 'usual'	j	jogo	**joh**goo
h	always silent	–	homem	o**meh**m̃
lh	lli in 'million'	ll	mulher	moo**ller**
nh	ni in 'onion'	ny	banho	**bah**ñnyoo
r	r in 'vertical'	r	carta	**kar**tah
rr; r (at the beginning of a word)	rolled	rr	carro	**ka**rroo
s (at the beginning of a word or after a consonant); ss	s in 'see'	s	sim	**see**m̃

pronunciation guide

s (between vowels)	z in 'zoo'	z	casa	**ka**zah
s (otherwise)	sh in 'shop'	sh	três	**trêh**sh
x	sh in 'shop'	sh	xadrez	shah**drêh**sh
or	z in 'zoo'	z	exemplo	ee**zehm**ploo
or	x in 'six'	ks	taxista	tak**seesh**tah
or	s in 'see'	s	proximi-dade	proseemee-**da**du
z	z in 'zoo'	z	zebra	**zêh**brah
z (at the end of a word)	sh in 'shop'	sh	faz	**fash**

* the Portuguese alphabet

The alphabet in Portuguese is the same as in English with the exception of the letters k, w and y, which are only found in foreign words used in Portuguese.

LETTER	PRONOUNCED	LETTER	PRONOUNCED
A	a	H	ah**ga**
B	bêh	I	ee
C	cêh	J	**jo**tah
D	dêh	K	**ka**pah
E	e	L	el
F	ef	M	em
G	jêh	N	en

O	*o*	U	*oo*
P	*pêh*	V	*vêh*
Q	*kêh*	W	*vêh **dooploo***
R	*err*	X	*sheesh*
S	*es*	Y	***eep**seelohn*
T	*têh*	Z	*zêh*

✳ spelling

There are times when it is useful to be able to spell words in Portuguese. For example, at a travel agency or a hotel you may need to spell your name or an address.

YOU MAY WANT TO SAY...

- How is it spelt?   Como se escreve?   ***koh**moo see eeshkrev*

- How do you spell your name?   Como se escreve o seu nome?   ***koh**moo see eeshkrev oo **sêh**oo nohm*

the basics

*essentials

Hello.	Olá.	*ola*
Goodbye.	Adeus.	*ahdêhoosh*
Yes.	Sim.	*seeñ*
No.	Não.	*nãhoo*
Please.	Por favor.	*poor fahvohr*
Thank you/thanks.	Obrigado/a.	*obreegadoo/ah*
Thank you very much.	Muito obrigado/a.	***mooee**nto obree**ga**doo/ah*
You're welcome.	Não tem de quê.	*nãhoo taheeñ du kêh*
I don't know.	Não sei.	*nãhoo sahee*
I don't understand.	Não compreendo.	*nãhoo kohmpree**ehn**doo*
I only speak a little bit of Portuguese.	Só falo um pouco de português.	*so **fa**loo ooñ **poh**koo du poortoo**gêh**sh*
Pardon?	Desculpe?	*dush**koolp***
Excuse me/Sorry.	Desculpe.	*dush**koolp***
I'm sorry.	Peço desculpa.	***pe**soo dush**kool**pah*
OK, fine.	Está bem.	*eesh**ta** baheeñ*
More slowly.	Mais devagar.	*maeesh duvah**gar***
Could you repeat that please?	Pode repetir, por favor?	*pod rupu**teer**, poor fah**vohr**?*

the basics

12

Do you speak English?	Fala inglês?	*fala eenglêhsh*
Is there anyone who speaks English?	Há alguém que fale inglês?	*a algaheem ku fal eenglêhsh?*
What's this?	O que é isto?	*o ku e eeshtoo*
Where is/are... ?	Onde é/são... ?	*ohnd e/sãhoo...*
Is there/are there...?	Há... ?	*a...*
What time... ?	A que horas... ?	*ah ku orahsh...*
I'd like...	Queria...	*kureeah...*
How much is... ?	Quanto é... ?	*kwahñtoo e...*
Is it possible to... ?	É possível... ?	*e pooseevel...*
Do you have... ?	Tem... ?	*taheem...*
Can I...	Posso...	*pos...*
have... ?	ter... ?	*têhr...*
go... ?	ir... ?	*eer...*
Can you...	Pode...	*pod...*
give me... ?	dar-me... ?	*darmu...*
tell me... ?	dizer-me... ?	*deezêhrmu...*
show me... ?	mostrar-me... ?	*mooshtrarmu...*
help me?	ajudar-me?	*ahjoodarmu*

the basics

13

* numbers

1	um/uma	*ooñ/oomah*
2	dois/duas	*doheesh/dooahss*
3	três	*trêhsh*
4	quatro	*kwatroo*
5	cinco	*seeñkoo*
6	seis	*saheesh*
7	sete	*set*
8	oito	*oheetoo*
9	nove	*nov*
10	dez	*desh*
11	onze	*ohñz*
12	doze	*dohz*
13	treze	*trêhz*
14	catorze	*kahtohrz*
15	quinze	*keeñz*
16	dezasseis	*duzahsaheesh*
17	dezassete	*duzahset*
18	dezoito	*duzahoheetoo*
19	dezanove	*duzahnov*
20	vinte	*veent*
21	vinte e um	*veent ee ooñ*
22...	vinte e dois...	*veent ee doheesh...*
30	trinta	*treeñtah*
40	quarenta	*kwahrehñtah*
50	cinquenta	*seeñkwehñtah*
60	sessenta	*susehñtah*
70	setenta	*setehñtah*
80	oitenta	*oheetehñtah*
90	noventa	*noovehñtah*
100	cem	*sehñ*
101	cento e um	*sehñtoo ee ooñ*
102	cento e dois	*sehñtoo ee doheesh*

200	duzentos	*doozehñtoosh*
250	duzentos e cinquenta	*doozehñtoosh ee seeñkwehñtah*
300	trezentos	*truzehñtoosh*
500	quinhentos	*keennyehñtoosh*
1000	mil	*meel*
100,000	cem mil	*sehm meel*
one million	um milhão	*oom meellãhoo*
one and a half million	um milhão e meio	*oom meellãhoo ee maheeoo*

✳ ordinal numbers

first	primeiro	*preemaheeroo*
second	segundo	*sugooñdoo*
third	terceiro	*tursaheeroo*
fourth	quarto	*kwartoo*
fifth	quinto	*keeñtoo*
sixth	sexto	*saheeshtoo*
seventh	sétimo	*seteemoo*
eighth	oitavo	*oheetavoo*
ninth	nono	*nohnoo*
tenth	décimo	*deseemoo*

✳ fractions

quarter	um quarto	*oom kwartoo*
half	metade	*mutad*
three-quarters	três quartos	*trêhsh kwartoosh*
a third	um terço	*oom têhrsoo*
two-thirds	dois terços	*doheesh têhrsoosh*

the basics

15

✳ days

Monday	a segunda-feira	*ah sugooñdah faheerah*
Tuesday	a terça-feira	*ah têhrsah faheerah*
Wednesday	a quarta-feira	*ah kwartah faheerah*
Thursday	a quinta-feira	*ah keeñtah faheerah*
Friday	a sexta-feira	*ah sêhshtah faheerah*
Saturday	o sábado	*oo sabahdoo*
Sunday	o domingo	*oo doomeeñgoo*

✳ months

January	Janeiro	*jahnaheeroo*
February	Fevereiro	*fuvuraheeroo*
March	Março	*marsoo*
April	Abril	*ahbreel*
May	Maio	*maeeoo*
June	Junho	*jooñnyoo*
July	Julho	*joolloo*
August	Agosto	*agohshtoo*
September	Setembro	*sutehm̃broo*
October	Outubro	*ohtoobroo*
November	Novembro	*noovehm̃broo*
December	Dezembro	*duzehm̃broo*

✳ seasons

spring	a Primavera	*ah preemahverah*
summer	o Verão	*oo vurãhoo*
autumn	o Outono	*oo ohtohnoo*
winter	o Inverno	*oo eeñvernoo*

* dates

- **What day is it today?** — Que dia é hoje? — *ku **dee**ah e ohj*

- **What date is it today?** — A quantos estamos? — *ah **kwahñ**toosh eesh**tah**moosh*

- **(It's) the fifteenth of April.** — É a quinze de Abril. — *e ah keeñz du ah**breel***

- **On the fifteenth of April.** — É no dia quinze de Abril. — *e noo **dee**ah keeñz du ah**breel***

* telling the time

- Use são to say 'it is' for numbers two and above: são duas horas (it's two o'clock). For 'one o'clock', use é: é uma hora (it's one o'clock).

To say 'half past' you have to add e meia (and a half) after the hour: são nove e meia (it's half past nine). To say 'quarter past' you have to add e um quarto (and a quarter) or e quinze (and fifteen) after the hour: é uma e um quarto/e quinze (it's quarter past one).

To say 'quarter to' you can add e quarenta e cinco (and three quarters) to the hour; alternatively, add um quarto para (a quarter to) or menos um quarto (less a quarter) to the next hour: são oito e quarenta e cinco/um quarto para as nove/nove menos um quarto (it's eight forty-five).

telling the time

- What time is it?   Que horas são?   *ku orahsh sãhoo*

- What time does it...   A que horas...   *ah ku orahsh...*
  - open?   abre?   *abru*
  - close?   fecha?   *fêhshah*
  - begin?   começa?   *koomesah*
  - finish?   acaba?   *ahkabah*

- It's 10 o'clock.   São dez horas.   *sãhoo desh orahsh*

- at half past nine   às nove e meia   *ash nov e maheeah*

- half past ten   dez e meia   *desh e maheeah*

- quarter past nine   nove e um quarto   *nov ee oom kwartoo*

- quarter to ten   um quarto para as dez   *oom kwartoo pahrah ash desh*

- twenty past ten   dez e vinte   *desh ee veent*

- twenty-five to ten   vinte e cinco para as dez   *veent ee seenkoo pahrah ash desh*

- It's...   É...   *e...*
  - midday   meio-dia   *maheeoo deeah*
  - midnight   meia-noite   *maheeah noheet*

- in...   daqui a...   *dahkee ah...*
  - ten minutes   dez minutos   *desh meenootoosh*
  - an hour   uma hora   *oomah orah*
  - half an hour   meia hora   *maheeah orah*

✳ time phrases

today	hoje	*ohj*
tomorrow	amanhã	*amahñnyāh*
the day after tomorrow	depois de amanhã	*dupoheesh du amahñnyāh*
yesterday	ontem	*ohntaheeñ*
the day before yesterday	anteontem	*ahntuohntaheeñ*
tonight	hoje à noite	*ohj a noheet*
on Friday	na sexta-feira	*nah sêhshtah faheerah*
every Friday	todas as sextas feiras	*tohdahs ahsh sêhshtahsh faheerahsh*
next week	na próxima semana	*nah proseemah sumahnah*
next month	no próximo mês	*noo proseemoo mehsh*
next year	no próximo ano	*noo proseemoo ahnoo*
a year ago	um ano atrás	*ooñ ahnoo ahtrash*

● this...	esta...	*eshtah...*
morning	manhã	*mahñnyāh*
afternoon	tarde	*tard*
evening	noite	*noheet*

● last...	na...	*nah...*
night	noite passada	*noheet pahsadah*
week	semana passada	*sumahnah pahsadah*

● since...	desde...	*dêhshd...*
last week	a semana passada	*ah sumahnah pahsadah*
last month	o mês passado	*oo mêhsh pahsadoo*
last year	o ano passado	*oo ahnoo pahsadoo*

the basics

19

✳ measurements

● Imperial measurements are not used in Portugal – you'll need to convert distances, weights, liquid measures, etc. from imperial to metric. Speed limits and distances are always in kilometres and metres. Food is sold in grammes and kilos. Liquids are measured in litres, etc.

MEASUREMENTS

centimetres	centímetros	*sehnteemutroosh*
metres	metros	*metroosh*
kilometres	quilómetros	*keelomutroosh*
a litre	um litro	*oom leetroo*
25 litres	vinte e cinco litros	*veent ee seeñkoo leetroosh*
gramme	a grama	*ah grahmah*
100 grammes	cem gramas	*sehm grahmahsh*
200 grammes	duzentas gramas	*doozehñtahsh grahmahsh*
kilo	o quilo	*oo keeloo*

CONVERSIONS

10cm = *4 inches*	1 inch = *2.45cm*
50cm = *19.6 inches*	1 foot = *30cm*
1 metre = *39.37 inches*	1 yard = *0.91m*
110 metres = *100 yards*	1 mile = *1.61km*
1km = *0.62 miles*	

1 litre = *1.8 pints*	1oz = *28g*
100g = *3.5oz*	¼ 1b = *113g*
200g = *7oz*	½ lb = *225g*
½ kilo = *1.1lb*	1 lb = *450g*
1 kilo = *2.2lb*	

To convert kilometres to miles, divide by 8 and multiply by 5 e.g. 16 kilometres (16 / 8 = 2, 2 x 5 = 10) = 10 miles.

For miles to kilometres, divide by 5 and multiply by 8 e.g. 50 miles (50 / 5 = 10, 10 x 8 = 80) = 80 kilometres.

✻ clothes and shoe sizes

WOMEN'S CLOTHES

UK	8	10	12	14	16	18	20
Continent	36	38	40	42	44	46	48

MEN'S CLOTHES

UK	36	38	40	42	44	46	48
Continent	46	48	50	52	54	56	58

MEN'S SHIRTS

UK	14	14½	15	15½	16	16½	17
Continent	36	37	38	39	41	42	43

SHOES

UK	2	3	4	5	6	7	8
Continent	35	36	37	38	39	40	42

UK	9	10	11	12
Continent	43	44	45	46

the basics

✳ national holidays and festivals

● On Liberation Day and other national holidays, there are street parties throughout Portugal. In small towns and villages during religious festivals, you may see procissões, parades in which people sing and pray and carry figures of saints.

Dia de Ano Novo	**New Year's Day**	1 January
Terça-feira de Carnaval	**Shrove Tuesday**	
Sexta-feira Santa	**Good Friday**	
Páscoa	**Easter**	
Segunda-feira de Páscoa	**Easter Monday**	
Dia da Liberdade	**Liberation Day**	25 April
Primeiro de Maio	**May Day**	1 May
Dia de Portugal	**National Day**	10 June
Corpo de Deus	**Corpus Christi**	(depends on the date of Easter)
Assunção de Nossa Senhora	**Assumption**	15 August
Implantação da República	**Republic Day**	5 October
Dia de Todos os Santos	**All Saints' Day**	1 November
Restauração da Independência	**Restoration of Independence**	1 December
Imaculada Conceição	**Immaculate Conception**	8 December
Dia de Natal	**Christmas Day**	25 December

general conversation

● Bom dia (meaning 'good morning' and 'good day') boa tarde (good afternoon) and boa noite (good evening/good night) can be used both as greetings or to say goodbye. Bom dia is used in the morning until lunch time, boa tarde from twelve until dusk and boa noite when it is dark.

● When you use expressions as greetings, you can also add Olá (hello): Olá, bom dia!

● When you use them to say goodbye, you can also add Adeus (goodbye): Adeus, boa noite.

● In Portugal, how you greet someone depends on how well you know them, their age and the type of situation. People in hotels, shops, restaurants will always be formal and will expect you to be formal in your greetings, even though you may know them very well. See page 150 for ways of saying 'you' in Portuguese and the relevant verb endings.

✳ greetings

YOU MAY WANT TO SAY...		
● Hello.	Olá.	*ola*
● Hello/Good morning.	Bom dia.	*bohm̃ deea*
● Hi!/'Bye!	Tchau!	*tshaoo*
● Good afternoon.	Boa tarde.	*bohah tard*
● Good evening/ night.	Boa noite.	*bohah noheet*

general conversation

24

- **Goodbye.** — Adeus. — *ahdehoosh*

- **'Bye.** — Tchau. — *tshaoo*

- **See you later.** — Até logo. — *ahte logoo*

- **How are you?**
  - (formal) — Como está? — *kohmoo eeshta*
  - (informal) — Como estás? — *kohmoo eeshtash*

- **How are things?** — Como vão as coisas? — *kohmoo vãhoo ash koheezahsh*

- **Fine, thanks.** — Bem, obrigado/a. — *baheem̃ obreegadoo/ah*

- **And you?**
  - (formal) — E o senhor/ a senhora? — *ee oo sehñyohr/ ah sehñyohrah*
  - (informal) — E você? — *ee vosêh*

✳ introductions

- **My name is...** — O meu nome é... — *oo mehoo nohm e..*

- **I am...** — Sou o... (male) — *soh oo...*
  Sou a... (female) — *soh ah...*

- **This is...** — Este é... — *ehsht e...*
  - David Brown — o David Brown — *oo David Brown*
  - my husband — o meu marido — *oo mehoo mahreedoo*
  - my partner — o meu companheiro — *oo mehoo kohmpah-nnyhaeeroo*

25

This is...	Esta é...	*eshtah e...*
Jane Clark	a Jane Clark	*ah Jane Clark*
my wife	a minha mulher	*ah **meen**nyah **mool**ler*
my partner	a minha companheira	*ah **meen**nyah kohmpahn-**nyhaee**rah*
Pleased to meet you.	Muito prazer em...	*moo**eeñ**too prah**zêhr** ahee**ñ***
(speaking to a man)	conhecê-lo	*koonnyeh**sêh**loo*
(speaking to a woman)	conhecê-la	*koonnyeh**sêh**lah*

✳ talking about yourself

I'm...	Sou...	*soh...*
English (male/female)	inglês/inglesa	*een**glêh**sh/ een**glêh**zah*
Irish	irlandês/irlandesa	*erlahn**dêh**sh/ eerlahn**dêh**zah*
Scottish	escocês/escocesa	*eeshkoo**sêh**sh/ eeshkoo**sêh**zah*
Welsh	galês/galesa	*ga**lêh**sh/ga**lêh**shah*
I come from...	Sou...	*soh...*
England	da Inglaterra	*dah eenglah**ter**rah*
Ireland	da Irlanda	*dah eer**lahn**dah*
Scotland	da Escócia	*dah eesh**ko**seeah*
Wales	do País de Gales	*doo pa**heesh** du **ga**lush*
I live in...	Moro em...	***mo**roo ahee**ñ**...*

I'm 30 years old.	Tenho trinta anos.	*taheennyoo treeñtah ahnoosh*
I'm a...	Sou...	*soh...*
web designer	web designer	*web deezaeenahr*
nurse	enfermeiro/a	*ehñfurmaheeroo/ah*
student	estudante	*eeshtoodahñt*
I work...	Trabalho...	*trahballo...*
for a bank	para um banco	*pahrah ooñ bahñkoo*
in a computer firm	numa empresa de computadores	*noomah ehñprehzah du kohmpootahdohrush*
I'm...	Sou...	*soh...*
unemployed	desempregado/a	*dehzehñ prugadoo/ah*
self-employed	empregado/a por conta própria	*ehñprugadoo/ah poor kontah propreeah*
I'm...	Sou...	*soh...*
married	casado/a	*kahzadoo/ah*
divorced	divorciado/a	*deevoorseeadoo/ah*
separated	separado/a	*supahradoo/ah*
single	solteiro/a	*soltaheeroo/ah*
I have...	Tenho...	*taheennyoo...*
three children	três filhos	*trêsh feelloosh*
one sister	uma irmã	*oomah eermãh*
I don't have any children.	Não tenho filhos.	*nãhoo taheennyoo feelloosh.*

● I'm on holiday here.	Estou cá de férias.	*eeshtoh ka deh fereeahs*
● I'm here on business.	Estou cá em negócios.	*eeshtoh ka aheeñ nehgoseeoosh*
● I'm with my...	Estou com...	*eeshtoh kohm...*
family	a minha família	*ah meennyah fahmeeleeah*
friend	a minha amiga/ o meu amigo	*ah meennyah ahmeegah/oo mehoo ameegoo*
● My wife/daughter is...	A minha mulher/ filha é...	*ah meennyah mooller/feellah e...*
● My husband/son is...	O meu marido/ filho é...	*oo mehoo mahreedoo/feelloo e...*

✱ asking about other people

● Where do you come from?	Donde é?	*dohnd e*
● What's your name?	Qual é o seu nome?	*kwal e oo sehoo nohm*
● Are you married?	É casado/a?	*e kazadoo/ah*
● Do you have...	Tem...	*taheeñ...*
any children?	filhos?	*feelloosh*
a boyfriend?	um namorado?	*ooñ nahmooradoo*
a girlfriend?	uma namorada?	*ooma nahmooradah*

- **How old are they?** Que idade têm? *keh eedadu*
  taheeaheem

- **How old are you?** Que idade tem? *keh eedadu taheem*

- **Where are** Onde vai? *ohnd vaee*
  you going?

- **Where are** Onde está? *ohnd eeshta*
  you staying?

- **Where do** Onde mora? *ohnd morah*
  you live?

✳ chatting

YOU MAY WANT TO SAY...

- **Portugal is very** Portugal é muito *poortoogal*
  beautiful. bonito. *e mooeentoo*
  booneetoo

- **It's the first time** É a primeira vez *e a primaheerah*
  I've been to que venho a Lisboa. *vehsh ku vaheennyo*
  Lisbon. *ah lishbohah*

- **Do you live here?** Mora aqui?/ *morah ahkee/*
  Mora cá? *morah ka*

- **Have you ever** Já foi a... *ja fohee ah...*
  been to...
  London? Londres? *lohndrush*
  Edinburgh? Edimburgo? *ehdeemboorgoo*

YOU MAY HEAR...

Gosta de Portugal?	*goshtah du poortoogal*	Do you like Portugal?
Já esteve em Portugal?	*ja eeshtêhveh aheem poortoogal*	Have you been to Portugal before?
Quanto tempo fica cá?	*kwahñtoo tehmpoo feekah ka*	How long are you here for?
O seu português é muito bom.	*oo sehoo poortoogêhsh e mooeentoo bohm*	Your Portuguese is very good.

✳ the weather

YOU MAY WANT TO SAY...

It's a beautiful day!	Está um dia muito bonito!	*eeshta oom deeah mooeentoo booneetoo*
What fantastic weather!	Está um tempo maravilhoso!	*eeshta oom tehmpoo mahrahveellohzoo*
It's (very)...	Está (muito)...	*eeshta (mooeentoo)...*
hot	calor	*kahlohr*
cold	frio	*freeoo*
humid	húmido	*oomeedoo*
windy	ventoso	*vehntohzoo*
cloudy	nublado	*noobuladoo*
raining	a chover	*ah shoovêhr*
snowing	a nevar	*ah nuvar*

general conversation

● What's the forecast?	Qual é a previsão?	*kwal e a pruhveezãhoo*
● It's raining!	Está a chover!	*eeshta a shoovêhr*

✳ likes and dislikes

● I like...
  strawberries
  beer
	Gosto de...
	  morangos
	  cerveja
		goshtoo du...
		  moorahngoosh
		  survehjah

● I love...
  sailing
	Adoro...
	  navegar
		ahdoroo...
		  nahvugar

● I don't like...
  tomatoes
	Não gosto de...
	  tomates
		nãhoo goshtoo du...
		  toomatush

● Do you like...
  walking?
  climbing?
	Gosta...
	  de andar?
	  de subir
	   montanhas?
		goshtah...
		  du ahndar
		  du soobeer
		   mohntahnnyash

● I quite like...
 	
  seafood risotto
	Eu gosto bastante de...
	  arroz de marisco
		ehoo goshtoo bashtahnt du...
		  ahrohsh du mahreeshkoo

● I really like...
 	
  lamb
	Eu gosto muito de...
	  carneiro
		ehoo goshtoo mooeentoo du...
		  kahrnaheeroo

● I don't really like...	Não gosto muito de...	*nãhoo goshto mooeentoo du...*

✳ feelings and opinions

● Are you...	Está...	eeshta...
all right?	bem?	baheeñ
happy?	feliz?	fuleesh
upset?	chateado?	shahteeadoo
● Are you (too)...	Está com (muito)...	eeshta koñ... (mooeentoo)
cold?	frio?	freeoo
hot?	calor?	kahlohr
● I'm (just)...	Estou (só)...	eeshtoh (so)...
tired	cansado/a	kahnsadoo/ah
sad	triste	treesht
embarrassed	envergonhado/a	ehnvuhrgoo-ñnyadoo/ah
● What do you think of... ?	Que acha de... ?	ku ashah du...
● I think it's...	Acho que...	ashoo ku...
great	é óptimo/a	e oteemoo/ oteemah
pathetic/awful	parvo/a	parvoo/ah
● Did you like it?	Gostou?	gooshtoh
● I thought it was...	Eu achei que era...	ehoo ahshahee ku erah...
beautiful	bonito/a	booneetoo
fantastic	fantástico/a	fahntashteekoo/ah
rubbish	uma porcaria	oomah poorkahreeah
● Don't you like it?	Não gosta?	nãhoo goshtah

What's your favourite film?	Qual é o seu filme favorito?	*kwal e oo **seh**oo feelm fahvoo**ree**too*
My favourite music is...	A minha música favorita é...	*ah **mee**nnyah **moo**zeeka fahvoo**ree**tah e...*

* making arrangements

What are you doing tonight?	O que faz hoje à noite?	*oo ku fash ohj a **noh**eet*
Would you like...	Quer...	*ker...*
a drink?	uma bebida?	***oo**mah bu**bee**dah*
something to eat?	alguma coisa para comer?	*al**goo**mah ko**hee**zah **pah**rah ko**mêh**r*
to come with us?	vir connosco?	*veer koh**nnohsh**koo*
Yes, please.	Sim, por favor.	*seem̃, poor fah**vohr***
No, thank you.	Não, obrigado/a.	*nãhoo obree**ga**doo/ah*
That'd be great.	Seria óptimo.	*su**ree**ah o**tee**moo*
What time shall we meet?	A que horas nos encontramos?	*ah ku **o**rahsh nosh ehncohn**trah**moosh*
Where shall we meet?	Onde nos encontramos?	*ohnd nosh ehncohn**trah**moosh*
See you...	Até...	*ah**te**...*
later	logo	*logo*
at seven	às sete	*ash set*

| Please go away. | Por favor vá-se embora. | *poor fahvohr vasu ehmborah* |
| Leave us alone! | Deixe-nos em paz! | **daheesh**noosh *aheem pash* |

✱ useful expressions
(see **essentials**, page 12)

Congratulations!	Parabéns	*pahrahbehñsh*
Happy birthday!	Parabéns/Feliz aniversário	*pahrahbehñsh/fuleesh ahneevursareeoo*
Happy Christmas!	Feliz Natal!	*fuleesh nahtal*
Happy New Year!	Feliz Ano Novo!	*fuleesh ahnoo nohvoo*
All the best!	Os meus cumprimentos!	*oosh mehoosh koompreemehntoosh*
That's... fantastic! terrible!	É... fantástico terrível	*e... fahntashteekoo turreevel*
What a pity!	Que pena!	*ku pêhnah*
Safe journey!	Boa viagem!	*bohah veeajaheem*
Enjoy your meal!	Bom apetite!	*bohm ahputeet*
Thank you, same to you!	Obrigado/a, e para o senhor/a senhora	*obreegad/ah, ee pahrah oo sunnyohr/ah sunnyohrah*
Cheers!	Saúde!	*sahood*

travel&transport

✳ arriving in the country

● EU citizens only need a passport to visit. If you stay more than six months you must apply for a residence permit. Anyone from outside the EU should check with the nearest Portuguese embassy or consulate before travelling.

YOU MAY SEE...

alfândega	customs
cidadãos europeus	EU citizens
cidadãos não europeus	non-EU citizens
controlo de passaportes	passport control
mercadorias a declarar	goods to declare
recolha de bagagem	baggage reclaim
saída	exit/way out

YOU MAY WANT TO SAY...

● I am here...   Estou aqui...   *eeshtoh ahkee...*
  on holiday   de férias   *du fereeahsh*
  on business   em negócios   *aheem*
                                          nugoseeooosh

● It's for my own   É para uso pessoal. *e pahrah oozoo*
  personal use.   *pusooahl*

YOU MAY HEAR...

● O seu passaporte,   *oo sehoo pasahport,*   Your passport,
  por favor.   *poor favohr*   please.

Os seus documentos, por favor.	*oosh sehoosh dookoomehñtoosh, poor fahvohr*	Your documents, please.
Qual é o objectivo da sua visita?	*kwal e oo objeteevoo dah sooah veezeetah*	What is the purpose of your visit?
Quanto tempo vai cá ficar?	*kwahñtoo tehñpoo vaee ka feekar*	How long are you going to stay here?
Onde vai ficar?	*ohnd vaee feekar*	Where are you going?
Por favor abra... esta mala o porta-bagagens	*poor fahvohr abrah... eshtah malah oo portah-bahgajaheeñsh*	Please open... this bag/suitcase the boot
Tem mais alguma bagagem?	*taheeñ maeesh algoomah bahgajaheeñ*	Do you have any other luggage?
Tem de pagar imposto por isto.	*taheeñ du pahgar eempohshtoo poor eeshtoo*	There is duty to pay on this.
Venha comigo/connosco, por favor.	*vaheennyah koomeegoo/ kohnnohshkoo, poor fahvohr*	Come along with me/with us, please.

✱ directions

● When you need to ask the way somewhere, the easiest thing is just to name the place you're looking for and add 'please', e.g. O Porto, por favor? Or you can start with 'where is...?': Onde é... ?

directions

● To ask the question 'where is the nearest...?', just ask 'is there a ... around here': Há um/uma ... aqui perto?

● If you need someone to repeat some directions, simply say outra vez (again).

YOU MAY SEE...

avenida	avenue
beco	alley
castelo	castle, fortress
catedral	cathedral
estação	station
galeria de arte	art gallery
igreja	church
mercado	market place
metro/metropolitano	underground
museu	museum
palácio	palace
paragem	bus stop
paragem de eléctricos	tram stop
passadeira	pedestrian crossing
peões	pedestrians
praça	square
privado	private
proibido a passagem	entry prohibited
rua	street
travessa	lane
zona pedestre	pedestrian precinct

travel and transport

YOU MAY WANT TO SAY...

- Excuse me, please. | Desculpe. | *dushkoolp*

- Where is... | Onde é... | *ohnd e...*
  - the town centre? | o centro da cidade? | *oo sehntroo dah seedadu*
  - the station? | a estação? | *ah eeshtahsãhoo*
  - the road to... ? | a rua para... ? | *ah rrooah pahrah...*

- Where are the toilets? | Onde são as casas de banho? | *ohnd sãhoo ahsh kazahsh du bahñnyoo*

- How do we get to... | Como se vai para... | *kohmoo su vaee pahrah...*
  - the airport? | o aeroporto? | *oo aeropohrtoo*
  - the beach? | a praia? | *ah praeeah*

- I'm lost. | Estou perdido/a. | *eeshtoh purdeedoo/ purdeedah*

- Is this the right way to... ? | É este o caminho para... ? | *e êhsht oo kahmeennyoo pahrah...*

- Can you show me on the map, please? | Pode mostrar-me no mapa, por favor? | *pod mooshtrarmu noo mapah, por fahvohr*

- Is it far? | Fica longe? | *feekah lohnj*

- Is there ... near here? | Há ... aqui perto? | *a ... ahkee pertoo*
  - a bank | um banco | *oõm bahnkoo*
  - a supermarket | um supermercado | *oõm soopermurkadoo*
  - an Internet café | um café com a internet | *oõm kahfe kohm a eenternet*

directions

YOU MAY HEAR... ❓

Estamos aqui.	*eeshtahmoosh ahkee*	We are here.
Por aqui/ali.	*poor ahkee/ahlee*	This way/that way.
Sempre em frente.	*sehmpru aheem frehnt*	Straight on.
Vá até...	*va ahte...*	Go on to...
ao fim da rua	*aoo feem dah rrooah*	the end of the street
aos semáforos	*aoosh sumafuroosh*	the traffic lights
Vire...	*veer...*	Turn...
à direita	*a deeraheetah*	(to the) right
à esquerda	*a eehskêhrdah*	(to the) left
Tome a primeira à esquerda.	*tomu ah preemaheera a eeshkêhrdah*	Take the first on the left.
É...	*e...*	It's...
em frente (de...)	*aheem frehnt (du...)*	in front (of...)
do lado oposto (de...)	*doo ladoo opohshtoo (du..)*	opposite
atrás (de...)	*ahtrash (du...)*	behind
perto (de...)	*pertoo (du...)*	close (to...)
ao lado (de...)	*aoo ladoo (du...)*	next to...
É muito perto daqui.	*e mooeentoo pertoo dahkee*	It's very near here.
É...	*e...*	It's...
a cinco minutos	*ah seeñkoo meenootoosh ah pe*	five minutes
a pé		on foot
Tem de apanhar o autocarro.	*taheem du ahpahnyar oo aootokarroo*	You have to take the bus.

✳ information and tickets
(see **telling the time**, page 17)

● Is there a... | Há (hoje) um... | a (ohj) ooᵐ...
  tram | eléctrico | *eeletreekoo*
  bus | autocarro | *aootokarroo*
  boat | barco | **barkoo**
  to... (today)? | para... ? | **pah**rah...

● What time is... | A que horas... | ah ku orahsh...
  the next train? | é o próximo comboio? | e oo **proseemoo** kohᵐ**boee**oo
  the last train? | é o ultimo comboio? | e oo **oolteemoo** kohᵐ**boee**oo
  the first bus? | é o primeiro autocarro? | e oo pree**mahee**roo aoto**ka**rroo

● Do they go often? | São frequentes? | *sãhoo frukooehntush*

● What time does it arrive in... ? | A que horas chega a... ? | *ah ku orahsh shêhgah ah...*

● Do I have to change? | Tenho de mudar? | **taheen**nyo du moo**dar**

● Which platform for... ? | Qual é a plataforma para... ? | *kwal e ah platah****for****mah* **pah**rah

● Can I get a ticket on the bus? | Posso comprar o bilhete no autocarro? | *pos kohᵐprar o beellêhtu noo aootokarroo*

● Where can I buy...
  a ticket? | Onde posso comprar... | *ohnd pos kohᵐprar...*
  a day pass? | um bilhete? | *ooᵐ beellêhtu*
  | um passe dum dia? | *ooᵐ pasu dooᵐ deeah*

information and tickets

- **One/two ticket(s) to ... please.** — Um/dois bilhete(s) para ... por favor. — *ooṁ/doheesh beellêht(ush) pahrah ... poor fahvohr*

- **single** — simples — *seeṁplush*

- **return** — de ida e volta — *du eedah ee voltah*

- **For two adults and a car.** — Para dois adultos e um carro. — *pahrah doheesh ahdooltoosh e ooṁ karroo*

- **I want to reserve...** — Quero reservar... — *keroo ruzurvar...*
  - **a seat** — um lugar — *ooṁ loogar*
  - **a cabin** — uma cabine — *oomah kahbeenu*

- **Is there...** — Tem... — *taheeṁ...*
  - **a supplement?** — suplemento? — *sooplumehntoo*
  - **a reduction for students?** — redução para estudantes? — *rudoosãhoo pahrah eeshtoo-dahntush*

YOU MAY HEAR...

Parte às...	*partu ash...*	It leaves at...
Chega às...	*shêhgah ash...*	It arrives at...
Tem de mudar em...	*taheeṁ du moodar aheeṁ...*	You have to change in...
Plataforma/cais número...	*plahtahformah/ kaeesh noomuroo...*	It's platform/pier number...
Pode comprar um bilhete...	*pod kohṁprar ooṁ beellêhtu...*	You can buy a ticket...
no autocarro	*noo aootokarroo*	on the bus
num kiosque	*noom keeoshku*	at a kiosk

travel and transport

42

Simples ou de ida e volta?	*seemplush oh du eedah e voltah*	Single or return?
Fumadores ou não fumadores?	*foomahdohrush oh nãhoo foomahdohrush*	Smoking or non-smoking?

✳ trains
(see **information and tickets**, page 41)

● Os Caminhos de Ferro Portugueses (CP) serve most of the country and offer inexpensive travel. The fastest service is the Alfa, which travels between Lisbon, Coimbra and Oporto. If you intend to travel a lot by train, there is a tourist ticket (bilhete turístico) which is valid for an unlimited number of journeys. Always enquire about travel passes as these are usually the best option for travelling within Portugal.

YOU MAY SEE...

acesso às plataformas	to the platforms
bilheteira	ticket office
bilhetes	tickets
cacifos	luggage lockers
carruagem-cama	sleeping-car
chegada	arrival
depósito de bagagem	left luggage
destino	destination
entrada	entrance
excepto aos domingos	except Sundays

horário dos comboios	train timetable
partida	departure
perdidos e achados	lost property office
plataforma	platform
reservas	reservations
saída	exit
sala de espera	waiting room
todos os dias	daily

YOU MAY WANT TO SAY...

- **Are there lifts to the platform?** — Há elevadores para a plataforma? — *a eeluvahdohrush pahrah ah plahtahformah*

- **Can I take my bicycle on the train?** — Posso levar a minha bicicleta no comboio? — *pos luvar ah meennyah beeseekletah noo kohm̃boeeo*

- **Does this train go to... ?** — Este comboio vai para... ? — *ehsht kohm̃boeeo vaee pahrah...*

- **Excuse me, I've reserved...** — Desculpe, reservei... — *dushkoolp, ruzurvahee...*
  - **that seat** — esse lugar — *ehs loogar*
  - **a couchette** — uma couchette — *oomah kooshet*

- **Is this seat free?** — Este lugar está vago? — *ehsht loogar eeshta vagoo*

- **May I...** — Posso... — *pos...*
  - **open the window?** — abrir a janela? — *ahbreer ah jahnelah*
  - **smoke?** — fumar? — *foomar*

- **Where are we?** — Onde estamos? — *ohnd eeshtahmoosh*

● **How long does the train stop here?**	Quanto tempo pára aqui o comboio?	*kwahñtoo tehm̃poo pahrah ahkee oo kohm̃boeeo*
● **Can you tell me when we get to... ?**	Pode dizer-me quando chegamos a... ?	*pod deezêhrmu kwahñdoo shegahmoosh ah...*

✱ buses and coaches
(see **information and tickets**, page 41)

YOU MAY WANT TO SAY...

● **Where does the bus to the town centre leave from?**	Donde sai o autocarro para o centro da cidade?	*dohnd saee oo aootokarroo pahrah oo sehñtroo dah seedadu*
● **Does the bus to the airport leave from here?**	O autocarro para o aeroporto parte daqui?	*oo aootokarroo pahrah oo aheropohrtoo partu dahkee*

45

● **What number is it?**	Que número é?	*ku **noo**muroo e*
● **Does this bus go to... ?**	Este autocarro vai para... ?	*ehsht aootokarroo vaee **pah**rah...*
● **Can you tell me where to get off, please?**	Pode dizer-me onde devo sair, por favor?	*pod dee**zehr**mu ohnd **deh**voo sa**heer**, poor fah**vohr***
● **The next stop, please.**	A próxima paragem, por favor.	*ah pro**seem**ah pahraja**heem**, poor fah**vohr***
● **Can you open the doors, please!**	Pode abrir as portas, por favor!	*pod ah**breer** ahsh **por**tahsh, poor fah**vohr***

✳ underground
(see **information and tickets**, page 41)

YOU MAY SEE...

entrada	entrance
informações	information
metro	underground
proibido fumar	no smoking
saída	exit

YOU MAY WANT TO SAY...

● **Do you have a map of the underground?**	Tem um mapa do metro?	*taheem oom **mapa**h doo **met**ro*

● Which line is it for... ?	Qual é a linha para... ?	*kwal e ah leennyah pahrah...*
● Which stop is it for... ?	Qual é a paragem para... ?	*kwal e ah pahrajaheem̃ pahrah...*
● Is this the right stop for... ?	Esta é a paragem certa para... ?	*eshtah e ah pahrajaheem̃ sertah pahrah...*
● Does this train go to... ?	Este comboio vai para... ?	*ehsht kohm̃boeeoo vaee pahrah...*

✶ boats and ferries
(see **information and tickets**, page 41)

YOU MAY SEE...

barco a vapor	steamer
cabines	cabins
cinto salva-vidas	lifebelt
cruzeiros	cruises
cais	pier, embarkation point
porto marítimo	port, harbour
viagens no rio	river trips

YOU MAY WANT TO SAY...

● Is there a car ferry to ... (today)?	Há (hoje) um ferry para... ?	*a ohj oom̃ feree pahrah...*

- **Are there any boat trips?** — Há passeios de barco? — *a pahsaheeoosh du barkoo*

- **How long is the cruise?** — Por quanto tempo é o cruzeiro? — *poor kwahñtoo tehmpoo e oo kroozaheeroo*

- **Is there wheelchair access?** — Tem acesso a cadeira de rodas? — *taheeñ ahsesoo ah kahdaheerah du rodahsh*

- **Can I go out on deck?** — Posso ir no convés? — *pos eer noo kohnvesh*

YOU MAY HEAR...

- Os barcos vão... — *oos barkoosh vãhoo...* — Boats go on...

  às terças e sextas — *ash têhrsahsh ee saheeshtahsh* — Tuesdays and Fridays
  todos os dias — *tohdoosh oosh deeahsh* — every day

- O mar está... — *oo mar eeshta...* — The sea is...
  calmo — *kalmoo* — calm
  bravo — *bravoo* — rough

✳ air travel
(see **information and tickets**, page 41)

YOU MAY SEE...

aluguer de automóveis	car hire
apertar os cintos	fasten seatbelts

travel and transport

chegadas	arrivals
não deixar a bagagem desacompanhada	do not leave luggage unattended
partidas	departures
recolha de bagagem	luggage reclaim
sala de partidas	departure lounge
segurança	security

YOU MAY WANT TO SAY...

I want to change/cancel my ticket.	Quero mudar/cancelar o meu bilhete.	*keroo moodar/kahnsular oo mehoo beellêhtu*
What time do I have to check in?	A que horas tenho de fazer o check-in?	*ah ku orahsh taheennyoo du fahzêhr oo shekeen*
Is there a delay?	Há algum atraso?	*a algoom ahtrazoo*
Which gate is it?	Qual é a porta?	*kwal e ah portah*
Have you got a wheelchair?	Tem uma cadeira de rodas?	*taheem oomah kahdaheerah du rodahsh*
My luggage hasn't arrived.	A minha bagagem não chegou.	*ah meennyah bahgajaheem nãhoo shugoh*
Is there a bus/train to the centre of town?	Há um autocarro/comboio para o centro da cidade?	*a oom aootokarroo/kohmboeeoo pahrah oo sehntroo dah seedadu*

WORDS TO LISTEN OUT FOR...

atraso	*ahtrazoo*	delay
cancelado	*kahnsuladoo*	cancelled
chamada	*shahmadah*	call
porta	*portah*	gate
última chamada	*oolteemah shahmadah*	last call
voo	*vohoo*	flight

✳ taxis
(see **directions**, page 37)

YOU MAY WANT TO SAY...

● Is there a taxi rank round here?	Há uma praça de táxis aqui perto?	*a oomah prasah du takseesh ahkee pertoo*
● Can you order me a taxi...	Pode mandar-me vir um táxi...	*pod mahndarmu veer oom taksee...*
● To this address, please.	Para esta morada, por favor.	*pahrah eshtah mooradah, poor fahvohr*
● How much will it cost?	Quanto vai custar?	*kwahñtoo vaee kooshtar*
● I'm in a hurry.	Estou com pressa.	*eeshtoh kohm presah*
● Stop here, please.	Páre aqui, por favor.	*paru ahkee, poor fahvohr*
● Can you wait for me, please?	Pode esperar por mim, por favor?	*pod eeshpurar poor meem, poor fahvohr*
● I think there's a mistake.	Acho que há um engano.	*ashoo ku a oom ehngahnoo*

travel and transport

• **On the meter it's €15.**	No taxímetro são €15.	noo *takseemutroo* sãhoo keeñz *e*roosh
• **Keep the change.**	Está bem assim.	eeshta baheeñ ah*seeñ*
• **Can you give me a receipt?**	Pode dar-me um recibo?	pod *dar*mu ooñ ru*seeboo*

• É a dez quilómetros daqui.	e ah desh *keelo*mutroosh *dahkee*	It's ten kilometres away.
• Tem um suplemento...	taheem ooñ *sooplumehn*too...	There's a supplement...
para a bagagem	*pah*rah ah *bahga*jaheeñ	for the luggage
por cada mala	poor *kahdah* malah	for each suitcase
para a viagem ao aeroporto	*pah*rah ah *veea*jaheeñ aoo *ahero*pohrtoo	for the journey to the airport

✳ hiring cars and bicycles

• **I'd like to hire...**	Quero alugar...	*ke*roo ahloogar...
two bicycles	duas bicicletas	*doo*ahsh beeseekuletahsh
a small car	um carro pequeno	ooñ *karro* pukehnoo
an automatic car	um carro automático	ooñ *karro* aootoomateekoo

hiring cars and bicycles

For...	Por...	poor...
a week	uma semana	**oo**mah su**mah**nah
How much is it...	Quanto é...	kwhañtoo e...
per day?	por dia?	poor **dee**ah
per week?	por semana?	poor su**mah**nah
Is kilometrage included?	Está incluída a quilometragem?	**eesh**ta eenkloo**ee**dah ah keelomu**tra**jaheeñ
Is insurance included?	O seguro está incluído?	oo su**goo**roo **eesh**ta eenkloo**ee**doo
My husband/ wife wants to drive too.	O meu marido/A minha mulher também quer conduzir.	oo **meh**oo ma**hree**doo/ah **meen**nyah **mool**ler tahm**ba**heeñ ker kohndoo**zeer**
Do you take...	Aceita...	ah**sahee**tah...
credit cards?	cartões de crédito?	kahr**tõee**sh du **kre**deetoo
travellers' cheques?	travellers cheques?	**trav**ulahrsh **she**kush

YOU MAY HEAR...

Que tipo de carro/ bicicleta quer?	ku **tee**poo du **ka**rroo/ beeseeku**le**tah ker	What kind of car/ bicycle do you want?
Por quanto tempo?	poor **kwahñ**too **teh**ñpoo	For how long?
A sua carta de condução, por favor.	ah **soo**ah **kar**tah du kohndoo**sãh**oo, poor fah**vohr**	Your driving licence, please.
Tem depósito de €100.	ta**heeñ** dupo**zee**too du sa**heeñ e**roosh	There's a deposit of €100.

Tem cartão de crédito?	*taheem̃ kahrtãhoo du kredeetoo*	Have you got a credit card?
Por favor devolva o carro com o depósito cheio.	*poor fahvohr duvohlvah oo karroo kohm̃ oo dupozeetoo shaheeoo*	Please return the car with a full tank.
Por favor devolva o carro/a bicicleta antes das (seis) horas.	*poor fahvohr duvohlvah oo karroo/ ah beeseekuletah ahntush dahsh (saheesh) orahsh*	Please return the car/bicycle before (six) o'clock.

✱ driving
(see **directions**, page 37)

● Traffic drives on the right-hand side of the road and traffic from the right has priority at junctions and crossroads. At roundabouts, traffic moves anti-clockwise. Seatbelts are compulsory. All motorways charge tolls so make sure you always have enough cash. Speed limits: **towns:** 60 kph (37 mph) **other roads:** 90 kph (55 mph) **motorways:** 120 kph (74 mph).

YOU MAY SEE...

auto-estrada	motorway
centro	town/city centre
conduza à esquerda/direita	drive on the left/right
curva perigosa	dangerous bend
dar prioridade	give way
desligar o motor	switch your engine off

travel and transport

desvio	diversion
devagar	slow
estação de serviço	service/petrol station
não estacionar	parking prohibited
obras na estrada	road works
parar	stop
peões	pedestrians
perigo	danger
portagem da auto-estrada	motorway toll
primeiros socorros	first aid
reduza a velocidade	reduce speed
rua sem saída	no through traffic
saída	exit
sentido único	one-way street

YOU MAY WANT TO SAY...

Where is the nearest petrol station?	Onde fica a estação de serviço mais próxima?	*ohnd feekah ah eeshtahsāhoo du surveesoo maeesh proseemah*
Fill it up with... unleaded	Encha com... gasolina sem chumbo	*ehnshah kohm... gahzooleenah saheem shoomboo*
diesel ...please.	gasóleo ...por favor.	*gazoleeoo ...poor fahvohr*
20 litres of super unleaded, please.	Vinte litros de gasolina sem chumbo super, por favor.	*veent leetroosh du gahzooleenah saheem shoomboo sooper, poor fahvohr*

A (litre) can of oil, please.	Uma lata (de litro) de óleo, por favor.	*oomah latah (du leetroo) du oleeoo, poor fahvohr*
Can you check the tyre pressure, please?	Pode ver a pressão dos pneus?	*pod vehr a prusãhoo doosh punehoosh*
Can you change the tyre, please?	Pode mudar o pneu, por favor?	*pod moodar oo punehoo, poor fahvohr*

✳ mechanical problems

YOU MAY WANT TO SAY...

My car has broken down.	O meu carro está avariado.	*oo mehoo karroo eeshta ahvahreeadoo*
I've run out of petrol.	Acabou a gasolina.	*ahkahboh ah gahzooleenah*
I have a puncture.	Tenho um furo.	*taheennyo oom fooroo*
Do you do repairs?	Faz reparações?	*fash rupahrahsõeesh*
I don't know what's wrong.	Não sei o que se passa.	*nãhoo sahee oo ku su pasah*
I think it's the...	Acho que é/são...	*ashoo ku e/sãhoo...*
I need...	Preciso de...	*pruseezoo du...*
The ... doesn't work.	O/A ... não trabalha.	*o/ah ... nãhoo trahballah*
Is it serious?	É sério?	*e sereeoo*
Can you repair it today?	Pode arranjar hoje?	*pod ahrrahnjar ohj*

| When will it be ready? | Quando está pronto? | *kwahñdoo eeshta prohntoo* |
| How much will it cost? | Quanto vai custar? | *kwahñtoo vaee kooshtar* |

* car parts

distributor	o distribuidor	*oo deetreebooeedohr*
exhaust pipe	o tubo de escape	*oo tooboo du eeshkap*
fanbelt	a correia de ventoinha	*ah koorraheeah du vehntooeeñnyah*
gears	as mudanças	*ahsh moodahñsahsh*
gearbox	a caixa das velocidades	*ah kaeeshah dahsh vulooseedadush*
headlights	os faróis	*oosh fahroeesh*
ignition	a ignição	*ah eegneesãhoo*
indicators	o pisca-pisca	*oo peeshkah-peeshkah*
points	os platinados	*oosh plahteenadoosh*
radiator	radiador	*radeeahdohr*
rear lights	os faróis de trás	*oosh fahroeesh du trash*
spare wheel	a roda sobresselente	*ah rodah soobrusulehnt*
spark plugs	as velas	*ahsh velahsh*
starter motor	o motor de arranque	*oo mootohr du ahrrahñk*
steering wheel	o volante	*oo voolahnt*
tyre	o pneu	*oo punehoo*
window	a janela	*ah jahnelah*
windscreen	o pára-brisas	*oo parah-breezahsh*

accommodation

accommodation

Accommodation in Portugal is varied, ranging from small, modest 1 or 2 star hotels and guest houses to luxury, state-owned hotels in old monasteries or annexes of palaces.

Hotéis	Hotels	1 to 5 stars
Hotéis apartamento	Apartment hotels	2 to 5 stars
Estalagens	Inns	4 to 5 stars
Albergarias	Inns	4 stars
Pensões	Guest houses	1 to 3 stars
Motéis	Road-side motels	2 to 3 stars
Pousadas	State-owned hotels (castles, etc.)	Regional and historic
Pousadas de juventude	Youth hostels	
Apartamentos turísticos	Tourist apartments	2 to 5 stars

Note: Hotéis and Pensões that offer bed and breakfast are also called Residenciais.

YOU MAY SEE...

água potável	drinking water
casa de banho	toilets
sala de jantar	dining room
cave	basement
chuveiros	showers
completo	full up

electricidade	electricity
elevador	lift
empregada de quarto	chambermaid
hotel de 5 estrelas	five-star hotel
lavandaria	laundry
lixo	rubbish
meia pensão	half board
não deitar lixo	do not dump rubbish
parque de campismo	campsite
pensão	guest house
pensão completa	full board
piscina	swimming pool
por favor toque à campainha	please ring the bell
porteiro	porter
pousada	state-owned luxury hotel
primeiro (1°)/segundo (2°) andar	first/second floor
proibido acampar	no (wild) camping
proibido fazer fogo	do not light fires
quartos vagos	vacant rooms
recepção	reception
recepcionista	receptionist
rés-do-chão	ground floor
saída (de emergência)	(emergency) exit
sala de estar	lounge
sala de televisão	television room
serviço de quarto	room service

✳ booking in advance
(see **telephones**, page 125)

Do you have...	Tem...	taheem̃...
a single room?	um quarto simples?	oom̃ kwartoo seem̃plush
a double room?	um quarto duplo?	oom̃ kwartoo dooploo
a family room?	um quarto de família?	oom̃ kwartoo du fahmeeleeah
a twin-bedded room?	um quarto de duas camas?	oom̃ kwartoo du dooahsh kahmahsh
space for a tent?	lugar para uma tenda?	loogar pahrah oomah tehñdah
space for a caravan?	lugar para uma caravana?	loogar pahrah oomah kahrahvahnah
I'd like to rent...	Queria alugar...	kureeah ahloogar...
an apartment	um apartamento	oom̃ ahpahrtahmehñtoo
a holiday home	uma casa de férias	oomah kazah du fereeahsh
For...	Por...	poor...
one night	uma noite	oomah noheet
two nights	duas noites	dooahsh noheetush
a week	uma semana	oomah sumahnah
From ... to ...	De ... a ...	du ... ah ...
With bath/shower.	Com banheiro/chuveiro.	kohm̃ bahnnyah-eeroo/shoovaheeroo

It's a two-person tent.	É uma tenda para duas pessoas.	e **oo**mah **teh**ndah **pah**rah **doo**ahsh pu**so**hahsh
How much is it... per night? per week?	Quanto é... por noite? por semana?	**kwahn**too e... poor **no**heet poor su**mah**nah
Is breakfast included?	O pequeno almoço está incluído?	oo pu**keh**noo al**moh**soo **eesh**ta eenkloo**ee**doo
Is there... a reduction for children?	Tem... desconto para crianças?	ta**heem**... dush**kohn**too **pah**rah kree**ahn**sahsh
a single room supplement?	suplemento o quarto simples?	sooplu**meh**ntoo oo **kwar**too **seem**plush
wheelchair access?	acesso a cadeira de rodas?	ah**se**soo ah kah**dahee**rah du **ro**dahsh
Can I pay by... credit card?	Posso pagar com... cartão de crédito?	pos pah**gar** kohm kahr**tah**oo du **kre**deetoo
traveller's cheques?	travellers cheques?	**tre**vulurs **she**kush
Can I book online?	Posso reservar pela internet?	pos rusur**var** **peh**lah een**ter**net
What's the address?	Qual é a morada?	kwal e ah moo**ra**dah
How do I find you?	Onde estão situados?	ohnd eesh**tah**oo seetoo**a**doosh

- **Can you recommend anywhere else?** | Pode recomendar outro lugar? | *pod rukoomehñdar ohtroo loogar*

YOU MAY HEAR...

- Por quantas noites? | *poor kwahntahsh noheetush* | For how many nights?

- Para quantas pessoas? | *pahrah kwahntahsh pusohahsh* | For how many people?

- Quarto simples ou duplo? | *kwartoo seemplush oh dooploo* | Single or double room?

- Quer cama de casal? | *ker kahmah du kahzal* | Do you want a double bed?

- Com... | *kohm...* | With...
  - banheira? | *bahnnyaheerah* | bath?
  - chuveiro? | *shoovaheeroo* | shower?

- Qual é o seu nome? | *kwal e oo sehoo nohm* | What's your name, please?

✱ checking in

YOU MAY WANT TO SAY...

- **I have a reservation for...** | Tenho uma reserva... | *taheennyoo oomah ruzervah*
  - **tonight** | para esta noite | *pahrah eshtah noheet*
  - **two nights** | por duas noites | *poor dooahsh noheetush*
  - **a week** | por uma semana | *poor oomah sumahnah*

It's in the name of...	Está no nome de...	*eeshta noo nohm du...*
Here's my passport.	Aqui está o meu passaporte.	*ahkee eeshta oo mehoo pasahport*

YOU MAY HEAR...

Tem um quarto/ um lugar reservado?	*taheem oom kwartoo/oom loogar rusurvadoo*	Have you reserved a room/space?
Posso ver o seu passaporte, por favor?	*pos vehr oo sehoo pasahport, poor fahvohr*	Can I have your passport, please?
Como deseja pagar?	*kohmoo duzêhjah pahgar*	How are you going to pay?

REGISTRATION CARD INFORMATION

Nome	First name
Sobrenome	Surname
Morada/Rua/Número	Home address/Street/Number
Código postal	Postcode
Nacionalidade	Nationality
Ocupação	Occupation
Data de nascimento	Date of birth
Local de nascimento	Place of birth
Número de passaporte	Passport number
Vem de/para	Coming from/going to
Emitido em	Issued at
Data	Date
Assinatura	Signature

accommodation

✳ hotels, B&Bs and hostels

- Where can I park? — Onde posso estacionar? — *ohnd pos eeshtahseeoonar*

- Can I see the room, please? — Posso ver o quarto, por favor? — *pos vehr oo kwartoo, poor fahvohr*

- Do you have... — Tem... — *taheem...*
  - a room with a view? — um quarto com vista? — *oorh kwartoo kohrh veeshtah*
  - a bigger room? — um quarto maior? — *oorh kwartoo maheeor*
  - a cot for the baby? — um berço para o bebé? — *oorh bêhrsoo pahrah oo bube*

- Is breakfast included? — O pequeno-almoço está incluído? — *oo pukehnoo almohsoo eeshta eenklooeedoo*

- What time... — A que horas... — *ah ku orahsh...*
  - is breakfast? — é o pequeno-almoço? — *e oo pukehnoo almohsoo*
  - do you lock the front door? — fecha a porta da frente? — *fehshah ah portah dah frehnt*

- Where is... — Onde é... — *ohnd e...*
  - the dining room? — a casa de jantar? — *ah kazah du jahntar*
  - the bar? — o bar? — *oo bar*

- Is there... — Há... — *a...*
  - 24 hour room service? — serviço de vinte e quatro horas? — *surveesoo du veent ee kwatro orahsh*
  - an Internet connection here? — aqui uma ligação à internet? — *ahkee oomah leegahsãhoo a eenternet*

| a business centre here? | aqui um centro de negócios? | *ahkee oom sehñtroo du nugoseeooosh* |

YOU MAY HEAR...

O pequeno-almoço (não) está incluído.	*oo pukehnoo almohsoo (nãhoo) eeshta eenklooeedoo*	Breakfast is(n't) included.
O pequeno-almoço é das ... às ...	*oo pukehnoo almohsoo e dahsh ... ash ...*	Breakfast is from ... to ...
Fechamos a porta da frente às...	*fushahmoosh ah portah dah frehnt ash...*	We shut the front door at...

* camping and caravanning
(see **directions**, page 37)

YOU MAY WANT TO SAY...

Is there a campsite/caravan site round here?	Há um parque de campismo/para caravanas aqui perto?	*a oom park du kahmpeeshmoo/ pahrah kahrahvah-nahsh ahkee pertoo*
Can we... camp here? park here?	Podemos... acampar aqui? estacionar aqui?	*poodehmoosh... akampar ahkee eeshtahseeoonar ahkee*
It's a two/four person tent.	É uma tenda para duas/quatro pessoas.	*e oomah tehndah pahrah dooahsh/ kwatro pusohahsh*

camping and caravanning

Where are...	Onde são...	*ohnd sãhoo...*
the toilets?	as casas de banho?	*ahsh kazahsh du bahñnyoo*
the showers?	os chuveiros?	*oosh shoovaheeroosh*
the dustbins?	os baldes do lixo?	*oosh baldush du leeshoo*
Do we pay extra for the showers?	Pagamos extra pelos chuveiros?	*pahgahmoosh aheeshtrah pêhloosh shuvaheeroosh*
Is the water OK for drinking?	A água é boa para beber?	*ah agooah e bohah pahrah bubêhr*
Where's the electricity?	Onde está a electricidade?	*ohnd eeshta ah eeletreeseedad*

YOU MAY HEAR...

O parque de campismo/ caravanas mais próximo é a ... quilómetros daqui.	*oo park du kahmpee-shmoo/kahrahvahn-ahsh maeesh prosee-moo e ah ... keelomutroosh dahkee*	The nearest campsite/caravan site is ... kilometres away.
Não pode acampar aqui.	*nãhoo pod akahmpar ahkee*	You can't camp here.
Os chuveiros são grátis.	*oosh shoovaheeroosh sãhoo grateesh*	The showers are free.
São ... euros por um duche.	*sãhoo... eroosh poor oom doosh*	It's ... euros for a shower.
A electricidade é ali.	*ah eeletreeseedad e ahlee*	The electricity is over there.

* requests and queries

- Are there any messages for me?
  Há algumas mensagens para mim?
  *a al**goo**mahsh meh**nsaj**ehnsh **pah**rah meem*

- I'm expecting...
  Estou à espera...
  *eesh**to** a eesh**perah**..*
  - a phone call
    de um telefonema
    *du oom tulufoo**neh**mah*
  - a fax
    de uma fax
    du oomah faks

- Can I...
  Posso...
  pos...
  - leave this in the safe?
    pôr isto no cofre?
    *pohr **eesh**too noo **ko**fru*

- Can you...
  Pode...
  pod...
  - give me my things from the safe?
    dar-me as coisas que tenho no cofre?
    ***dar**mu ahsh **koh**eezahsh ku ta**heen**nyoo noo **ko**fru*
  - wake me up at eight o'clock?
    acorda-me às oito horas?
    *ah**koor**damu ash **ohee**too orahsh*
  - order me a taxi?
    chama-me um táxi?
    ***shah**mamu oom **tak**see*

- Do you have...
  Tem...
  taheem...
  - a babysitting service?
    um serviço de babysitter?
    *oom sur**vee**soo du **bahee**bee **see**tahr*
  - a baby alarm?
    um alarm de bebé?
    *oom ah**larm** du bube*

- I need...
  Preciso...
  *pru**see**zoo...*
  - another pillow
    doutra almofada
    ***doh**trah almoo**fa**dah*
  - an adaptor
    um adaptador
    *oom ahdahputah**dohr***

I've lost my key. | Perdi a minha chave. | *purdee ah meennyah shav*

I've left my key in the room. | Deixei a minha chave no quarto. | *daheeshaee ah meennyah shav noo kwart*

* problems and complaints

YOU MAY WANT TO SAY...

● Excuse me... | Desculpe... | *dushkoolp*

● The room is... | O quarto é... | *oo kwart e...*
  too hot | muito quente | *mooeentoo kehnt*
  too cold | muito frio | *mooeentoo freeoo*

● There isn't any... | Não há nenhum... | *nãhoo a nunnyoom̃...*
  toilet paper | papel de casa de banho | *pahpel du kasha du bahnnyoo*

● There isn't any... | Não há nenhuma... | *nãhoo a nunnyoomah...*

  hot water | água quente | *agooah kehnt*
  electricity | electricidade | *eeletreeseedad*

● There aren't any... | Não há nenhumas... | *nãhoo a nunnyoomahsh...*

  towels | toalhas | *tooallahsh*

● I can't... | Não consigo... | *nãhoo kohnseegoo...*
  open the window | abrir a janela | *ahbreer ah jahnelah*
  turn the tap off | fechar a torneira | *fêhshar ah toornaheerah*

  work the TV | fazer trabalhar a televisão | *fahzêhr trahbahllar ah tuluveezãhoo*

● The bed is uncomfortable. | A cama é desconfortável. | *ah kahmah e dushkohnfoortavel*

● The bathroom is dirty.	A casa de banho está suja.	ah *kazah* du *bahñnyoo* *eeshta* *soojah*
● The toilet doesn't flush.	A sanita não funciona.	ah *sahneetah* nãhoo *foonseeohnah*
● The drain is blocked.	O cano está entupido.	oo *kahnoo* eeshta *enhtoopeedoo*
● It's very noisy.	Está muito barulho.	eeshta *mooeentoo* *bahroolloo*
● ... doesn't work.	... não funciona.	... nãhoo *foonseeohnah*
The light	A luz	ah *loosh*
The key	A chave	ah *shav*
The oven	O fogão	oo *foogãhoo*
● There's a smell of gas.	Cheira a gás.	*shaheerah* ah *gash*
● I want to see the manager!	Quero ver o gerente!	*keroo* vêhr oo *jurehnt*

✳ checking out

● The bill, please.	A conta, por favor.	ah *kohntah*, por *favohr*
● I'd like to...	Queria...	*kureeah*...
check out	pagar	*pahgar*
stay another night	ficar mais uma noite	*feekar* maeesh *oomah* *noheet*
● What time is check out?	A que horas temos de deixar os quartos?	ah ku *orahsh* *tehmoosh* du *daheeshar* oosh *kwartoosh*

self-catering/second homes

Can I leave my bags here?	Posso deixar as malas aqui?	*posdaheeshar ahsh malahsh ahkee*
There's a mistake in the bill.	Há um erro na conta.	*a oom êhrroo nah kohntah*
I've had a great time here.	Diverti-me imenso aqui.	*deevurteemu eemehnsoo ahkee*

YOU MAY HEAR...

Saída às...	*saheedah ash...*	Check out is at...
Pode ficar com o quarto até às...	*pod feekar kohm oo kwartoo ahte ash...*	You can have the room till...
Quantas malas?	*kwahntahsh malahsh*	How many bags?
Deixe-as aqui.	*daheeshuahsh ahkee*	Leave them here.
Deixe-me ver.	*daheeshmu vêhr*	Let me check it.
Volte outra vez!	*volt ohtrah vêhsh*	Come again!

✳ self-catering/second homes
(see **problems and complaints**, page 68)

YOU MAY WANT TO SAY...

I've rented...	Aluguei...	*ahloogahee...*
a chalet	um chalet	*oom shale*
an apartment	um apartamento	*oom ahpahrtahmehntoo*
My name is...	O meu nome é...	*oo mehoo nohm e...*

- We're in number... Estamos no número... *eeshtahmoosh noo noomuroo...*

- Can you give me the key, please? Pode dar-me a chave, por favor? *pod darm ah shav, poor fahvohr*

- Where is... Onde é... *ond e...*
    the fusebox? a caixa dos fusíveis? *ah kaeeshah doo foozeevaheesh*

    the stopcock? a torneira de segurança? *ah toornaheerah du sugoorahnsah*

- How does the cooker/hot water work? Como trabalha o fogão/a água quente? *kohmoo trahballah oo foogãhoo/ah agooah kehnt*

- Is there... Há... *a...*
    air-conditioning? ar condicionado? *ar kohndeeseeoo-nadoo*
    another gas bottle? outra botija de gás? *ohtrah booteejah du gash*

- Are there... Há... *a...*
    any more blankets? mais cobertores? *maeesh kooburtohrush*
    any shops round here? lojas aqui perto? *lojahsh ahkee pertoo*

- Where do I put the rubbish? Onde ponho o lixo? *ohnd pohnnyoo oo leeshoo*

- When do they collect the rubbish? Quando tiram o lixo? *kwahndoo teerahm̃ oo leeshoo*

- When does the cleaner come? Quando vem a mulher da limpeza? *kwahndoo vaheem ah mooller dah leempêhzah*

accommodation

71

self-catering/second homes

Can I borrow...	Empresta-me...	*aheempreshtee-mahmu...*
a drill?	um brocador?	*oom bookahdohr*
a corkscrew?	um saca-rolhas?	*oom sakah-rohllahsh*
We need...	Precisamos de...	*pruseezahmoosh du...*
an (emergency) plumber	um canalizador (de emergência)	*oom kahnah-leezahdohr (du eemurgehnseeah)*
an electrician	um electricista	*oom eeletruseeshtah*
help	ajuda	*ahjoodah*
How can I/we contact you?	Como posso contactá-lo/la?	*kohmoo pos kohntahtaloo/ kohntahtalah*

YOU MAY HEAR... ?

Ponha o lixo...	*pohnnyah oo leeshoo...*	Put the rubbish...
no caixote de lixo	*noo kaeeshot du leeshoo*	in the dustbin
na rua	*nah rrooah*	on the street
Tiram o lixo à...	*teerahm oo leeshoo a*	The rubbish is collected on....
A mulher da limpeza vem à...	*ah mooller dah leempehzah vaheem a...*	The cleaner comes on...
O número do meu telemóvel é o...	*oo noomuroo doo mehoo tulumovel e oo...*	My mobile number is...

accommodation

72

food&drink

● Lunch in Portugal is usually between 12 noon and 2.30pm and dinner between 7pm and 9.30 pm. In the afternoon, between about 4pm and 5pm, the Portuguese have a lanche (afternoon tea), which can consist of a sandwich or a cake and coffee or tea.

● A Portuguese meal often starts with a sopa (soup), the most famous of which is the caldo verde (cabbage soup). With such a long sea coast, Portugal is rich in dishes which have a sea flavour, such as as caldeiradas (fish stew) and a sardinha assada (grilled sardines). The Portuguese national dish, however, is the cozido, similar to Irish stew. O bacalhau (dried cod) also has a special place at the Portuguese table.

YOU MAY SEE...

aceitamos cartões de crédito	we take credit cards
adega	wine cellar
bebidas	drinks
cachorros e hamburguers	hot dog and burger stand
café	café
caixa	till
casas de banho	toilets
cervejaria	pub
ementa turista	tourist menu
geladaria	ice-cream parlour
marisqueira	seafood restaurant
restaurante	restaurant
pronto-a-comer	fast food

✳ making bookings
(see **telling the time**, page 17)

- I'd like to reserve a table for...

  Queria reservar uma mesa para...

  kureeah rusurvar ooma mehzah pahrah...

  - two people

    duas pessoas

    dooahsh pusohahash

  - tomorrow evening

    amanhã à noite

    amahñnyãh a noheet

  - at half past eight

    às oito e meia

    ahsh oheetoo ee maheeah

  - this evening at seven o'clock

    esta noite às sete horas

    eshtah noheet ash set orahsh

- My name is...

  O meu nome é...

  oo mehoo nohm e...

- My telephone/ mobile number is...

  O número do meu telefone/telemóvel é...

  oo noomuroo doo mehoo tulufon/ tulumovel e...

- Could you squeeze us in earlier/later?

  Podia arranjar lugar para mais cedo/tarde?

  poodeeah ahrrahñjar loogar pahrah maeesh sêhdoo/tard

- Para quando quer a mesa?

  pahrah kwahñdoo ker a mêhzah

  When would you like the table for?

- Para quantas pessoas?

  pahrah kwahñtahsh pusohahsh

  For how many?

- Qual é o seu nome?

  kwal e oo sehoo nohm

  What's your name?

food and drink

75

at the restaurant

| Desculpe mas estamos cheios. | dushkoolp mahsh eeshtahmoosh shaheeoosh | I'm sorry, we're fully booked. |

✳ at the restaurant

YOU MAY WANT TO SAY...

- **I've booked a table.** — Reservei uma mesa. — rusurvahee oomah mêhzah

- **My name is...** — O meu nome é... — oo mehoo nohm e...

- **We haven't booked.** — Não reservamos. — nãhoo rusurvamoosh

- **Have you got a table for four, please?** — Tem uma mesa para quatro pessoas, por favor? — taheem oomah mêhzah pahrah kwatroo pusohahss, poor fahvohr

- **Outside/on the terrace if possible.** — Lá fora/na esplanada, se possível. — la forah/nah eeshplahnadah, su pooseevel

- **Have you got a high chair?** — Tem uma cadeira alta? — taheem oomah kahdaheerah altah

- **How long do we have to wait?** — Quanto tempo temos de esperar? — kwahntoo tehmpoo tehmoosh du eeshpurar

- **Do you take credit cards?** — Aceitam cartões de crédito? — ahsaheetahm kahrtõheesh du kredeetoo

food and drink

76

food and drink

YOU MAY HEAR...

Tem uma reserva?	*taheeḿ oomah ruzervah*	Have you got a reservation?
Onde deseja/ desejam sentar?	*ohnd duzêhjah/ duzêhjahḿ sehntar*	Where would you like to sit?
Fumadores ou não fumadores?	*foomahdohrush oh nãhoo foomahdohrush*	Smoking or non-smoking?
Só um momento.	*so ooḿ moomehñtoo*	Just a moment.
Deseja/Desejam esperar?	*duzêhjah/duzêhjahḿ eeshpurar*	Would you like to wait?
Nós (não) aceitamos cartões de crédito.	*nosh (nãhoo) ahsaheetahmoosh kahrtõheesh du kredeetoo*	We (don't) accept credit cards.

✳ ordering your food

Ordering food or drinks in Portugal is straightforward: just name what you want and add por favor (please). To order more than one of the same thing, add an s at the end of the word: uma sopa de tomate/duas sopas de tomate.

YOU MAY WANT TO SAY...

Excuse me!	Faz favor!	*fash fahvohr*
The menu, please.	A ementa, por favor.	*ah eemehñtah, poor fahvohr*

- Do you have...
  vegetarian food?

  a tourist menu?

Tem...
  comida
    vegetariana?
  uma ementa
    turista?

taheem̃...
  koomeedah
    vugutahreeahnah
  oomah eemeh̃tah
    too**reesh**tah

- Is it self-service?

É self-service?

e self serveesu

- We're ready to
  order.

Estamos prontos.

eeshtahmoosh
proh̃toosh

- Can I have... ?

Posso ter... ?

pos tehr...

- I'd like...
  for starters
  for main course

  for dessert

Queria...
  para entrada
  para prato principal

  para sobremesa

kureeah...
  pahrah eh̃tradah
  pahrah pratoo
    preenseepal
  pahrah
    soobrumêhzah

- Does that come
  with vegetables?

Isso vem com
vegetais?

eesoo vaheem̃ kohm̃
vugutaeesh

- What's this,
  please?

O que é isto, por
favor?

oo ku e eeshtoo, poor
fahvohr

- What are your
  specials today?

Qual é a especialidade
para hoje?

kwal e ah
eeshpuseeahleedad
pahrah ohj

- What's the local
  speciality?

Qual é o prato
regional?

kwal e oo pratoo
rugeeoonal

- I'll have the same
  as him/her/them.

Quero o mesmo que
ele/ela/eles.

keroo oo mehshmoo
ku ehl/êhlah/ehlush

- Excuse me, I've
  changed my mind.

Desculpe,
mudei de ideias.

dushkoolp,
moodahee du
eedaheeahsh

YOU MAY HEAR... ⃝

Já decidiu/ decidiram?	*ja dusee**deeoo**/ dusee**deer**ahm̃*	Have you decided?
Que deseja para...	*ku du**zêh**jah pahrah...*	What would you like for...
entrada?	*ehñ**tra**dah*	starters?
prato principal?	***pra**too preensee**pal***	main course?
sobremesa?	*soobru**mêh**zah*	dessert?
Aconselhamos...	*ahkohnsullah**moosh**...*	We recommend...
Mais alguma coisa?	*maeesh al**goo**mah **koh**eezah*	Anything else?

✳ ordering your drinks

YOU MAY WANT TO SAY... 💬

Can I see the wine list, please?	Posso ver a lista dos vinhos, por favor?	*pos vehr ah **leesh**tah doosh vee**ñny**oosh, poor fa**vohr***
A bottle of this, please.	Uma garrafa deste, por favor.	*oomah gah**rra**fah dêhsht, poor fah**vohr***
Half a litre of this, please.	Meio litro deste, por favor.	*ma**hee**oo **lee**troo dêhsht, poor fah**vohr***
A glass of the ... please.	Um copo de ... por favor.	*oom̃ **ko**poo du ... poor fah**vohr***
We'll have the house red/white, please.	Queremos o vinho branco/tinto da casa, por favor.	*ku**reh**moosh oo vee**ñny**oo brah**ñk**oo/ **teeñ**too dah **ka**zah, poor fah**vohr***

ordering your drinks

- **What beers do you have, please?** — Que cervejas tem, por favor? — *ku survêhjahsh taheem, poor fahvohr*

- **Is that a bottle or draught?** — É em garrafa ou imperial? — *e aheem gahrrafah oh eempureeal*

- **Can I have...** — Dá-me... — *damu...*
  - a gin and tonic — um gin tónico — *oom jeen toneekoo*
  - a whisky — um whisky — *oom wishki*
  - a vodka and Coke — um vodka com Coca Cola — *oom vodkah kohm kokah kolah*

- **Do you have any liqueurs?** — Tem licores? — *taheem leekohrush*

- **A bottle of mineral water, please.** — Uma garrafa de água mineral, por favor. — *oomah gahrrafah du agooah meenural, poor fahvohr*

- **What soft drinks do you have, please?** — Que bebidas sem álcool tem, por favor? — *ku bubeedahsh saheem alcohol taheem, poor fahvohr*

YOU MAY HEAR... (?)

Gelo e limão?	*jehloo ee leemãhoo*	Ice and lemon?
Deseja com água?	*duzêhjah kohm agooah*	Do you want water with it?
Água com ou sem gás?	*agooah kohm oh saheem gash*	Fizzy or still water?
Uma garrafa grande ou pequena?	*oomah gahrrafah grahñdu oh pukehnah*	A large or small bottle?

* bars, cafés and snack bars

I'll have...	Quero...	*keroo...*
A coffee, please.	Um café, por favor.	*oom kahfe, poor fahvohr*
A milky coffee, please.	Um café com bastante leite, por favor.	*oom kahfe kohm bahshtahnt laheet, poor fahvohr*
A black coffee, please.	Um café sem leite, por favor.	*oom kahfe saheem laheet, poor fahvohr*
A cup of tea, please.	Um chá, por favor.	*oom sha, poor fahvohr*
With milk/lemon.	Com leite/limão.	*kohm laheet/leemãhoo*
A fruit/herbal tea please.	Um chá de frutos/de ervas, por favor.	*oom sha du frootoosh/du ervahsh, poor fahvohr*
A glass of... tap water	Um copo de... água da torneira	*oom kopoo du... agooah dah toornaheerah*
wine apple juice ...please.	vinho sumo de maçã ...por favor.	*veennyoo soomoo du mahsãh ...poor fahvohr*
No ice, thanks.	Sem gelo, por favor.	*saheem jehloo, poor fahvohr*
A bottle of water, please.	Uma garrafa de água.	*oomah gahrrafah du agooah*

food and drink

- A piece of... / Uma fatia de... / *oomah fahteeah du...*

    apple tart / torta de maçã / *tortah du mahsāh*
    chocolate cake / bolo de chocolate / *bohloo du shookoolat*

...please. / ...por favor. / *...poor fahvohr*

- What kind of ... do you have? / Que ... tem? / *ku ... taheem̃*

- Is there any... / Tem... / *taheem̃...*
    tomato ketchup? / ketchup? / *ketshahp*
    pepper and salt? / sal e pimenta? / *sal ee peemehñtah*

- It's my round. / É a minha vez. / *e ah meennyah vêhsh*

- How much is that? / Quanto é isso? / *kwahñtoo e eesoo*

YOU MAY HEAR...

- Que deseja? / *ku duzêhjah* / What can I get you?

- Grande ou pequeno? / *grahñd oh pukehnoo* / Large or small?

- Com gás ou sem gás? / *kohm̃ gash oh sehm̃ gash* / Fizzy or still?

- Com gelo? / *kohm̃ gehloo* / With ice?

- Pagam junto ou separado? / *pagahm̃ jooñtoo oh supahradoo* / Are you paying together or separately?

* special requirements

- I'm/he/she is diabetic. — Sou/Ele/Ela é diabético/a. — *soh/el/êhlah/ e deeahbeteekoo/ deeahbeteekah*

- I'm/he/she is allergic to... — Sou/Ele/Ela é alérgico/a a... — *soh/el/êhlah/e ahlerjeekoo/ ahlerjeekah a...*

  - nuts — nozes — *nozush*
  - cow's milk — leite de vaca — *laheet du vakah*
  - MSG — glutamato de monossódio — *glootahmatoo du monosodeeoo*
  - shellfish — marisco — *mahreeshkoo*

- I'm... — Sou... — *soh...*
  - vegetarian — vegetariano/a — *vujutahreeahnoo/ nah*
  - vegan — naturalista — *nahtoorahleeshtah*

- I can't eat... — (Eu) não posso comer... — *(ehoo) nãhoo pos koomehr...*

- He/she can't eat... — Ele/Ela não pode comer... — *el/êhlah nãhoo pod koomêhr...*
  - dairy products — produtos com leite — *proodootoosh kohm laheet*
  - wheat products — produtos com trigo — *proodootoosh kohm treegoo*

- Do you have... ? — Tem... ? — *taheem... ?*
  - halal — halal — *ahlal*
  - kosher — kosher — *kohshahr*
  - free-range — de capoeira — *du kahpooaheerah*

food and drink

low sodium	com pouco sódio	*kohm* **pohk***oo* *so***dee***oo*
low fat	com poucas gorduras	*kohm* **pohk***ahsh* *goor***door***ajsj*
organic	orgânico	*or***gah***neecoo*
Is that cooked with (butter)?	É feito com (manteiga)?	*e* **fah***eetoo kohm* (*mahn***tah***eegah*)

✳ comments and requests

This is delicious.	Isto está delicioso.	**eesh***too eesh***ta** *du***lee***see***ooh***zoo*
Can I have more ... please?	Queria mais ... por favor.	*ku***ree***ah* *maeesh* ... *poor* *fah***vohr**
bread	pão	*pã***hoo**
water	água	*a***gooah**
Can I have ... please?	Queria ... por favor.	*ku***ree***ah* ... *poor* *fah***vohr**
a knife	uma faca	*oo***mah** **fak***ah*
a fork	um garfo	*oom* **gar***foo*
a spoon	uma colher	*oo***mah** **kool***ler*
a napkin	um guardanapo	*oom* *gooahrdah***nap***oo*
another bottle of wine	outra garrafa de vinho	**oh***trah gah***rraf***ah du* **veen***nyo*
another glass	outro copo	**oh***troo* **kop***oo*
I can't eat another thing.	Já não consigo comer mais.	*ja* **nã***hoo kohn***see***goo koo***mêhr** *maeesh*

- Vou perguntar à cozinha. — *voh purgooñtar a koozeeñnyah* — I'll check with the kitchen.

- Tem tudo (manteiga). — *taheeñ toodoo (mahñtaheegah)* — It's all got (butter) in.

✱ problems and complaints

- **Excuse me.** Desculpe. *dushkoolp*

- **This is...** Isto está... *eeshtoo eeshta...*
  cold — frio — *freeoo*
  underdone — mal cozinhado — *mal koozeennyadoo*
  burnt — queimado — *kaheemadoo*

- **I didn't order this.** Não pedi isto. *nãhoo pudee eeshtoo*

- **I ordered the...** Pedi o/a... *pudee oo/ah...*

- **Is our food coming soon?** A nossa comida está a vir? *ah nosah koomeedah eeshta ah veer*

✱ paying the bill

- **The bill, please.** A conta, por favor. *ah kohñtah, poor fahvohr*

- **Is service included?** O serviço está incluído? *oo surveesoo eeshta eenklooeedoo*

food and drink

- **There's a mistake here.** · Está aqui um erro. · *eeshta ahkee oom êhrroo*

- **That was great, thank you.** · Estava óptimo, obrigado/a. · *eeshtavah oteemoo, obreegadoo/ah*

YOU MAY HEAR...

- O serviço não está incluído. · *oo surveesoo nãhoo eeshta eenklooeedoo* · **Service isn't included.**

- Desculpe, mas só aceitamos dinheiro. · *dushkoolp, mahsh so ahsaheetahmoosh deennyaheeroo* · **Sorry, we only accept cash.**

✳ buying food

YOU MAY WANT TO SAY...

I'd like...	Queria...	*kureeah...*
some of that	alguns desses/ daqueles	*algoonsh dêhsush/ dahkêhlush*
some of those	algumas dessas/ daquelas	*algoomahsh desahsh/ dahkêlahsh*
a kilo (of...)	um quilo (de...)	*oom keeloo (du...)*
half a kilo (of...)	meio quilo (de...)	*maheeoo keeloo (du...)*
two hundred grammes of that	duzentos gramas disso/daquilo	*doozehñtahsh grahmahsh deesoo/ dahkeeloo*
a piece of that	um pedaço disso/ daquilo	*oom pudasoo deesoo/dahkeeloo*

food and drink

- How much is...   Quanto é...   *kwahntoo e ...*
    that?   aquilo/isso?   *ahkeeloo/eesoo*
    a kilo of cheese?   um quilo de   *oom keeloo du*
                             queijo?   *kaheejoo*

- What's that,   O que é isso, por   *oo ku e eesoo, poor*
    please?   favor?   *fahvohr*

- Have you got...   Tem...   *taheem...*
    any bread?   pão?   *pãhoo*
    any more?   mais?   *maeesh*

- A bit more/less,   Um pouco mais/   *oom pohkoo maeesh/*
    please.   menos, por favor.   *mehnoosh, poor*
                                                   fahvohr

- That's enough,   Chega, obrigado/a.   *shêhgah,*
    thank you.   *obreegadoo/ah*

- That's all, thank   É tudo, obrigado/a.   *e toodoo,*
    you.   *obreegadoo/ah*

- I'm looking   Estou à procura   *eeshtoh a prokoorah*
    for...   de...   *du...*
    frozen food   congelados   *kohnguladoosh*
    dairy products   produtos com leite   *proodootoosh*
                                                   kohm laheet
    the fruit and   da secção de   *dah seksãhoo du*
    vegetable   frutas e vegetais   *frootahsh ee*
    section   *vujutaeesh*

- Can I have a bag,   Dá-me um saco, por   *damu oom sakoo,*
    please?   favor?   *poor fahvohr*

menu reader

DRINKS

água com gás **fizzy water**
água mineral **mineral water**
água sem gás **still water**
aguardente **spirit**
bagaceira **grape spirit**
batido de leite **milk shake**
bebidas **drinks**
bica **small, strong, black coffee**
café **coffee**
café descafeinado **decaffeinated**
carioca **small, weak, black coffee**
carta de vinhos **wine list**
cerveja **beer**
cerveja de barril **draught beer**
cerveja preta **dark beer**
chá **tea**
chá com leite **with milk**
chá com limão **with lemon**
chá de camomila **camomile tea**
chá de ervas **herbal tea**
chá de ortlã pimenta **peppermint tea**
conhaque **cognac, brandy**
galão **large, white coffee in a glass**
garoto **small black coffee with milk**
gin **gin**
ginjinha **cherry liqueur**
laranjada **orangeade**
leite com chocolate **hot chocolate**
licores **spirits, liqueurs**
limonada **lemonade**
medronho **arbutus berry liqueur**
meia de café **black coffee in a large cup**

meia de leite **white coffee in a large cup**
mosto **grape juice**
refrigerantes **soft drinks**
sumo **fruit juice**
sumo de laranja **orange juice**
sumo de maçã **apple juice**
sumo de manga **mango juice**
sumo de pêra **pear juice**
sumo de tomate **tomato juice**
sumo de uvas **grape juice**
vermute **vermouth**
vinho **wine**
vinho branco **white wine**
vinho branco com limonada ou água mineral **white wine with lemonade or mineral water**
vinho da Madeira **Madeira wine**
vinho da região demarcada **wine of delimited region**
vinho de mesa **table wine**
vinho de reserva **specially selected wine (appears on bottles)**
vinho do porto **port wine**
vinho doce **sweet wine**
vinho moscatel **muscatel**
vinho rosé **rosé wine**
vinho seco **dry wine**
vinho tinto **red wine**
vinho verde **green/young wine**

FOOD

A

aceitamos cartões de crédito **we accept credit cards**

acepipes **hors d'oeuvres**

aipo **celery**

alcachofra **artichoke**

alguns dos nossos pratos contêm traços de nozes **some of our dishes may contain traces of nuts**

alho **garlic**

almoço **lunch**

almôndegas **meatballs**

alperce **apricot**

amêijoa **cockle**

amêijoa à bulhão pato **cockles with garlic and coriander**

amêijoas na cataplana **cockles with cured ham and spiced sausage in a special dish**

amêndoas **almonds**

amoras **blackberries**

ananás **pineapple**

arroz **rice**

arroz branco **plain rice**

arroz de ervilhas **rice with peas**

arroz de pato **duck rice**

arroz de pimentos **rice made with peppers**

arroz de tomate **tomato rice**

arroz doce **rice pudding**

atum **tuna**

aves **fowl**

azeitonas **olives**

B

bacalhau **cod**

bacalhau à brás **cod with eggs, onions and potatoes**

bacalhau à gomes de sá **cod with onions, potatoes and black olives**

bacalhau cozido **boiled cod with boiled vegetables**

bacon fumado **smoked bacon**

bananas **bananas**

batata cozida **boiled potatoes**

batata cozida com casca **potatoes boiled in their skins**

batatas **potatoes**

batatas fritas **chips**

beringela **aubergine**

bifana **small steak in bread**

bife **beef/rump steak**

bola de berlim **custard doughnut**

bolacha **biscuit**

bolinha **bread roll**

bolo **cake**

bolo rei **cake with almonds, nuts and candied and dried fruits (often eaten at Christmas)**

bolo de chocolate **chocolate cake**

bolo de coco **coconut cake**

bolo de laranja **orange cake**

borrego **lamb**

broa de milho **bread made with maize**

C

cabreiro **strong goat cheese**

cachorro **hot dog**

caldeirada **fish stew**

caldo verde **green cabbage soup**

camarão **prawns**

canela **cinnamon**

caracóis **snails**

caranguejo **crab**

carapau **horse-mackerel**

caril **curry**

carne **meat**

food and drink

89

carne assada **roast meat**
carne picada **mince**
carneiro **mutton**
caseiro **home-made**
castanhas **chestnuts**
cavala **mackerel**
cebola **onion**
cenouras **carrots**
cerejas **cherries**
cherne **turbot**
chocolate **chocolate**
chouriço **smoked pork sausage**
chouriço preto **black pudding**
coelho **hare, rabbit**
cogumelos **mushrooms**
costeletas de porco **pork chops**
couve **cabbage**
couve galega **spring cabbage**
couves de bruxelas **brussels sprouts**
cove flor **cauliflower**
cozido à portuguesa **a stew made**
  of pork and beef/veal with
  vegetables and sausage
cozido a vapor **steamed**
cozinhado em ovo e miolo de pão
  cooked in egg and breadcrumbs
cozinhado no forno **cooked in the oven**
croquetes **croquettes**

D
doces **sweets, desserts**
dose **portion**

E
eiroz **conger eel**
ementa turista **set menu (tourist)**
empadão de carne **large meat-pie**
enguia **eel**
entradas **starters**
entrecosto **rib**
ervas **herbs**

ervilhas **peas**
escalopes **scallops**
escalopes de vitela **veal escalope**
espargo **asparagus**
esparguete **spaghetti**
especialidades **specialities**
espetada **roasting spit**
espinafre **spinach**

F
falcão **pheasant**
febras de porco **lean pork slices**
feijão **beans**
feijão verde **green (French) beans**
feijoada **bean and beef stew**
feijões brancos **butter beans**
fiambre **ham**
fígado **liver**
figos **figs**
filete **fillet**
framboesa **raspberry**
frango **chicken**
frango no churrasco **barbecued**
  chicken
frito **fried**
fruta **fruit**

G
gaspacho **cold soup made with dry**
  bread, garlic, oilve oil, vinegar,
  tomatoes, cucumber, oregano
gelado **ice cream**
gelatina **jelly**
gengibre **ginger**
grão **chick peas**
gratinado **melted**
grelhado **grilled**
guisado **stew**

H
hamburguer **hamburger**

food and drink

I

IVA incluído VAT inclusive

J

jantar dinner

L

lagosta lobster
lagostim crayfish
lampreia lamprey
laranja orange
legumes vegetables
leitão sucking pig
limão lemon
língua tongue
linguado sole
lombo loin
lombo de boi (vaca) sirloin
lombo de porco pork loin
lombo de vitela veal loin
lula squid

M

maçã apple
maçãs assadas baked apples
marisco sea food
massa pasta, dough
melancia watermelon
melão melon
mexilhões mussels
milho sweetcorn
molho sauce
morangos strawberries

N

nabo turnip
não aceitamos cartões de crédito
   we don't accept credit cards
natas cream
natas batidas whipped cream
nóz nut
nóz muscada nutmeg

O

omelete de cebola onion omelette
omelete de cogumelos mushroom
   omelette
omelete de fiambre ham omelette
omelete simples plain omelette
ostras oysters
o serviço está incluído service
   included
ovos eggs
ovos cozidos boiled egg
ovos estrelados fried egg
ovos mexidos scrambled egg
ovos moles egg sauce (Hollandaise)

P

panquecas pancakes
pão bread
pão de ló light sponge cake
pão de trigo wholemeal bread
pastéis de nata small custard cakes
pastel (pl. pastéis) de bacalhau cod
   fish cakes
pato duck
peixe fish
peixe espada swordfish
pepino cucumber
pequeno-almoço breakfast
pêra pear
perdiz partridge
perú turkey
pescada whiting
pêssego peach
petiscos snacks
picante spicy
pimenta pepper
piripiri chilli and olive oil seasoning
polvo octopus
porco pork
pratos combinados set menu

pratos do dia **dishes of the day**
prego **steak sandwich**
presunto **smoked ham**
pudim flan **crème caramel**
puré de batata **mashed potatoes**

Q

queijos **cheeses**
queijo da serra **sheep cheese from Serra da Estrêla**
queijo de azeitão **small creamy cheese**
queijo **cheese**
queijo da ilha **from the Azores, used grated like 'parmesan'**

R

rabanadas **French toast**
recheada **stuffed**
requeijão **curd cheese**
rim, rins **kidney(s)**
rissol (pl. rissóis) **rissole**
robalo **rock bass**
rosmaninho **rosemary**

S

salada **salad**
salada de alface **lettuce salad**
salada de frutas **fruit salad**
salada de tomate **tomato salad**
salada mista **mixed salad**
salada russa **Russian salad**

salmão **salmon**
salmonete **red mullet**
salsa **parsley**
salsicha **sausage**
salteado **dipped**
sampaio **cured ham**
santola **spider-crab**
sapateira **crab/kingcrab**
sardinha **sardine**
serpa **sweet and unctuous cheese**
sobremesas **desserts**
sopa **soup**
sopa de feijão **bean soup**
sopa de lentilhas **lentil soup**
sopa de peixe **fish soup with dry bread**
sopa de tomate **tomato soup**
sorvet **sherbet**

T

tomatada com ovos **eggs cooked in a tomato sauce, sometimes served with fried bread**
tomates **tomatoes**
torta de amêndoa **almond tart**
tripas **tripe**
truta **trout**

V

viado **veal**
vinagre **vinegar**

sightseeing
&activities

✳ at the tourist office

To find out information about all the sights, nightlife and tours, visit the Centro de Turismo.

Do you speak English?	Fala inglês?	*falah eenglêhsh*
Do you have...	Tem...	*taheeṁ...*
a map of the town?	um mapa da cidade?	*ooṁ mapah dah seedadu*
a list of hotels?	uma lista de hotéis?	*oomah leeshtah du otaheesh*
Can you recommend...	Pode recomendar...	*pod rukoomehndar...*
a cheap hotel?	um hotel barato?	*ooṁ otel bahratoo*
a good campsite?	um bom parque de campismo?	*ooṁ bohṁ park du kaṁpeeshmoo*
Do you have information...	Tem informações...	*taheeṁ een-foormahsõheesh...*
in English?	em inglês?	*aheeṁ eenglêhsh*
about opening times?	sobre o horário de abertura?	*sohbru oo orareeoo du ahburtoorah*
Can you book...	Pode reservar-me...	*pod ruzurvarmu...*
a hotel room for me?	um quarto de hotel?	*ooṁ kwarto du otel*
this day trip for me?	esta viagem de um dia?	*eshtah veeajaheeṁ du ooṁ deeah*
Where is...	Onde é...	*ohnd e...*
the old town?	a parte velha da cidade?	*ah part vellah dah seedadu*

the art gallery?	a galeria de arte?	*ah gahlureeah du art*
the ... museum?	o museu ... ?	*oo moozehoo...*
Is there...	Há...	*a...*
a swimming pool?	uma piscina?	*oomah peesseenah*
a bank?	um banco?	*ooñ bahñkoo*
Is there a post office near here?	Há um correio aqui perto?	*a ooñ kooraheeoo ahkee pertoo*
Can you show me on the map?	Pode mostrar-me no mapa?	*pod mooshtrarmu noo mapah*

✳ opening times
(see **telling the time**, page 17)

Museums opening times vary but most are closed for lunch (usually from 12 noon to 2pm or 12.30pm to 2.30pm) or do not open on Mondays or public holidays. Major churches do not have a fixed timetable but smaller churches and those in rural places may only open for services. You may have to find the key holder to visit the church.

Most museums charge a small entrance fee (from one to three euros). Young people (under 14) and pensioners may obtain a considerable discount. Those under 26 with an International Student Identity Card or Cartão Jovem (youth card) may also obtain a reduction.

YOU MAY WANT TO SAY...

- **What time does the ... open?** — A que horas abre...? — *ah ku orahsh abru...*
  - museum — o museu — *oo moozehoo*
  - palace — o palácio — *oo pahlaseeoo*

- **What time does the ... close?** — A que horas fecha... ? — *ah ku orahsh fehshah...*

- **When does the exhibition open?** — Quando abre a exibição? — *kwahñdoo abru ah ehzeebeesãhoo*

- **Is it open...** — Está aberto/a... — *eeshta ahbertoo/ ahbertah...*

  - on Mondays? — à segunda-feira? — *a sugooñdah faheerah*

  - at the weekend? — ao fim-de-semana? — *aoo feem du sumahnah*

- **Can I/we visit (the monastery)?** — Pode-se visitar (o mosteiro)? — *podusu veezeetar (oo mooshtaheeroo)*

- **Is it open to the public?** — Está aberto/a ao público? — *eeshta ahbertoo/ ahbertah aoo poobleekoo*

YOU MAY HEAR...

Está aberto/a das ... às...	*eeshta ahbertoo/ah dahsh ... ash...*	It's open from ... to...
Está fechado/a...	*eeshta fushadoo/ah...*	It's closed...
à segunda-feira	*a sugooñdah faheerah*	on Monday
ao domingo	*aoo doomeengoo*	on Sunday

Está fechado/a...	*eeshta fushadoo/ah...*	It's closed for...
para o inverno	***pah***rah oo *eenver*noo	the winter
para obras	***pah***rah *ob*rahsh	repairs

✳ visiting places

YOU MAY SEE...

aberto	open
é proibido mexer	do not touch
é proibido tirar fotografias com flash	no flash photography
entrada proibida	no entry
fechado (para obras)	closed (for restoration)
horário de abertura	opening hours
privado	private
visitas guiadas	guided tours

YOU MAY WANT TO SAY...

How much does it cost to get in?	Quanto custa a entrada?	*kwahñto kooshtah ah ehntradah*
Two adults, please.	Dois adultos, por favor.	*doheesh ahdooltoosh, poor fahvohr*
One adult and two children, please.	Um adulto e duas crianças, por favor.	*ooñ ahdooltoo ee dooahsh kreeahnsahsh, poor fahvohr*

sightseeing and activities

A family ticket, please.	Um bilhete de família.	*oom beellêhtu du fahmeeleeah*
Is there a reduction for...	Há redução para...	*a rudoosãhoo pahrah...*
students?	estudantes?	*eeshtoodahntush*
pensioners?	pensionistas?	*pehnseeooneeshtahsh*
children?	crianças?	*kreeahnsahsh*
Is there...	Há...	*a...*
wheelchair access?	acesso a cadeira de rodas?	*ahsesoo ah kahdaheerahsh du rodahsh*
an audio tour?	uma visita guiada gravada?	*oomah veezeetah geeadah grahvadah*
Are there guided tours (in English)?	Há visitas guiadas (em inglês?)	*a veezeetahsh geeadahsh (aheem eenglêhsh)*
Can I/we take photos?	Pode-se tirar fotografias?	*podusu teerar footoograhfeeahsh*
Could you take a photo of us, please?	Podia tirar-nos uma fotografia?	*poodeeah teerarnoosh oomah footoograhfeeah*
When was this built?	Quando foi construido?	*kwahñdoo fohee kohñshtrooeedoo*
Who painted that?	Quem pintou aquilo?	*kaheem peentohoo ahkeeloo*
How old is it?	Quantos anos tem?	*kwahñtoosh ahnoosh taheem*

YOU MAY HEAR...

Custa ... euros por pessoa.	*kooshtah ... eroosh poor pusohah*	It costs ... euros per person.
Há redução para estudantes/ pensionistas.	*a rudoosãhoo pahrah eeshtoodahntush/ pehnseeoneeshtahsh*	There's a reduction for students/ pensioners.
Entrada grátis para crianças com menos de...	*ehntradah grateesh pahrah kreeahnsahsh kohm mehnoosh du...*	Free entrance to children under...
Há rampas para cadeiras de rodas.	*a rahmpahsh pahrah kahdaheerahsh du rodahsh*	There are wheelchair ramps.

* going on tours and trips

YOU MAY WANT TO SAY...

I'd like to join the tour to...	Desejo seguir a visita a...	*duzêhjoo sugeer ah veezeetah a...*
What time... does it leave? does it get back?	A que horas... parte? regressa?	*ah ku orahsh... part rugresah*
How long is it?	Quanto tempo demora?	*kwahñtoo tehmpoo dumorah*
Where does it leave from?	Donde parte?	*dohnd part*
Does the guide speak English?	O/a guia fala inglês?	*oo/ah geeah falah eenglêhsh*

- How much is it?   Quanto custa?   *kwahñtoo kooshtah*

- Is lunch/ accommodation included?   O almoço/ alojamento está incluído?   *oo almohsoo/ ahloojahmehntoo eeshta eenklooeedoo*

- When's the next...   Quando é a próxima viagem...   *kwahñdoo e ah proseemah veeajaheeñ...*

  boat trip?   de barco?   *du barkoo*
  day trip?   de um dia?   *du ooñ deeah*

- Can we hire...   Podemos alugar...   *poodehmoosh ahloogar...*

  a guide?   um guia?   *ooñ geeah*
  an English-speaking guide?   um guia que fale inglês?   *ooñ geeah ku falu eenglêhsh*

- How much is it (per day)?   Quanto é (por dia)?   *kwahnto e (poor deeah)*

- I'm with a group.   Estou com um grupo.   *eeshtoh kohm ooñ groopoo*

- I've lost my group.   Perdi-me do meu grupo.   *purdeemu doo mehoo groopoo*

YOU MAY HEAR...

Parte às...	*part ash...*	It leaves at...
Regressa às...	*rugresah ash...*	It gets back at...
Parte de...	*part du...*	It leaves from...
Qual é o nome do seu grupo?	*kwal e oo nohm doo sehoo groopoo*	What's the name of your group?

✳ entertainment

● Throughout the country, and in particular in the cities, you'll find a varied programme of culture: rock and pop festivals, classical and popular music events, opera, theatre, cinemas, dance and football games and bullfighting.

Nightlife in Portugal can start late: from 9pm onwards. Usually theatres will have performances starting at 9pm or 9.30pm and discos can go on until 5am or 6am. Films are usually shown in their original language with Portuguese subtitles. On Mondays many cinemas offer reductions.

YOU MAY SEE...

balcão	dress circle
bancadas	stand, grandstand
bilhetes para a sessão de hoje	tickets for today's performance
camarotes	boxes
cinema	cinema
concerto	concert hall
discoteca	disco
entrada	entry
esgotado	sold out
fila	row, tier
hipódromo	racecourse
não permitida a entrada a menores de 18	no admittance to under-18s

sightseeing and activities

não permitida a entrada uma vez que a sessão tenha começado	no entry once the performance has begun
ópera	opera house
plateia	stalls
reservas com antecedência	advance booking
sem intervalo	no interval
teatro	theatre

YOU MAY WANT TO SAY...

- **Is there anything for children?** — Há alguma coisa para crianças? — *a algoomah koheezah pahrah kreeahnsahsh*

- **Is there...** — Há... — *a...*
  - **a cinema round here?** — um cinema aqui perto? — *oom seenehmah ahkee pert*
  - **a good club round here?** — um bom clube aqui perto? — *oom bohm kloob ahkee pert*

- **What's on...** — O que há... — *oo ku a...*
  - **tonight?** — esta noite? — *eshtah noheet*
  - **tomorrow?** — amanhã? — *amahnnyãh*
  - **at the theatre?** — no teatro? — *noo teeatroo*
  - **at the cinema?** — no cinema? — *noo seenehmah*

- **When does the game/performance start?** — Quando começa o jogo/o espectáculo? — *kwahndoo koomesah oo johgoo/oo eeshpetakooloo*

- **What time does it finish?** — A que horas acaba? — *ah ku orahsh ahkabah*

● How long is it?	Quanto tempo demora?	*kwahñtoo tehmpoo dumorah*
● Do we need to book?	Precisamos reservar?	*pruseezahmoosh ruzurvar*
● Where can I get tickets?	Onde posso comprar bilhetes?	*ohnd pos kohmprar beellêhtush*
● Is it suitable for children?	É apropriado para crianças?	*e ahproopreeadoo pahrah kreeahnsahsh*
● Has the film got subtitles?	O filme tem legendas?	*oo feelm taheeñ lugehndahsh*
● Is it dubbed?	É dobrado?	*e doobradoo*

YOU MAY HEAR...

● Pode-se comprar bilhetes aqui.	*podusu kohmprar beellêhtush ahkee*	You can buy tickets here.
● Começa às...	*koomesah ash...*	It starts at...
● Acaba às...	*ahkabah ash...*	It finishes at...
● É melhor reservar com antecedência.	*e mullor ruzurvar kohñ ahntusudehnseeah*	It's best to book in advance.
● É dobrado.	*e doobradoo*	It's dubbed.
● Tem legendas (em inglês).	*taheeñ lugehndahsh (aheeñ eenglêhsh)*	It's got (English) subtitles.

✳ booking tickets

YOU MAY WANT TO SAY...

- Can you get me tickets for...
  - the ballet?
  - the football match?
  - the theatre?

  Pode arranjar-me bilhetes para...
  - o ballet?
  - o jogo de futebol?
  - o teatro?

  pod ahrrahnjarmu beellehtush pahrah...
  - *o bale*
  - *oo johgoo du footubol*
  - *oo teeatroo*

- Are there any seats left for Saturday?

  Ainda há lugares para sábado?

  aheendah a loogarush pahrah sabahdoo

- I'd like to book...
  - a box
  - two seats in the stalls

  Queria reservar...
  - um balcão
  - dois lugares na plateia

  kureeah ruzurvar...
  - *oom balkāhoo*
  - *doheesh loogarush nah plahtaheeah*

- Is there wheelchair access?

  Tem acesso a cadeira de rodas?

  taheem ahsesoo ah kahdaheerah du rodahsh

YOU MAY HEAR...

Quantos?	*kwahñtoosh*	How many?
Para quando?	*pahrah kwahñdoo*	When for?
Tem cartão de crédito?	*taheem kahrtāhoo du kredeetoo*	Do you have a credit card?
Lamento mas estamos esgotados para essa noite/ esse dia.	*lahmehntoo mahsh eeshtahmoosh eeshgootadoosh pahrah esah noheet/ ehs deeah*	I'm sorry, we're sold out that night/day.

✳ at the show

What film/play/opera is on tonight?	Que filme/peça/ópera é esta noite?	ku feelm/**pe**sah/**o**purah e **esh**tah **noh**eet
One adult and two children, please.	Um adulto e duas crianças, por favor.	ooṁ ah**dool**too ee **doo**ahsh kreeahnsahsh, poor fah**vohr**
How much is that?	Quanto é isso?	**kwahn**too e **ee**soo
We'd like to sit...	Queríamos sentar...	ku**ree**ah**moosh** sehn**tar**...
at the front	à frente	a **frehnt**
at the back	atrás	ah**trash**
in the middle	no centro	noo **sehn**troo
We've reserved seats.	Temos lugares reservados.	**teh**moosh loo**ga**rush ruzur**va**doosh
My name is...	Chamo-me ...	**shah**moomu...
Is there an interval?	Tem intervalo?	ta**heeṁ** eentur**va**loo
Where...	Onde...	ohnd...
are the stalls?	é a plateia?	e ah plah**ta**heeah
is the bar?	é o bar?	e oo bar
Where are the toilets?	Onde são as casas de banho?	ohnd **sã**hoo ahsh **ka**zahsh du **bah**ñnyoo
Can you stop talking, please?	Pode parar de falar, por favor?	pod pah**rar** du fah**lar**, poor fah**vohr**

105

✳ sports and activities

aluguer de barcos	boat hire
campo	countryside
campo de futebol	football pitch
campo de golfe	golf course
centro desportivo	sports hall
court de ténis	tennis court
eléctrico	cable car
perigo	danger
piscina (ao ar livre/coberta)	swimming pool (outdoor/indoor)
praia	beach
primeiros socorros	first aid
proibido nadar	no swimming
proibido passar	entry prohibited
proibido pescar	no fishing

YOU MAY WANT TO SAY...

- Can I...   Posso...   pos...
    go riding?   andar a cavalo?   ahndar ah kahvaloo
    go fishing?   pescar?   pushkar
    go skiing?   fazer esqui?   fahzêhr eeshkee
    go swimming?   nadar?   nahdar

- Where can I   Onde posso...   ohnd pos...
    play tennis?   jogar ténis?   joogar teneesh
    play golf?   jogar golfe?   joogar gohlf

- I'm a beginner. Sou principiante. *soh preenseepeeahnt*

- I'm quite experienced. Tenho bastante experiência. *taheennyoo bahshtahnt aheeshpureeehñseeah*

- How much does it cost... Quanto custa... *kwahñtoo kooshtah...*
    - per hour? por hora? *poor orah*
    - per day? por dia? *poor deeah*
    - per week? por semana? *poor sumahnah*
    - per round? por volta? *poor voltah*

- Can I hire... Posso alugar... *pos ahloogar...*
    - equipment? equipamento? *ehkeepahmehntoo*
    - clubs? clubes? *kloobush*
    - racquets? raquetas? *raketahsh*

- Can I have lessons? Posso ter lições? *pos tehr leesōheesh*

- Do I have to be a member? Tenho de ser sócio/a? *taheennyoo du sehr soseeoo/ah*

- Can children do it too? As crianças também podem tomar parte? *ahsh kreeahnsahsh tahmbaheeñ podaheeñ toomar part*

- Is there a reduction for children? Há um preço reduzido para crianças? *a ooñ prehsoo rudoozeedoo pahrah kreeahnsahsh*

- What's... Como... *kohmoo...*
    - the water like? está a água? *eeshta ah agooah*
    - the snow like? está a neve? *eeshta ah nev*

YOU MAY HEAR...

Custa ... euros por hora.	*kooshtah ... eroosh poor orah*	It costs ... euros per hour.
Tem um depósito reembolsável de ... euros.	*taheem oom dupozeetoo rreeaheembohlsavel du ... eroosh*	There's a refundable deposit of ... euros.
Estamos cheios neste momento.	*eeshtahmoosh shaheeoosh nêhsht moomehntoo*	We're booked up at the moment.
Que tamanho é?	*ku tahmahnnyoo e*	What size are you?
Precisa de... uma foto seguro	*pruseezah du... oomah fotoo sugooroo*	You need... a photo insurance

* at the beach, river or pool

YOU MAY WANT TO SAY...

Can I swim here?	Posso nadar aqui?	*pos nahdar ahkee*
Is it dangerous?	É perigoso?	*e pureegohzoo*
Is it safe for children?	É seguro para crianças?	*e sugooroo pahrah kreeahnsahsh*
When is high tide?	Quando está maré alta?	*kwahndoo eeshta mahre altah*
Is the water clean?	A água é limpa?	*ah agooah e leempah*

shops&services

* shopping

In Portugal you'll find more small individual shops than large department stores. In the last few years, however, one of the most popular developments throughout Portugal has been the shopping malls, os centros comerciais.

Shops are generally open between 9am and 7pm on Mondays to Fridays, and close for lunch between 1pm and 3pm. On Saturdays, they are open from 9am to 1pm.

YOU MAY SEE...

aberto (todo o dia)	open (all day)
aberto todos os dias	open every day
artigos de desporto	sports goods
brinquedos	toys
cabeleireiro/a	hairdresser's
caixa	cashier
calçado	footwear
centro comercial	shopping centre
charcutaria	delicatessen
correios	post office
discos	records
doces	sweet shop
drogaria	drugstore
electrodomésticos	electrical goods
entrada	entrance
farmácia	chemist

farmácia/médico de serviço	duty chemist (or doctor)
fechado/encerrado	closed
florista	florist
gabinete de provas	fitting rooms
hipermercado	hypermarket
lembranças	souvenirs
liquidação	closing down sale
livraria	bookshop
loja de bolos	cake shop
mercearia	groceries
mobiliário	furniture shop
moda	fashion
não mexer	please do not touch
oculista	optician's
ourivesaria	jeweller's
padaria	baker's
papelaria	stationer's
pastelaria	cake shop/café
peixaria	fishmonger's
perfumaria	perfumery
relojoaria	watchmaker's
roupas	clothes/fashions
saldos	sale
sapataria	shoe shop
supermercado	supermarket
tabacaria	tobacconist's
talho	butcher's

YOU MAY WANT TO SAY...

Where is...	Onde é...	*ohnd é...*
the shopping street?	a rua das lojas?	*ah rrooah dahs lojahs*
the post office?	o correio?	*oo koorraheeoo*
Where can I buy...	Onde posso comprar...	*ohnd pos kohm prar...*
walking boots?	botas para andar ?	*botahsh pahrah ahndar*
a map?	um mapa ?	*oom mapah*
I'd like...	Queria...	*kureeah...*
that one there, please	aquele ali, por favor	*ahkehl ahlee poor fahvohr*
this one here, please	este aqui, por favor	*ehsht ahkee poor fahvohr*
two of those, please	dois desses por favor	*doheesh dêhsush poor fahvohr*
Have you got... ?	Tem... ?	*taheem...*
How much does it cost?	Quanto custa?	*kwahñtoo kooshtah*
How much do they cost?	Quanto custam?	*kwahñtoo kooshtahm*
Can you write it down, please?	Pode escrever, por favor?	*pod eeshkruvêhr, poor fahvohr*
I'm just looking.	Estou só a ver.	*eehstoh so ah vêhr*
There's one in the window.	Há um/uma na montra.	*a oom/oomah nah mohñtrah*
I'll take it.	Levo-o/a.	*levoo-oo/levoo-ah*

- Is there a guarantee? — Tem garantia? — *taheem̃ gahrahnteeah*

- Can you... — Pode... — *pod...*
  - keep it for me? — guardar-mo/ guardar-ma? — *gooahrdarmoo/ gooahrdarmah*
  - order it for me? — mandar vir? — *mahndar veer*

- I need to think about it. — Preciso pensar. — *pruseezoo pehnsar*

YOU MAY HEAR...

- Precisa de ajuda? — *pruseezah du ahjoodah* — Can I help you?

- Custa ... euros. — *kooshtah ... eroosh* — It costs ... euros.

- Lamento, mas acabaram. — *lahmehntoo, mahsh ahkahbarahm̃* — I'm sorry, we've sold out.

- Podemos mandar vir. — *poodehmoosh mahndar veer* — We can order it for you.

* paying

YOU MAY WANT TO SAY...

- Where do I pay? — Onde posso pagar? — *ohnd pos pahgar*

- Do you take credit cards? — Aceita cartões de crédito? — *ahsaheetah kahrtõheesh du kredeetoo*

- Can you wrap it, please? — Pode embrulhar, por favor? — *pod ehmbroollar, poor fahvohr*

113

buying clothes and shoes

- Can I have...
  - the receipt?
  - a bag, please?

  - my change?

- Pode dar-me...
  - um recibo?
  - um saco, por favor?

  - troco?

- pod **dar**mu...
  - ooṁ rru**see**boo
  - ooṁ **sa**koo, poor fah**vohr**

  - **troh**koo

- Sorry, I haven't got any change.
- Lamento, mas não tenho troco.
- lah**mehn**too, mahsh nãhoo **taheen**nyoo **troh**koo

YOU MAY HEAR...

- Deseja que embrulhe?
- du**zê**jah ku ehm**broo**llu
- Do you want it wrapped?

- Como paga?
- **koh**moo **pa**gah
- How do you want to pay?

- Posso ver...
  - o bilhete de identidade, por favor?
  - o seu passaporte, por favor?

- pos **vêhr**...
  - oo bee**llêh**tu du eedehntee**dad**, poor fah**vohr**
  - oo **seh**oo pasah**port**, poor fah**vohr**

- Can I see...
  - some ID, please?

  - your passport, please?

✷ buying clothes and shoes
(see **clothes and shoe sizes**, page 21)

YOU MAY WANT TO SAY...

- Have you got...
  - the next size down/up?

  - another colour?

- Tem...
  - o número abaixo/ acima?

  - outra cor?

- ta**heeṁ**...
  - oo **noo**muroo ah**bae**eshoo/ ah**see**mah

  - **oh**trah kohr

What size is this in British sizes?	Que tamanho é em inglês?	*ku tahmahñnyoo e aheeñ eenglêhsh*
I'm size...	Sou tamanho...	*soh tahmahñnyoo...*
I'm looking for...	Estou à procura de...	*eeshtoh a prokoorah du...*
a shirt	uma camisa	*oomah kahmeezah*
a pair of jeans	um par de jeans	*ooñ par du jeens*
a jumper	um pulover	*ooñ poolover*
a jacket	um casaco	*ooñ kahzakoo*
a skirt	uma saia	*oomah saeeah*
a t-shirt	uma t-shirt	*oomah t-shirt*
a hat	um chapéu	*ooñ shahpeeoo*
A pair of...	Um par de...	*ooñ par du...*
trainers	ténis	*teneesh*
shoes	sapatos	*sahpatoosh*
sandals	sandálias	*sahndaleeahsh*
Where are the changing rooms, please?	Onde estão os gabinetes de provas?	*ond eeshtãhoo oosh gahbeenehtush du provahsh*

* changing rooms

Can I try this on, please?	Posso provar, por favor?	*pos proovar, poor fahvohr*
It's too big/small.	É muito grande/ pequeno.	*e mooeentoo pukehnoo*
It doesn't suit me.	Não me fica bem.	*nãhoo mu feekah baheeñ*

115

Quer provar?	*ker proovar*	Would you like to try it/them on?
Qual é o tamanho?	*kwal e oo tahmahñnyoo*	What size are you?
Trago-lhe outro/outra.	*tragoollu ohtroo/ohtrah*	I'll get you another one.
Lamento, mas é o último.	*lahmehntoo, mahsh e oo oolteemoo*	Sorry, that's the last one.

* exchanges and refunds

● Shops that don't like exchanging goods show the sign: Não fazemos trocas or Não fazemos reembolsos (we don't give refunds). Always check with the shop assistant and keep the receipt, o recibo. To ask if they do returns, say Fazem trocas? To ask if you can return it, Posso devolver?

Excuse me...	Desculpe...	*dushkoolp...*
this is faulty	isto está estragado	*eeshtoo eeshta eeshtrahgadoo*
this doesn't fit	não serve	*nãhoo serv*
I'd like...	Queria...	*kureeah...*
a refund	reembolso	*rreeehmbohlsoo*
a new one	outro	*ohtroo*
I'd like to ... this.	Queria ... este/esta.	*kureeah ... êhsht/eshtah*
return	devolver	*duvolvêhr*
exchange	trocar	*trookar*

Tem...	*taheem̃...*	Have you got...
o recibo?	*oo rruseeboo*	the receipt?
a garantia?	*ah gahrahnteeah*	the guarantee?
Lamento, mas não trocamos.	*lahmehntoo, mahsh nãhoo trookahmoosh*	Sorry, we don't give refunds.

✳ bargaining

Is this your best price?	Este é o melhor preço que pode fazer?	*ehsht e oo mehllor prêhsoo ku pod fahzêhr*
It's too expensive.	É muito caro.	*e mooeentoo karoo*
Is there a reduction for cash?	Não há desconto por pagar com dinheiro?	*nãhoo a duskohñtoo poor pahgar kohm̃ deennyaheeroo*
I'll give you...	Dou-lhe...	*doh-llu...*
That's my final offer.	É a minha última oferta.	*e ah meennyah oolteemah ofertah*

✳ photography

Can you develop this film for me?	Pode revelar este filme?	*pod ruvular ehsht feelm*

I have a digital camera.	Tenho uma máquina fotográfica digital.	*taheennyoo oomah makeenah footoografeekah deegeetal*
Can you print from this memory card?	Pode imprimir deste cartão de memória?	*pod ehmpreemeer dêhsht kahrtãhoo du memoreeah*
When will it/they be ready?	Quando está pronto/a Quando estão prontos/as?	*kwahndoo eeshta prohntoo/prohntah kwahndoo eeshtãhoo prohntoosh/ prohntahsh*
Do you have an express service?	Tem serviço rápido?	*taheeñ surveesoo rrapeedoo*
Does it cost extra?	Custa mais?	*kooshtah maeesh*
How much does it cost... per film? per print?	Quanto custa... por filme? por foto?	*kwahñtoo kooshtah... poor feelm poor foto*
I need... a colour film	Preciso de... um rolo a cores	*pruseezoo du... ooñ rohloo ah kohrush*
a black and white film	um rolo a preto e branco	*ooñ rohloo ah prêhtoo ee brahnkoo*
a memory card	um cartão de memória	*oom kahrtãhoo de mumoreeah*
I'd like... a 24 exposure film	Queria... um rolo de vinte e quatro	*kureeah... ooñ rohloo du veent ee kwatro*

a 36 exposure film	um rolo de trinta e seis	*oom rohloo du treeñtah ee saheesh*
a disposable camera, please	uma máquina fotográfica descartável, por favor	*oomah makeenah footoografeekah dushkahrtavel, poor fahvohr*
● My camera is broken.	A minha máquina fotográfica não funciona.	*ah meennyah makeenah footoografeekah nãhoo foonseeohnah*
● Do you do repairs?	Arranja máquinas fotográficas?	*ahrrahñjah makeenahsh footoografeekahsh*

YOU MAY HEAR...

● De que tamanho deseja as fotos?	*du ku tahmahññyoo duzêhjah ahsh fotosh*	What size do you want your prints?
● Deseja papel semi-mate ou brilhante?	*duzêhjah pahpel semee-mat oh breellahnt*	Do you want them semi-matt or glossy?
● Volte... amanhã daqui a uma hora	*volt... amahnnyãh dahkee ah oomah orah*	Come back... tomorrow in an hour
● Quantas fotos quer?	*kwahntahsh fotosh ker*	How many exposures do you want?

✳ at the tobacconist

● A tabacaria used to be a shop that sold mainly cigarettes, cigars, matches and lighters. Nowadays tabacarias also sell newspapers, magazines, postcards, pens, paper, lottery tickets and bus tickets. If you need to buy stamps, go to the post office.

YOU MAY WANT TO SAY...

● Can I have a packet of cigarettes?	Quero um maço de cigarros.	*keroo oom masoo du seegarroosh*
● Do you have matches/lighters?	Tem fósforos/ isqueiros?	*taheem foshfooroosh/ eeshkaheeroosh*
● Do you have any cigars?	Tem charutos?	*taheem shahrootoosh*
● Do you have bus tickets for Carris?	Tem cadernetas de bilhetes da Carris?	*taheem kahdurnêhtahsh du beellêhtush dah kahrreesh*

✳ at the post office

● Post office (Correios) opening times are from 8.30am to 6pm Monday to Friday. Major cities will also have one post office open on a Saturday. Stamps are available from hotels and stationers as well. Look for the sign with a red horse on a white circle.

YOU MAY WANT TO SAY...

- A stamp for ... please.
  - Um selo para ... por favor.
  - ooῆ *sêhloo para ...* *poor fahvohr*
    - the UK
      - o Reino Unido
      - oo *rraheenoo* *ooneedoo*
    - America
      - a América
      - ah *ahmereekah*
    - Ireland
      - a Irlanda
      - ah *eerlahndah*

- Can I send this...
  - Posso mandar isto...
  - pos *mahndar eeshtoo...*
    - registered, please?
      - registado, por favor?
      - *rrujeeshtadoo,* *poor fahvohr*
    - airmail, please?
      - por via aérea, por favor?
      - *poor veeah ahereeah,* *poor fahvohr*

- It contains...
  - Tem...
  - *taheem...*

- Do you change money here?
  - Troca dinheiro aqui?
  - *troka deennyaheeroo* *ahkee*

- Can I have a receipt, please?
  - Dá-me um recibo, por favor?
  - *damu ooῆ rruseeboo,* *poor fahvohr*

YOU MAY HEAR...

- Ponha na balança, por favor.
  - *pohnnyah nah* *bahlahnsah, poor* *fahvohr*
  - Put it on the scales, please.

- O que tem dentro?
  - *oo ku taheeῆ* *dehntroo*
  - What's in it?

- Por favor preencha este formulário para a alfândega.
  - *poor fahvohr* *preeehnshah ehsht* *foomoolareeoo* *pahrah ah alfahῆdugah*
  - Please fill in this customs declaration form.

✳ at the bank

● Banks open from 8.30am to 3pm Monday to Friday.

● Excuse me, where's the foreign exchange counter?
Desculpe, onde é o balcão do câmbio?
dushkoolp, ond e oo balkāhoo doo kahm̃beeoo

● Is there a cashpoint machine here?
Há uma caixa aqui?
a oomah kaeeshah ahkee

● The cashpoint machine has eaten my card.
A caixa ficou com o meu cartão.
ah kaeeshah feekoh kohm̃ oo mehoo kahrtāhoo

● I've forgotten my pin number.
Esqueci-me do código pessoal.
eeshkeseemu doo kodeegoo pusooal

● Can I check the balance of my account, please?
Posso verificar o saldo da minha conta, por favor?
pos vureefeekar oo saldoo dah meennyah kohñtah, poor fahvohr

● My account number is...
O número da minha conta é...
oo noomuroo dah meennyah kohñtah e...

● My name is...
O meu nome é...
oo mehoo nohm e...

● I'd like to...
withdraw some money
pay some money in
cash this cheque
Queria...
levantar dinheiro
depositar dinheiro
trocar este cheque por dinheiro
kureeah...
luvahntar deennyaheeroo
dupoozeetar deennyaheeroo
trookar ehsht shek poor deennyaheeroo

YOU MAY HEAR...

Os documentos de identidade, por favor.	*oosh dookoo**mehn**toosh du eedehntee**dad**, poor fah**vohr***	**ID, please.**
O passaporte, por favor.	*oo pasah**port**, poor fah**vohr***	**Passport, please.**
O seu saldo é...	*oo sehoo **sal**doo e...*	**Your balance is...**
Está sem fundos.	*ee**shta** sa**heem** **foon**doosh*	**You're overdrawn.**

✴ changing money

● It is rare for hotels or shops to accept travellers' cheques as payment and commissions can be very high. Cash machines are common throughout the country and offer a cheaper and more convenient alternative to counter service. Use a credit card or debit card at a cash machine for a cheaper exchange rate.

YOU MAY WANT TO SAY...

● I'd like to change...	Queria cambiar...	*ku**ree**ah kahm**bee**ar...*
travellers' cheques	travellers' cheques	*tra**vu**lursh **she**kush*
one hundred pounds	cem libras esterlinas	*sa**heem** **lee**brahsh eeshtur**lee**nahsh*
... please.	... por favor.	*... poor fah**vohr***

123

changing money

Can I have...	Dá-me...	*damu...*
small notes	notas pequenas	*notahsh pukehnahsh*
new notes	notas novas	*notahsh novahsh*
some change	trocos	*trokoosh*
... please?	... por favor.	*... poor fahvohr*

Can I get money out on my credit card?	Posso levantar dinheiro com o meu cartão de crédito?	*pos luvahntar deennyaheeroo kohm̃ oo mehoo kahrtãhoo du kredeetoo*

What's the rate today...	Qual é o câmbio hoje...	*kwal e oo kahm̃beeoo oj...*
for the pound?	para a libra esterlina?	*pahrah ah leebrah eeshturleenah*
for the dollar?	para o dólar?	*pahrah oo dolahr*
for the euro?	para o euro?	*pahrah oo eeroo*

YOU MAY HEAR...

Quanto?	*kwahñtoo*	How much?
O passaporte, por favor.	*oo pasahport, poor fahvohr*	Passport, please.
Assine aqui, por favor.	*ahseenu ahkee, poor fahvohr*	Sign here, please.
Está a ... euros a libra esterlina.	*eeshta ah ... eeroosh ah leebrah eeshturleenah*	It's at ... euros to the pound.

shops and services

124

✳ telephones

International phone calls can be made direct from any telephone booth or post office in the country. Public pay phones take both coins and cards. They are found in booths in the streets, in shopping centres and also in bars and restaurants. The cheapest way of making a phone call is with a card. Credifone (phone cards) are available from post offices, kiosks or newsagents and vary in price depending on the latest offer. Cheap-rate international calls are between 8.00pm and 8.00am.

When answering the phone the Portuguese say Estou, literally 'I am'. To say, 'It's John speaking', you say, Daqui fala and add o plus your name if you're a man, or a plus your name if you're a woman: Daqui fala o John/a Jill.

YOU MAY WANT TO SAY...

- **Where's the (nearest) phone?**
  Onde fica o telefone mais próximo?
  ond feekah oo tulufon maeesh proseemoo

- **Is there a public phone?**
  Há um telefone público?
  a oom tulufon poobleekoo

- **Have you got change for the phone, please?**
  Tem moedas para o telefone, por favor?
  taheem mooedahsh pahrah oo tulufon, poor fahvohr

- **I'd like to...**
  Queria...
  kureeah...

  buy a phone card
  comprar um credifone
  kohmprar oom kredeefon

call England	ligar para a Inglaterra	*leegar pahrah ah eenglahterrah*
make a reverse charge call	fazer uma chamada a cobrar no destinatário	*fahzêhr oomah shahmadah ah koobrar noo dusteenahtareeoo*
The number is...	O número é...	*oo noomuroo e ...*
How much does it cost per minute?	Quanto é por minuto?	*kwahñtoo e poor meenootoo*
What's the area code for... ?	Qual é o indicativo da área de...?	*kwal e oo eendeekahteevoo dah areeah du...*
What's the country code for... ?	Qual é o indicativo de...?	*kwal e oo eendeekahteevoo du...*
How do I get an outside line?	Como obtenho linha?	*kohmoo obtaheennyoo leennyah*
Hello.	Estou.	*eeshtoh*
It's ... speaking.	Daqui fala o/a...	*dahkee falah oo/ah...*
Can I have extension ... please?	Dá-me a extensão ... por favor?	*damu ah ehshtehnsãhoo ... poor fahvohr*
Can I speak to... ?	Posso falar com...?	*pos fahlar kohm̃...*
When will he/she be back?	Quando volta?	*kwahñdoo voltah*
I'll ring back.	Volto a ligar.	*voltoo ah leegar*

- **Can I leave a message?** — Posso deixar mensagem? — *pos daheeshar mehnsajehm̃*

- **Can you say ... called?** — Pode dizer que o/a ... telefonou? — *pod deezêhr ku oo/ah ... tulufoonoh*

- **My number is...** — O meu número é o... — *oo mehoo noomuroo e oo...*

- **Sorry, I've got the wrong number.** — Desculpe, é engano. — *dushkulp, e ehñgahnoo*

- **It's a bad line.** — A linha não presta. — *ah leennyah nãhoo prêshtah*

- **I've been cut off.** — Cortaram-me a ligação. — *koortarahm̃mu ah leegahsãhoo*

YOU MAY HEAR...

- Estou. — *eeshtoh* — Hello.

- Quem fala? — *kaheem̃ falah* — Who's calling?

- Desculpe, mas não está. — *dushkulp, mahsh nãhoo eehsta* — Sorry, he/she's not here.

- Qual é o seu número? — *kwal e oo sehoo noomuroo* — What's your number?

- Está ocupado. — *eeshta okoopadoo* — It's engaged.

- Não atende. — *nãhoo ahtehnd* — There's no answer.

- Quer esperar? — *ker eeshpurar* — Do you want to hold?

- Desculpe, é engano. — *dushkulp, e ehñgahnoo* — Sorry, wrong number.

✳ mobiles

Have you got...	Tem...	taheeñ...
a charger for this phone?	um recarregável para este telefone?	ooñ rrukahrrugavel pahrah ehsht tulufon
a SIM card for the local network?	um cartão SIM para o network local?	ooñ kahrtãhoo seem pahrah oo netwahrku lookal
a pay-as-you-go phone?	um telefone recarregável?	ooñ tulufon rrukahrrugavel
Can I hire a mobile?	Posso alugar um telemóvel?	pos ahloogar ooñ telemovel
What's the tariff?	Qual é o tarifário?	kwal e a tahreefareeoo
Are text messages included?	As mensagens a texto estão incluídas?	ahsh mehnsagehñsh ah têhshtoo eeshtãhoo eenklooeedahsh
How do you make a local call?	Como se faz uma ligação local?	kohmoo su fash oomah leegahsãhoo lookal
Is there a code?	Tem indicativo?	taheeñ eendeekahteevoo
How do you send text messages?	Como se manda mensagens a texto?	kohmoo su mahñdah mehnsagehñsh ah têhshtoo

✳ the Internet

● The Internet is growing and becoming very popular, with cyber-cafés appearing in busy towns and tourist areas. Some major post offices also now have Internet booths. Cards can be purchased behind the counter.

● Computing terms in Portuguese tend to be very similar to their English equivalent, both in spelling and pronunciation. So if you don't know a word, just say it in English. Chances are that it is the same or very similar, so people will understand it.

YOU MAY WANT TO SAY...

● Is there an Internet café near here?

Há um café com a internet aqui perto?

a oom kahfe kohm ah eenternet ahkee pertoo

● I'd like to...
  log on

Queria...
  entrar na internet

kureeah...
  ehntrar nah eenternet

  check my emails

  ver os meus emails

  vêhr oosh mehoosh eemaheelsh

● How much is it per minute?

Quanto é por minuto?

kwahñtoo e poo meenootoo

● I can't...
  get in
  log on

Não consigo...
  entrar
  entrar na internet

nãhoo kohnseegoo...
  ehntrar
  ehntrar nah eenternet

● It's not connecting.

Não faz conexão.

nãhoo fash koonesãhoo

It's very slow.	É muito lenta.	*e **mooee**ntoo **leh**ntah*
Can you...	Pode...	*pod...*
print this?	imprimir isto?	*eempree**meer** **eesh**too*
scan this?	fazer o scan?	*fah**zêhr** oo skahn*
Do you have...	Tem...	*taheem̃...*
a CD rom?	um CD rom?	*oom̃ she dêh rrom*
a zip drive?	uma zip drive?	***oo**mah zeep draeev*
a USB lead?	uma tomada USB?	***oo**mah to**ma**dah oo-es-beh*

* faxes

YOU MAY WANT TO SAY...

What's your fax number?	Qual é o seu número de fax?	*kwal e oo **seh**oo **noo**muroo du faks*
Can you send this fax for me, please?	Pode-me mandar esta fax?	*po**du**mu mahn**dar eesh**tah faks*
How much is it?	Quanto é?	*kwah**ñto** e*

health&safety

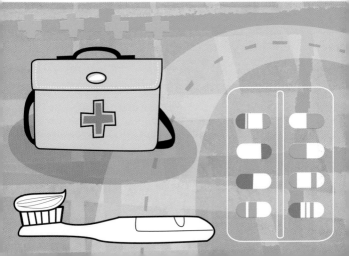

✱ at the chemist's

Have you got something for...	Tem alguma coisa para...	taheeñ algoomah koheezah pahrah...
sunburn?	as queimaduras solares?	ahsh kaheemahdoo-rahsh soolarush
diarrhoea?	a diarreia?	ah deeahrraheeah
period pains?	as dores do período?	ahsh dohrush doo pureeoodoo
headaches?	as dores de cabeça?	ahsh dohrush du kahbêhsah
stomach ache?	as dores de estômago?	ahsh dohrush du eeshtohmahgoo
a sore throat?	as dores de garganta?	ahsh dohrush du gahrgahñtah
I need some ... please.	Preciso de ... por favor.	pruseezoo du ... poor fahvohr
aspirin	aspirina	ahshpeereenah
plasters	pensos rápidos	pehñsoosh rapeedoosh
insect repellent	repelente para insectos	rupulehnt pahrah eensetoosh
suntan lotion	loção do sol	loosãhoo do sol
travel sickness pills	comprimidos para o enjoo	kohmpreemeedoosh pahrah oo ehnjohoo
condoms	preservativos	pruzurvahteevoosh
shampoo	champô	shahmpoh
shower gel	gel de banho	jel du bahñnyoo
deodorant	desotorizante	duzotooreezahnt
toothpaste	pasta dos dentes	pashtah doosh dêhntush
tampons	tampões	tahmpõheesh
sanitary towels	toalhetes	tooahllêhtush

✳ at the doctor's
(see **medical complaints and conditions**, page 135)

● I need a doctor (who speaks English).	Preciso dum médico (que fale inglês).	*pru**see**zoo doo**m̄** **me**deekoo (ku falu een**glêh**sh)*
● Can I make an appointment for...	Posso fazer uma marcação para...	*pos fah**zêhr** oomah mahrkah**sāhoo pah**rah...*
today?	hoje?	*ohj*
tomorrow?	amanhã?	*amah**ññyāh***
● I've run out of my medication.	Acabei os meus medicamentos.	*ahkah**bahee** oosh **me**hoosh mudeekah**mehn**toosh*
● I'm on medication.	Estou a tomar medicamentos	*eesh**toh** ah too**mar** mudeekah**mehn**toosh*
● I've had a ... jab.	Levei uma injecção contra...	*lu**vahee** oomah eenje**sāhoo koh̄n**trah...*
tetanus	o tétano	*oo **te**tahnoo*
typhoid	a tifóide	*ah tee**foeed***
rabies	a raiva	*rra**ee**vah*
● He/she has had a ... vaccination.	Ele/Ela levou uma vacina contra...	*el/**êh**lah lu**voh** oomah vah**see**nah **koh̄n**trah...*
polio	a polio	*ah **pol**leeoo*
measles	o sarampo	*oo sha**rahm̄**poo*
mumps	a papeira	*ah pah**pahee**rah*
● Can I have a receipt for my health insurance, please?	Pode dar-me um recibo para o meu seguro, por favor?	*pod **dar**mu oo**m̄** ru**see**boo **pah**rah oo **me**hoo su**goo**roo, poor fah**vohr***

✳ describing your symptoms

● To indicate where the pain is, you can simply point and say 'it hurts here' (Dói aqui). Otherwise you'll need to look up the Portuguese for the appropriate part of the body, see page 137.

YOU MAY WANT TO SAY...

● I don't feel well.   Não me sinto bem.   *nãhoo mu **seen**too baheem̃*

● It's my...   É o meu/a minha...   *e oo **meh**oo/ah **meen**nyah...*

● My ... hurts.   Dói-me o meu/ a minha...   ***do**eemu oo **meh**oo/ ah **meen**nyah...*
     stomach   estômago   *eesh**toh**mahgoo*
     head   cabeça   *kah**beh**sah*

● I feel...   Sinto-me...   ***seen**toomu...*
     sick   enjoado/a   *ehnjoo**a**doo/ah*
     dizzy   com tonturas   *kohm̃ tohn**too**rahs*

● I can't ... properly.   Não consigo ... normalmente.   *nãhoo kohn**see**goo ... normal**mehnt***
     breathe   respirar   *rush**pee**rar*
     sleep   dormir   *doo**meer***

● I've cut myself.   Cortei-me.   *koor**tah**eemu*

● I've burnt myself.   Queimei-me.   *kahee**mah**eemu*

● I've been sick.   Vomitei.   *voomee**tah**ee*

health and safety

✳ medical complaints and conditions

I am...	Sou...	soh...
asthmatic	asmático/a	ahshmateekoo/ah
diabetic	diabético/a	deeahbeteekoo/ah
blind	cego/a	segoo/ah
deaf	surdo/a	soordoo/ah
epileptic	epiléptico/a	ehpeeleteekoo/ah
HIV positive	HIV positivo	ahga ee veh poozeeteevoo
I am a wheelchair user.	Ando numa cadeira de rodas.	ahndoo noomah kahdaheerah du rrodahs
I have...	Tenho...	taheennyoo...
difficulty walking	dificuldade em andar	deefeekooldad aheeῆ ahndar
a heart condition	um problema de coração	ooῆ prooblehmah du koorahsãhoo
arthritis	artrite	ahrtreet
high/low blood pressure	a tensão alta/ baixa	ah tehnsãhoo altah/baeeshah
I am pregnant.	Estou grávida.	eehstoh graveedah
I am allergic to...	Sou alérgico/a...	soh ahlergeekoo/ah
antibiotics	a antibióticos	ah ahnteebeeoo-teekoosh
penicillin	a penicilina	puneeseeleenah
cortisone	a cortisona	koorteezohnah
I suffer from...	Sofro de...	sohfroo du...
angina	angina	ahngeenah
migraines	enchaquecas	ehnshakekahs

135

medical complaints

Onde dói?	*ohnd doee*	Where does it hurt?
Está a tomar medicamentos?	*eeshta ah toomar mudeekahmehntoosh...*	Are you on medication?
Preciso medir-lhe a temperatura.	*pruseezoo mudeerllu ah tehmpurahtoorah*	I need to take your temperature.
Dispa-se, por favor.	*deeshpahsu, poor fahvohr*	Get undressed, please.
Não é nada de grave.	*nãhoo e nadah du grav*	It's nothing serious.
Tem uma infecção.	*taheem oomah eenfesãhoo*	You've got an infection.
Está infectado/a.	*eehsta eenfetadoo/ eenfetadah*	It's infected.
Preciso de uma análise...	*pruseezoo du oomah ahnaleezu...*	I need a ... sample.
ao sangue	*aoo sahng*	blood sample
à urina	*a ooreenah*	urine
às fezes	*ash fezush*	stool
Precisa duma radiografia.	*pruseezah doomah radeeoograhfeeah*	You need an X-ray.
Vou dar-lhe uma injecção.	*voh darllu oomah eenjesãhoo*	I'm going to give you an injection.
Tome isto ... vezes ao dia.	*tomu eeshtoo ... vêhzush aoo deeah*	Take this ... times a day.
Precisa de descansar.	*pruseezah du duskahnsar*	You must rest.

Não deve beber.	*nãhoo dev bubêhr*	You mustn't drink.
Precisa ir ao hospital.	*pruseezah eer aoo oshpeetal*	You need to go to hospital.
Torceu o...	*toorsehoo oo...*	You've sprained your...
Partiu o...	*pahrteeoo o...*	You've broken your...
Tem...	*taheem̃...*	You've got...
uma gripe	*oomah greep*	flu
uma apendicite	*oomah apehndeeseet*	appendicitis
uma bronquite	*oomah brohnkeet*	bronchitis
uma fractura	*oomah fratoorah*	a fracture
É um ataque de coração.	*e oom̃ ahtak du koorahsãhoo*	It's a heart attack.

✳ parts of the body

ankle	tornezelo	*toornuzêhloo*
appendix	apêndice	*ahpehndeesu*
arm	braço	*brasoo*
artery	artéria	*ahrtereeah*
back	costas	*koshtahsh*
bladder	bexiga	*busheegah*
blood	sangue	*sahng*
body	corpo	*kohrpoo*
bone	osso	*ohsoo*
bottom	rabo	*raboo*
bowels	intestino	*eentusteenoo*
breast	seio	*saheeoo*

health and safety

137

buttock	nádegas	*nadugahsh*
cartilage	cartilagem	*kahrteelajaheem̃*
chest	peito	*paheetoo*
chin	queixo	*kaheeshoo*
collar bone	clavícula	*klahveekoolah*
ear	orelha (outside)	*orehllah*
	ouvido (inner ear)	*ohveedoo*
elbow	cotovelo	*kootoovêhloo*
eye	olho	*ohllo*
face	cara	*karah*
finger	dedo	*dêhdoo*
foot	pé	*pe*
genitals	genitais	*guneetaeesh*
gland	glândula	*glahndoolah*
hair	cabelo	*kahbêhloo*
hand	mão	*māhoo*
head	cabeça	*kahbêhsah*
heart	coração	*koorahsãhoo*
heel	calcanhar	*kalkahnnyar*
hip	anca	*ahnkah*
jaw	maxilar	*makseelar*
joint	articulação	*ahrteekoolahsãhoo*
kidney	rim	*rreem̃*
knee	joelho	*jooehlloo*
leg	perna	*pernah*
ligament	ligamento	*leegahmehntoo*
lip	lábio	*labeeoo*
liver	fígado	*feegahdoo*
lung	brônquio	*brohnkeeoo*
mouth	boca	*bohkah*
muscle	músculo	*mooshkooloo*
nail	unha	*oonnyah*
neck	pescoço	*puskohsoo*

nerve	nervo	*nehrvoo*
nose	nariz	*nahreesh*
penis	pénis	*peneesh*
private parts	partes privadas	*partush privadahsh*
rib	costela	*kooshtelah*
shoulder	ombro	*ohm̃broo*
skin	pele	*pel*
spine	espinha	*eeshpeennyah*
stomach	estômago	*eeshtohmahgoo*
tendon	tendão	*tehndāhoo*
testicle	testículo	*tushteekooloo*
thigh	coxa	*kohshah*
throat	garganta	*gahrgahntah*
thumb	polgar	*polgar*
toe	dedo do pé	*dêhdoo doo pe*
tongue	língua	*leengooah*
tonsils	amígdalas	*ahmeegdahlahsh*
tooth	dente	*dent*
vagina	vagina	*vajeenah*
vein	veia	*vaheeah*
wrist	pulso	*poolsoo*

✳ at the dentist's

YOU MAY WANT TO SAY...

- I've got toothache. Tenho dores de dentes. *taheennyoo dohrush du dehntush*

- It really hurts. Dói muito. *doee mooeentoo*

- It's my wisdom teeth. É o meu dente do sizo. *e oo mehoo dehnt doo seezoo*

at the dentist's

- I've lost...   Perdi...   *purdee...*
  - a filling   um chumbo   *oom shoomboo*
  - a crown/cap   uma coroa   *oomah koorohah*

- I've broken a tooth.   Parti um dente.   *pahtee oom dehnt*

- Can you fix it temporarily?   Pode arranjá-lo temporariamente?   *pod ahrrahnjaloo tehmpoorarreeahmehnt*

YOU MAY HEAR...

- Abra bem (a boca).   *abrah baheem (ah bohkah)*   Open (your mouth) wide.

- Cerre os dentes.   *serr oosh dehntush*   Bite your jaws together.

- Precisa dum chumbo.   *pruseezah doom shoomboo*   You need a filling.

- Tenho de tirá-lo.   *taheennyoo du teeraloo*   I'll have to take it out.

- Vou dar-lhe uma injecção.   *voh darllu oomah eenjesãhoo*   I'm going to give you an injection.

- Vou pôr-lhe...   *voh pohrllu...*   I'm going to give you...
  - um chumbo temporário   *oom shoomboo tehmpoorareeoo*   a temporary filling
  - uma coroa temporária   *oomah koorohah tehmpoorareeah*   a temporary crown

✳ emergencies

I need...	Preciso...	pruseezoo...
a doctor	dum médico	doom medeekoo
an ambulance	duma ambulância	doomah ahmboolahnseah
the fire brigade	dos bombeiros	doosh bohmbaheeroosh
the police	da polícia	dah pooleeseeah
Immediately!	Imediatamente!	eemudeeatahmehnt
Help!	Ajude-me!/Socorro!	ahjoodumu/ sohkohrroo
Please help me.	Por favor ajude-me.	poor fahvohr ahjoodumu
There's a fire.	Há um incêndio.	a oom eensehndeeoo
There's been an accident.	Houve um acidente.	ohv oom ahseedehnt
I have to use the phone.	Tenho de usar o telefone.	taheennyoo du oozar oo tulufon
I'm lost.	Estou perdido/a.	eeshtoh purdeedoo/ purdeedah
I've lost my...	Perdi...	purdee...
son	o meu filho	oo mehoo feelloo
daughter	a minha filha	ah meennyah feellah
friends	os meus amigos	oosh mehoosh ahmeegoosh
friends (female only)	as minhas amigas	ahsh meennyahsh ahmeegahsh

● Stop!   Pare!   *paru*

✳ police

● Sorry, I didn't realise it was against the law.

Desculpe, não sabia que era contra a lei.

dushkoolp, nãhoo sahbeeah ku erah kohñtrah a lahee

● Here are my documents.

Aqui estão os meus documentos.

ahkee eeshtãhoo oosh mehoosh dookoomehntoosh

● I haven't got my passport on me.

Não tenho o meu passaporte comigo.

nãhoo taheennyoo oo mehoo pasahport koomeegoo

● I don't understand.

Não compreendo.

nãhoo kohñpreeehndoo

● I'm innocent.

Estou inocente.

eeshtoh eenoosehnt

● I need a lawyer (who speaks English).

Preciso dum advogado (que fale inglês).

pruseezoo dooñ ahduvoogadoo (ku falu eenglehsh)

● I want to contact my embassy/ consulate.

Quero contactar a minha embaixada/o meu consulado.

keroo kohñtahtar ah meennyah aheeñbaeeshadah

● Tem de pagar uma multa.

taheeñ du pahgar oomah mooltah

You have to pay a fine.

Os documentos, por favor.	*oosh dookoomehn-toosh, poor fahvohr*	Your documents, please.
Venha comigo.	*vaheennyah koomeegoo*	Come with me.
Está preso.	*eeshta prêhzoo*	You're under arrest.

✳ reporting crime

I want to report a theft.	Quero participar um furto.	*keroo pahrteeseepar ooم̃ foortoo*
My ... has been stolen.	O meu/A minha ... foi roubado/a.	*oo mehoo/ah meennyah ... fohee rohbadoo/rohbadah*
purse	bolsa	*bohlsah*
wallet	carteira	*kahrtaheerah*
suitcase	mala	*malah*
Our car has been broken into.	O nosso carro foi assaltado.	*oo nosoo karroo fohee ahsaltadoo*
I've lost my...	Perdi...	*purdee...*
credit cards	os meus cartões de crédito	*oosh mehoosh kahtõheesh du kredeetoo*
luggage	a minha bagagem	*ah meennyah bahgajaheeم̃*
I've been...	Fui...	*fooee...*
mugged	roubado	*rrohbadoo*
attacked	atacado	*ahtahkadoo*

YOU MAY HEAR...

Quando aconteceu?	*kwahñdoo ahkohtusehoo*	When did it happen?
Onde?	*ohnd*	Where?
O que aconteceu?	*oo ku ahkohntusehoo*	What happened?
Tem de preencher este impresso.	*taheem du preeehñshêhr êhsht eempresoo*	You'll have to fill in this form.
Como era ele/ela?	*kohmoo erah el/êhlah*	What did he/she look like?

YOU MAY WANT TO SAY...

It happened...	Aconteceu...	*ahkohntuseho...*
this morning	esta manhã	*eshtah mahñnyã*
on the beach	na praia	*nah praeeah*
... minutes ago	há ... minutos	*a ... meenootoosh*
He/She had...	Ele/Ela tinha...	*el/elah teennyah...*
blonde hair	cabelo louro	*kahbêhloo lohroo*
a knife	uma faca	*oomah fakah*
He/She was...	Ele/Ela era...	*el/elah erah...*
tall	alto/a	*alto/altah*
young	novo/a	*nohvoo/novah*
short	baixo/a	*baeeshoo/baeeshah*
He/She was wearing...	Ele/Ela tinha...	*el/êhlah teennyah...*
jeans	jeans	*jeens*
a shirt	uma saia	*oomah saeeah*

basic grammar

✳ nouns

Portuguese nouns (names of people or things) are either masculine or feminine. Words that are very similar to English are usually masculine: o designer, o email, o self-service.

Masculine nouns usually end in o and feminine nouns usually end in a, são, ção, gião, stão, gem, ade, ude and ie.

o carro	car
a cama	bed
a canção	song
a paragem	(bus) stop
a cidade	city

some exceptions:

o dia	day
o telegrama	telegram

Any other endings can be either masculine or feminine.

✳ plurals

Words that end in a, o, u, or e, add an s:

a batata	as batatas	potatoes
o vestido	os vestidos	dresses
o museu	os museus	museums
o estudante	os estudantes	students

For words ending in a consonant (except l or m), add es:

professor	professores	teachers
francês	franceses	French (people)

Words ending in al, el, ol, change to ais, éis or óis:

postal	postais	postcards
pastel	pastéis	cake, pastry
rissol	rissóis	rissoles

Words ending in m, change to ns:

paragem	paragens	(bus) stop

Words ending in ão, change to ões:

peão	peões	pedestrians

✳ articles (a, an, the)

Articles (o, a, os, as, for 'the' and um, uma, uns, umas, for 'a, an') are used with nouns and depend on whether the noun is masculine or feminine.

	MASCULINE	FEMININE
singular	o, um	a, uma
plural	os, uns	as, umas

a camioneta the coach   as sardinhas the sardines
o batido the milkshake   os livros the books
uma mesa a table   um quarto a bedroom

uns/umas often mean 'some':

uns livros some books   umas canetas some pens
uns ovos some eggs   umas revistas some magazines

The articles o, a, os, as when followed by a (to), de (of, from) and em (in, on) change to combine both words:

	SINGULAR	PLURAL
a	a+o = ao	a+os = aos
	a+a = à	a+as = às
de	de+o = do	de+os = dos
	de+a = da	de+as = das
em	em+o = no	em+os = nos
	em+a = na	em+as = nas

Vou *ao* teatro *(Vou a+o teatro)* I'm going to the theatre.
Diga *às* crianças *(Diga a+as crianças)* Tell the children.

Sou *do* Porto *(Sou de+o Porto)* I'm from Oporto.
Esqueci-me *dos* selos *(Esqueci-me de+os selos)* I forgot the stamps

Entre *na* camioneta *(Entre em+a camioneta)* Get on the coach
Moro *nos* arredores de Lisboa *(Moro em+os arredores de Lisboa)* I live on the outskirts of Lisbon

Sometimes de and em are followed by the articles um, uma, uns or umas. When this happens, the two words are combined:

Preciso *duma* *(de+uma)* toalha. I need a towel.
Moro *numa* *(em+uma)* casa de campo. I live in a country house.

✳ adjectives

Adjectives (describing words) usually come after the noun to which they refer:
A rapariga *portuguesa* the Portuguese girl
O rapaz *alto* the tall boy

Exceptions are common adjectives:

bom/boa (good)   *boa ideia*   good idea
primeiro (first)   *o primeiro ano*   the first year
bastante (a lot)   *bastante carne*   a lot of meat

Adjectives have a masculine and a feminine:

A casa nova the new house
O carro novo the new car

Note that adjectives ending in e are both masculine
and feminine:

Uma caixa *grande* a big box
Um gelado *grande* a large ice-cream

If the noun is in the singular, the adjective has to be singular:

A camisa branca the white shirt

If the noun is in the plural, the adjective has to be plural.

As camisas brancas the white shirts

✳ possessives (my, your, his, her, etc.)

Possessives have a masculine and feminine and are used
with the article 'the' (o, a, os, as).

	SINGULAR		PLURAL	
	m	f	m	f
my	o meu	a minha	os meus	as minhas
your (informal)	o teu	a tua	os teus	as tuas
our	o nosso	a nossa	os nossos	as nossas
your (pl)	o vosso	a vossa	os vossos	as vossas
your (formal)/ his/her/their	o seu	a sua	os seus	as suas

A minha casa my house
O meu passaporte my passaport
Os nossos filhos our children
Os seus documentos your documents

To say 'Mary's book' in Portuguese you use de:
O livro da Mary (O livro de+a Mary)

✳ demonstratives (this, that)

SINGULAR		
	m	f
this	este	esta
that	esse	essa
that (over there)	aquele	aquela

PLURAL		
	m	f
these	estes	estas
those	esses	essas
those (over there)	aqueles	aquelas

esse/essa and esses/essas are used when the thing you are referring to is near the person you are speaking to, but away from you. aquele/aquela and aqueles/aquelas are used when the thing you are referring to is away from both of you.

Isto, isso and aquilo are used when you are not referring to anything in particular or when you are not using a noun:

Isto é incrível This is incredible
Aquilo faz calor That makes you hot

✳ subject pronouns (I, you, he, she, etc.)

Subject pronouns are not used much in Portuguese, except when you want to give emphasis or to ensure there is no confusion:

Eu quero peixe com batatas. I want fish and chips.
Ele é americano. He is American.

I	eu
you (singular informal)	tu
you (singular informal)	você
you (singular formal)	o senhor (man)
	a senhora (woman)
you (plural informal)	vocês
you (plural formal)	os senhores (men)
	as senhoras (women)
he	ele
she	ela
they	eles (men)
	elas (women)

✳ you

In Portuguese, there are several ways of saying 'you'. The one you use depends on the degree of formality and politeness required. The most formal is o senhor/os senhores and a senhora/as senhoras. You usually use these forms with people you don't know very well or who are older to show respect.

Você/vocês shows more familiarity and is used with people you know well, for example, work colleagues, family and neighbours. Tu is very informal and is used with children, very close friends and relatives.

✳ object pronouns (me, him, her, it, etc.)

me	me	us	nos
you (informal, singular)	te	you (informal, plural)	vos
you (formal) /him/her/it (direct)	o, a	you (formal) /them (direct)	os, as
you (formal) /him/her/it (indirect)	lhe	you (formal) /them (indirect)	lhes

Object pronouns usually come after the verb with a hyphen:

Dê-*me* um casaco Give me a coat

Traga-*as* Bring them

Compre-*o* Buy it

If you use words such as que, onde, como or não, the pronoun comes before the verb:

Não *lhe* diga Don't tell him/her

O vestido não *te* fica bem The dress does not suit you

Onde *o* ponho? Where do I put it?

Sometimes pronouns are not necessary:

Posso provar? May I try it?

Gosta? Do you like it?

✳ reflexives

Reflexive verbs have a se (the reflexive pronoun) after them, which could be translated into English as 'oneself': lavar-se (to wash *oneself*); sentar-se (to sit *oneself* down); chamar-se (to call *oneself*).

myself	me	ourselves	nos
yourself (inf., sing.)	te	yourself (inf., plural)	vos
yourself (form., sing.)/ him/her/itself	se	yourself (form., sing.)/ themselves	se

Chamo-me Carla My name is Carla (Literally, 'I call myself Carla')

Sentem-se Sit down (literally, 'Sit yourselves down')

✳ verbs

Verbs (action words) are recognised in English by the 'to' in front: to work, to say. In Portuguese, verbs end in ar, er and ir. Some verbs are regular, which means that they all follow a similar pattern; others are irregular and you'll need to learn them individually.

Regular verbs follow the pattern below:

	PAGAR	**BATER**	**PARTIR**
Eu	pago	bato	parto
Tu	pagas	bates	partes
Você/Ele/Ela	paga	bate	parte
Nós	pagamos	batemos	partimos
Vocês/Eles/Elas	pagam	batem	partem

The most common irregular verb is the verb 'to be'.
In Portuguese there are two verbs for 'to be': ser and estar.

	SER	**ESTAR**
Eu	sou	estou
Tu	és	estás
Você/Ele/Ela	é	está
Nós	somos	estamos
Vocês/Eles/Elas	são	estão

basic grammar

Ser is used to say where something is:
O cinema é ali The cinema is over there
Onde é a paragem do 33? Where is the stop for number 33?

describe someone or something:
Ela é muito amável She is very kind (helpful)
O vestido é vermelho e azul The dress is red and blue

Estar is used for temporary states:
Estou em Lisboa I'm in Lisbon
Ele *está* com fome He is hungry

Other common irregular verbs are: ter (to have), ir (to go),
vir (to come):

	TER	IR	VIR
Eu	tenho	vou	venho
Tu	tens	vais	vens
Você/Ele/Ela	tem	vai	vem
Nós	temos	vamos	vimos
Vocês/Eles/Elas	têm	vão	vêm

At this stage it is sufficient to know that some verbs are
only irregular in the 'I' form: dizer: digo (I say), trazer: trago
(I bring), saber: sei (I know), poder: posso (I can/may).

✳ tenses

The use of the present tense in Portuguese is similar in most
cases to English. It is used to say that something is true at
the time of speaking or will happen in the near future:
Falo um pouco de português I speak a little Portuguese
Estou no hotel Praia do Mar I'm in the Praia do Mar hotel
Vou jogar golfe I'm going to play golf

To say that something is happening now, use estar+a+*verb*:
Estou a fazer jogging no park I'm jogging in the park
Ele está a jogar golfe He is playing golf

A few other verb tenses you may find useful:

ser (to be)	era	I was/used to be
	éramos	we were/used to be
estar (to be)	estive	I was/have been
	estivemos	we were/have been
ter (to have)	tive	I had/have had
	tinha	I had/I used to have
	tivemos	we had/have had
	tínhamos	we had/used to have
ir (to go)	fui	I went/have been
	ia	I used to go
	fomos	we went/have been
	íamos	we used to go

For talking about the future, you can use the present tense:
No domingo voltamos a Londres We return to London
on Sunday

'I'm going to' in Portuguese is the verb ir+*verb*:
Vou visitar Coimbra. I'm going to visit Coimbra.

✳ negative

To make a negative, put the word não before the verb:
Não sei I don't know
Não sou casado I'm not married

Portuguese has double negatives:
Não compro nada I'm not buying anything (nothing)

English – Portuguese dictionary

There's a list of **car parts** on page 56 and **parts of the body** on page 137. See also the **menu reader** on page 88, and **numbers** on page 14.

Portuguese nouns are given with their gender in brackets: (m) for masculine and (f) for feminine, (m/f) for those which can be either. (pl) is for plural.

Adjectives which have different endings for masculine and feminine are shown like this: branco/a (i.e. branco for masculine, branca for feminine). See **basic grammar**, page 147, for further explanation.

A

a, an um/uma *oom̃/oomah*
abbey abadia (f) *ahbahdeeah*
about *(relating to)* sobre du *sohbru du; (approximately)* mais ou menos *maeesh oh mehnoosh*
above acima *ahseemah*
abroad estrangeiro (m) *eeshtrahnjaheeroo*
abscess abcesso (m) *abusesoo*
to **accept** *(take)* aceitar *ahsaheetar*
accident acidente (m) *ahseedehntu*
accommodation alojamento (m) *ahloojahmehntoo*
account *(bank)* conta (f) *kohntah*
ache dor (f) *dohr*
acid *(adj)* ácido/a *aseedoo/ah*
across do outro lado de *doo ohtroo ladoo du*
adaptor adaptador (m) *ahdahputahdohr*
address morada (f) *mooradah*
admission entrada (f) *ehntradah*
admission charge preço de entrada (m) *prehsoo du ehntradah*
adopted adotado/a *ahdotadoo/ah*
adult adulto/a *ahdooltoo/ah*

advance: in advance com antecedência *kohm̃ ahntusudehnseeah*
advanced (level) (nível) avançado (m) *neevel ahvahnsadoo*
advertisement publicidade (f) *poobuleeseedadu*
aerial antena (f) *ahntehnah*
aeroplane avião (m) *ahveeãhoo*
afford: I can't afford it é muito caro e *mooeentoo karoo*
afraid: I'm afraid *(fear)* tenho medo *taheennyoo mehdoo*
after depois de *dupoheesh du*
afterwards depois *dupoheesh*
afternoon tarde (f) *tardu*
aftershave aftershave (m) *afturshahvu*
again outra vez *ohtrah vehsh*
against contra *kohntrah*
age idade (f) *eedadu*
agency agência (f) *ahjehnseeah*
ago atrás *ahtrash*
to **agree** concordar *kohnkoordar*
AIDS SIDA (f) *seedah*
air ar (m) *ar*
» **by air** por avião *poor) ahveeãhoo*

air conditioning ar condicionado (m) *ar kohndeeseeoonadoo*

air force força aérea (f) *fohrsah ahereeah*

airline linha aérea (f) *leennyah ahereeah*

airport aeroporto (m) *aheropohrtoo*

aisle corredor (m) *koorrudohr*

alarm alarme (m) *ahlarmu*

alarm clock despertador (m) *duspurtahdohr*

alcohol álcool (m) *alkol*

alcoholic *(drink)* com álcool *kohm alkol;* *(person)* alcoólico/a *alkoleekoo/ah*

alive vivo/a *veevoo/ah*

all todo/toda (f) *tohdoo/ah*

allergic to alérgico/a *ahlerjeekoo/ah ah*

alley beco (m) *behkoo*

to allow permitir *purmeeteer*

allowed permitido/a *purmeeteedoo/ah*

all right *(OK)* está bem *eeshta baheem*

alone só, sozinho/a *so, sozeennyoo/ah*

along por *poor*

already já *ja*

also também *tahmbaheem*

although embora *ehmborah*

always sempre *sehmpru*

ambassador embaixador (m) *aheemaeeshahdohr*

ambition ambição (f) *ahmbeesãhoo*

ambulance ambulância (f) *amboolahnseeah*

among entre *ehntru*

amount *(money)* quantia (f) *kwahnteeah*

amusement park feira popular (f) *faheerah poopoolar*

anaesthetic anestésico (m) *ahnushtezeecoo*

and e *ee*

angry zangado/a *zahngadoo/ah*

animal animal (m) *ahneemal*

ankle tornozelo (m) *toornoozehloo*

anniversary aniversário (m) *ahneevursareeoo*

annoyed irritado/a *eerreetadoo/ah*

another outro/a *ohtro/ah*

answer resposta (f) *rushposhtah*

to answer responder *rushpohndehr*

antibiotic antibiótico (m) *ahnteebeeooteekoo*

antifreeze anticongelante (m) *ahnteekohnjulahntu*

antique antiguidade (f) *ahnteegooeedadu*

antiseptic anti-séptico (m) *ahntiseteekoo*

anxious ansioso/a *ahnseeohzoo/ ahnseeozah*

any algum/alguma *algoom/algoomah*

anyone alguém *algaheem*

anything qualquer coisa *kwalker koheezah*

anything else mais alguma coisa *maeesh algoomah koheezah*

anyway de qualquer maneira *du kwalker mahnaheerah*

anywhere em qualquer parte *aheem kwalker part*

apart (from) para além de *pahrah alaheem du*

apartment apartamento (m) *ahpahrtahmehntoo*

appendicitis apendicite (f) *ahpehndeeseetu*

apple maçã (f) *mahsãh*

appointment *(interview)* entrevista (f) *ehntruveeshtah; (doctor)* consulta (f) *kohnsooltah*

approximately aproximadamente *aproseemadahmehnt*

archaeology arqueologia (f) *ahrkeeooloojeeah*

architect arquitecto/a *ahrkeetetoo/ah*

area área (f) *areeah*

argument argumento (m) *ahrgoomehntoo*

arm braço (m) *brasoo*

armbands *(swimming)* braçadeiras (fpl) *brahsahdaheerahs*

army exército (m) *eezerseetoo*

around ao redor de *aoo rudor du*

to **arrange** *(fix)* organizar *orgahneezar*

arrest: under arrest preso/a *prehzoo/ah*

arrival chegada (f) *shugadah*

to **arrive** chegar *shugar*

art arte (f) *artu*

art gallery galeria de arte (f) *gahlureeah du art*

» **fine arts** belas artes (fpl) *belahsh artush*

arthritis artrite (f) *ahrtreet*

article artigo (m) *ahrteegoo*

artificial artificial *ahrteefeeseeal*

artist artista (m/f) *ahrteeshtah*

as *(like)* como *kohmoo*

ashtray cinzeiro (m) *seenzaheeroo*

to **ask** pedir *pudeer*

aspirin aspirina (f) *ahshpeereenah*

assistant assistente (m/f) *ahseeshtehnt*

» **shop assistant** empregado/a *aheemprugadoo/ah*

asthma asma (f) *ashmah*

at a, em *ah, aheem*

athletics atletismo (m) *ahtuleteeshmoo*

atmosphere atmosfera (f) *ahtumooshferah*

to **attack** atacar *ahtahkar*

(mug) roubar *rohbar*

attendant *(bathing)* salva-vidas (m/f) *salvah veedahs*

attractive atraente *ahtrahehnt*

aunt tia (f) *teeah*

automatic automático/a *aootoomateekoo/ah*

autumn Outono (m) *ohtohnoo*

avalanche avalanche (f) *ahvahlahnshah*

to **avoid** evitar *ehveetar*

away (kilometres) a … (quilómetros) *ah …(kilomutroosh)*

awful terrível *turreevel*

baby bebé (m/f) *bube*

baby food comida de bebé (f) *koomeedah du bube*

baby wipes toalhetes de bébé (mpl) *tooahllehtush du bube*

baby's bottle biberão (m) *beeburãhoo*

babysitter ama (f) *ahmah*

back *(reverse side)* traseira (f) *trahzaheerah*

» **at the back** atrás *ahtrash*

backwards para atrás *pahrah trash*

bacon toucinho fumado (m) *tohseennyoo foomadoo*

bad mau *maoo*

bag saco (m) *sakoo*

baggage bagagem (f) *bahgajaheem*

baker padeiro/a *padaheeroo/ah*

baker's padaria (f) *padahreeah*

balcony *(theatre)* varanda (f) *varahndah*

bald careca *kahrekah*

ball bola (f) *bolah*

ballet ballet (m) *bale*

banana banana (f) *bahnahnah*

band *(music)* banda (f) *bahndah*

bandage penso (m) *pehnsoo*

bank *(money)* banco (m) *bahñkoo*

bar bar (m) *bar*

barber's barbeiro (m) *bahrbaheeroo*

bargain pechincha (f) *pusheenshah*

baseball baseball (m) *baheezubol*

basement cave (f) *kav*

basin *(sink)* bacia (f) *bahseeah*

basket cesto (m) *sehshtoo*

basketball basketball (m) *bashketubol*

bath banho (m) *bahnnyoo*

bathing costume fato de banho (m) *fatoo du bahnnyoo*

bathroom casa de banho (f) *kazah du bahñnyoo*

battery pilha (f) *peellah*

bay baía (f) *baheeah*

to **be** ser, estar *sehr, eeshtar*

beach praia (f) *praeeah*

beans feijões (mpl) *faheejoheesh*

beard barba (f) *barbah*

beautiful bonito/a *booneetoo/ah*

because porque *poorku*

bed cama (f) *kahmah*

bedroom quarto (m) *kwartoo*

bee abelha (f) *ahbehllah*

beef carne de vaca (f) *karnu du vakah*

beer cerveja (f) *survehjah*

before antes *ahntush*

to **begin** começar *koomusar*

beginner principiante (m/f) *preenseepeeahnt*

beginning começo (m) *koomehsoo*

behind atrás *ahtrash*

beige bege *bej*

to **believe** acreditar *ahkrudeetar*

bell campainha (f) *kahmpaheennyah*

to **belong to** pertencer *purtehnsehr*

below por baixo *poor baeeshoo*

belt cinto (m) *seentoo*

bend curva (f) *koorvah*

berry baga (f) *bagah*

berth beliche (m) *buleeshu; (on ship)* camarote (m) *kahmahrot*

best o melhor *oo mullor*

better melhor *mullor*

between entre *ehntru*

beyond para além de *pahrah alaheem du*

bib babete (m) *bahbetu*

Bible Bíblia (f) *beebuleeah*

bicycle bicicleta (f) *beeseekuletah*

big grande *grahnd*

bigger maior *maheeor*

bill conta (f) *kohntah*

bin *(rubbish)* caixote (do lixo) (m) *kaishot (doo leeshoo)*

bin liners sacos do lixo (mpl) *sakoosh doo leeshoo*

binoculars binóculos (mpl) *beenokooloosh*

bird pássaro (m) *pasahroo*

birthday aniversário (m) *ahneevursareeoo*

biscuit bolacha (f) *boolashah*

bit um pouco *oom pohkoo*

to **bite** morder *moordehr*

bitter amargo/a *ahmargoo/ah*

black preto/a *prehto/ah*

blackcurrant groselha preta (f) *grozehllah prehtah*

blanket cobertor (m) *kooburtohr*

beach praia (a) *praeeah*

to **bleed** sangrar *sahngrar*

blind cego/a *segoo/segah*

blister bolha (f) *bohllah*

to **block** *(road)* impedir *eempudeer*

blocked bloqueado/a *bulookeeadoo/ah; (road)* impedido/a *eempudeedoo/ah*

blonde louro/a *lohroo/ah*

blood sangue (m) *sahng*

blouse blusa (f) *buloozah*

to **blow** soprar *sooprar*

to **blow-dry** secar *sukar*

blue azul *ahzool*

to **board** embarcar *aheembahrkar*

boarding card cartão de embarque (m) *kahrtãhoo du aheembahrk*

boat barco (m) *barkoo*

boat trip viagem de barco (f) *veeajaheem du barkoo*

body corpo (m) *kohrpoo*

to **boil** cozer *koozehr*

 » **boiled egg** ovo cozido (m) *ovoo koozeedoo*

boiler caldeira (f) *kaldaheerah*

bomb bomba (f) *bohmbah*

bone osso (m) *ohsoo*

book livro (m) *leevroo*

to **book** reservar *ruzurvar*

booking reserva (f) *ruzervah*

booking office bilheteira (f) *beellutaheerah*

booklet *(bus tickets)* caderneta (f) *kahdurnehtah*

bookshop livraria (f) *leevrahreeah*

boot *(shoe)* bota (f) *botah*

border *(edge)* borda (f) *bordah; (frontier)* fronteira (f) *frohntaheerah*

boring aborrecido/a *ahboorru**seedoo**/ah*

both os dois/as duas *oosh do**heesh**/ahsh
  dooahsh

bottle garrafa (f) *ga**hrrafah***

bottle opener abregarrafas (m)
  *abruga**hrrafahsh***

bottom fundo (m) *foondoo*

bow (ship) proa (f) *prohah*

bowl bacia (f) *bah**seeah***

box caixa (f) *kaee**shah**; (theatre)
  camarote (m) *kahma**hrot***

box office bilheteira (f) *beellu**taheerah***

boy rapaz (m) *rrah**pash***

boyfriend namorado (m) *nahmoo**radoo***

bra soutien (m) *sootee**ahñ***

bracelet bracelete (f) *brasu**let***

brain cérebro (m) *se**rubroo***

branch (bank, etc.) ramo (m) *rrah**moo***

brand marca (f) *markah*

brandy conhaque (m) *kon**yak***

brass latão (m) *lah**tãhoo***

brave valente *vah**lehnt***

bread pão (m) *pãhoo*

bread roll bolinha (f) *bo**leenyah***

to break (inc. limb) partir *pah**rteer***

to break down avariar *ahvah**reear***

breakdown truck reboque (m) *rru**boku***

breakfast pequeno almoço *puke**hnoo**
  al**mohsoo***

breast seio (m) *sa**heeoo***

to breathe respirar *ruspee**rar***

bridge ponte (f) *pohnt*

briefcase mala (f) *malah*

bright (colour) vivo/a *veevo/ah*;
  (light) claro/a *klaroo/klarah*

to bring trazer *trah**zehr***

British Británico/a *bree**tahneekoo**/ah*

broad largo/a *largo/ah*

brochure brochure (f) *broo**shoorah***

broken partido/a *pah**rteedoo**/ah*

bronchitis bronquite (f) *brohn**keet***

bronze bronze (m) *brohnzu*

brooch broche (m) *brosh*

broom vassoura (f) *vah**sohrah***

brother irmão (m) *eer**mãhoo***

brother-in-law cunhado (m)
  *koon**nyadoo***

brown castanho/a *kahsh**tahnnyoo**/ah*

bruise negra (f) *nehgrah*

brush escova (f) *eesh**kohvah***

bucket balde (m) *baldu*

buffet buffet (m) *boofeh*

to build construir *kohnsh**trooeer***

building prédio (m), edifício (m)
  *predeeoo, ehdee**feeseeoo***

bulb (light) lâmpada (f) *lahm**pahdah***

bull (fighting) touro (ɪɪ) *tohroo*

burn (on skin) queimadura (f)
  *kaheema**hdoorah***

burnt (food) queimado/a *ka**heemado**/ah*

bus autocarro (m) *aooto**karroo***

  » **by bus** de autocarro *du aooto**karroo***

bus-driver motorista (m/f)
  *mootoo**reeshtah***

bush arbusto (m) *ahr**booshtoo***

business negócios (mpl) *nugo**seeoosh***

  » **on business** em negócios *aheeñ*
  *nugo**seeoosh***

bus station estação de autocarros (f)
  *eeshtah**sãhoo** du aooto**karroosh***

bus stop paragem de autocarros (f)
  *pah**rajaheeñ** du aooto**karroosh***

busy ocupado/a *okoo**padoo**/ah*

but mas *mahsh*

butane gas gás butano (m) *gash*
  *boo**tahnoo***

butcher's talho (m) *talloo*

butter manteiga (f) *mahn**taheegah***

butterfly borboleta (f) *boorboo**lehtah***

button botão (m) *boo**tãhoo***

to buy comprar *kohm**prar***

by (author, etc.) por *poor*

C

cabin cabine (f) *ka**beenu***

cable car eléctrico (m) *ee**letreekoo***

café café (m) *kahfe*

cake bolo (m) *bohloo*

cake shop pastelaria (f) *pahshtulah**reeah***

calculator calculador (m) *kalkoolah**dohr***

to **call** telefonar *tulufoo**nar***

» **to be called** chamar-se *shah**mar**su*

calm calmo/a, tranquilo/a *kal**moo**/ah, trahn**kwee**loo/ah*

camera máquina fotográfica (f) *ma**keen**ah footoo**graf**eekah*

to **camp** acampar *ahkahm**par***

camping campismo (m) *kahm**peesh**moo*

campsite parque de campismo (m) *park du kahm**peesh**moo*

can (to be able) poder *poo**dehr***

can (tin) lata (f) *latah*

can opener abre-latas (m) *abru**lat**ahsh*

to **cancel** cancelar *kansu**lar***

cancer cancro (m) *kahn**kroo***

candle vela (f) *velah*

canoe canoa (f) *kah**noh**ah*

capital (city) capital (f) *kahpee**tal***

captain (boat) capitão (m) *kahpee**tãhoo***

car carro (m) *karroo*

» **by car** de carro *du karroo*

car hire aluguer de carros (m) *ahloo**ger** du karroosh*

car park parque de estacionamento (m) *park du eeshtahseeoonah**mehn**too*

carafe jarra (f) *jarrah*

caravan caravana (f) *kahrah**vah**nah*

caravan site parque de campismo (m) *park du kahm**peesh**moo*

cardigan casaco de malha (m) *kah**zak**oo du mallah*

care: I don't care não me importa *nãhoo mu eem**por**tah*

careful cuidadoso/a *kooeedah**dohz**oo/ kooeedah**doz**ah*

carpet alcatifa (f) *alkah**teef**ah*

carriage (rail) carruagem (m) *kahrrooaja**heñ***

carrier bag saco de compras (m) *sakoo du kohm**prahsh***

to **carry** levar *luvar*

to **carry on** (walking/driving) continuar *kohnteenoo**ar***

car wash lavagem automática (f) *lah**va**jaheeñ aootoo**mat**eekah*

case: in case no caso de *noo kazoo du*

cash dinheiro (m) *deen**nyah**eeroo*

» **to pay cash** pagar com dinheiro *pah**gar** kohñ deen**nyah**eeroo*

to **cash** cobrar *koo**brar***

cash desk (cashier) caixa (f) *kaeeshah*

cassette cassette (f) *kaset*

castle (palace) castelo (m) *kahsh**teloo***; (fortress) forte (m) *fort*

cat gato (m) *gatoo*

catalogue catálogo (m) *kah**taloogoo***

to **catch** (train/bus) apanhar *ahpahn**nyar***

cathedral cathedral (f) *kahtu**dral***

Catholic católico/a *kah**tol**eekoo/ah*

to **cause** causar *kaoo**zar***

caution cuidado (m) *kooee**da**doo*

cave gruta (f) *grootah*

ceiling tecto (m) *tetoo*

cellar cave (f) *kavu*

cemetery cemitério (m) *sumee**te**reeoo*

centimetre centímetro (m) *sehn**teem**utroo*

central heating aquecimento (m) *ahkesee**mehn**too*

centre centro (m) *sehntro*

century século (m) *sekooloo*

certain seguro/a *su**goor**oo/ah*

certainly com certeza *kohñ sur**teh**zah*

certificate certificado (m) *surteefee**ka**doo*

chain cadeia (f) *ka**dah**eeah*

chair cadeira (f) *kah**dah**eerah*

chair lift elevador cadeira (m) *eeluvah**dohr***

chalet chalé (m) *shale*

champagne champanhe (m) *shahm**pahn**nyu*

change (small coins) troco (m) *trohkoo*

to **change** (clothes) trocar *troo**kar***; (money) cambiar *kahm**beear***; (trains) mudar de *moo**dar** du*

chapel capela (f) *kah**pela***

charcoal carvão (m) *karvãhoo*

charge *(money)* preço (m) *prehsoo*

charter flight voo charter (m) *vohoo sharter*

cheap barato/a *bahratoo/ah*

to **check** controlar *kohntroolar*

check-in (desk) (balcão) de check-in (m) *(balkãhoo) du shekin*

to **check in** fazer o check-in *fahzehr oo shekin*

cheek bochecha (f) *booshehshah*

cheers! saúde *sahood*

cheese queijo (m) *kaheejoo*

chef chefe (m) *shefu*

chemist farmácia (f) *fahrmaseeah*

cheque cheque (m) *sheku*

chewing gum pastilha elástica (f) *pahshteellah eelashteekah*

chicken galinha (f) *gahleennyah*

chickenpox varicela (f) *vahreeselah*

child criança (f) *kreeahnsah*

children crianças (fpl) *kreeahnsahsh*

chimney *(exterior)* chaminé (f) *shahmeene*

chin queixo (m) *kaheeshoo*

chips batatas fritas (fpl) *bahtatahsh freetahsh*

chocolate chocolate (m) *shookoolat*

to **choose** escolher *eeshkoollehr*

Christian Cristão/Cristã *kreeshtãhoo/ kreeshtãh*

Christmas Natal (m) *nahtal*

church igreja (f) *eegraheejah*

cigar charuto (m) *shahrootoo*

cigarette cigarro (m) *seegarroo*

cigarette paper papel de cigarro (m) *pahpehl du seegarroo*

cinema cinema (m) *seenehmah*

circle círculo (m) *seerkooloo (theatre)* balcão (m) *balkãhoo*

city cidade (f) *seedadu*

class classe (f) *klasu*

classical music música clássica (f) *moozeekah klaseekah*

claustrophobia claustrophobia (f) *klaooshtroofoobeeah*

to **clean** limpar *leempar*

clean limpo/a *leempoo/ah*

cleaner mulher da limpeza (f) *mooller dah leempehzah*

clear claro/a *klaroo/klarah*

clever inteligente *eentuleejehnt*

cliff rochedo (m) *rooshehdoo*

climate clima (m) *kleemah*

to **climb** subir *soobeer*

climber alpinista (m/f) *alpeeneeshtah*

clinic clínica (f) *kleeneekah*

clock relógio (m) *rulojeeoo*

close *(by)* perto *pertoo*

to **close** fechar *fushar*

closed fechado/a *fushadoo/ah*

clothes roupa (f) *rrohpah*

clothes pegs pegas (fpl) *pegahsh*

cloud núvem (f) *noovaheem*

cloudy nublado *noobuladoo*

club clube (m) *kloob*

coach autocarro (m), camioneta (f) *aootokarroo, kameeoonetah; (railway)* carruagem (f) *kahrrooajaheem*

coast costa (f) *koshtah*

coat casaco (m) *kahzakoo*

coat-hanger cabide (m) *kahbeed*

cocktail cocktail (m) *kokutaheel*

coffee café (m) *kahfe*

coin moeda (f) *mooedah*

cold frio/a *freeoo/ah*

» **to have a cold** estar constipado/a *eeshtar kohnshteepadoo/ah*

collar colarinho (m) *koolahreennyoo*

colleague colega (m/f) *koolegah*

to **collect** recolher *rukoollehr*

collection *(postal)* recolha (f) *rukohllah*

college colégio (m) *koolejeeoo*

colour cor (f) *kohr*

colour-blind daltónico/a *daltoneekoo/ah*

comb pente (m) *pehnt*

to **come** vir *veer*

» **to come back** voltar *voltar*

» **to come in** entrar *ehntrar*

comedy comédia (f) *koomedeeah*

comfortable comfortável *kohmfoortavel*

commercial comercial *koomurseeal*

common (usual) familiar *fahmeeleear*; (shared) comum *koomoom*

communism comunismo (m) *koomooneeshmoo*

company companhia (f) *kohmpahnyeeah*

compared with comparado/a com *kohmpahradoo/kohmpahradah kohm*

compartment compartimento (m) *kohmpahrteemehntoo*

compass bússola (f) *boosoolah*

to **complain** reclamar *ruklahmar*

complaint reclamação (f) *ruklahmahsãhoo*

complete (finished) acabado (m) *ahkahbadoo;* (whole) completo (m) *kohmpletoo*

complicated complicado/a *kohmpleekadoo/ah*

compulsory obrigatório/a *obreegahtoreeoo/ah*

composer compositor (m)/ora (f) *kohmpozeetohr/kohmpozeetohrah*

computer computador (m) *kohmpootahdohr*

concert concerto (m) *kohnsehrtoo*

concert hall sala de concertos (f) *salah du kohnsehrtoosh*

concussion concussão (f) *kohnkoosãhoo*

condition (state) condição (f) *kohndeesãhoo*

conditioner amaciador (m) *ahmahseeahdohr*

condom preservativo (m) *pruzurvahteevoo*

conference conferência (f) *kohnfurehnseeah*

to **confirm** confirmar *kohnfeermar*

conjunctivitis conjuntivite (m) *kohnjoonteeveet*

connection ligação (f) *leegahsãhoo*

conscious consciente *kohnsseeehnt*

conservation conservação (f) *kohnsurvahsãhoo*

constipation prisão de ventre (f) *preezãhoo du vehntru*

consulate consulado (m) *kohnsooladoo*

consultant consultor (m) *kohnsooltohr*

contact lenses lentes de contacto (fpl) *lehntush du kohntatoo*

continent continente (m) *kohnteenehnt*

contraceptive contraceptivo (m) *kohntrahseteevoo*

contract contracto (m) *kohntratoo*

control (passport) controle (m) *kohntrol*

convent convento (m) *kohnvehntoo*

convenient conveniente *kohnvuneeehnt*

cook cozinheiro (m) *koozeennyaheeroo*

to **cook** cozinhar *koozeennyar*

cooked cozinhado *koozeennyadoo*

cooker fogão (m) *foogãhoo*

cool fresco/a *frehshkoo*

cool box geleria (f) *gahlureeah*

copper cobre (m) *kobru*

copy cópia (f) *kopeeah*

corkscrew saca-rolhas (m) *sakah-rrohllahsh*

corner (outside) esquina (f) *eeshkeenah*

correct correcto/a *koorretoo/ah*

cosmetics cosméticos (mpl) *koshmeteekoosh*

to **cost** custar *kooshtar*

cot berço (m) *behrsoo*

cottage casa de campo (f) *kazah du kahmpoo*

cotton (material) algodão (m) *algoodãhoo*

cotton wool algodão (m) *algoodãhoo*

cough tosse (f) *tos*

to **cough** tossir *tooseer*

to **count** contar *kohntar*

counter (post office) balcão (m) *balkãhoo*

country país (m) *paheesh*

country(side) campo (m) *kahmpoo*

couple (pair) par (m) *par*

course *(lessons)* curso (m) **koor**soo

court *(law)* tribunal (m) treeboo**nal**;
(tennis) campo de ténis (m) **kahm**poo
du te**neesh**

cousin primo/a **pree**moo/ah

cover *(lid)* tampa (f) **tahm**pah

cow vaca (f) **va**kah

crab caranguejo (m) kahrahn**ga**heejoo

cramp cãibra (f) **kã**eebrah

crazy louco/a **loh**kah

cream *(lotion)* creme (m) krem; *(colour)*
creme krem

credit card cartão de crédito (m)
kahr**tã**hoo du **kre**deetoo

cross cruz (f) kroosh

to cross *(border)* atravessar ahtrah**vusar**

crossing *(sea)* travessia (f) trahvu**see**ah

crossroads cruzamento (m)
kroozah**mehn**too

crowd multidão (f) moolteedã**hoo**

crowded cheio/a sha**hee**oo/ah

crown coroa (f) koo**roh**ah

cruise cruzeiro (m) krroza**hee**roo

crutch muleta (f) moo**leh**tah

to cry chorar shoo**rar**

crystal cristal (m) kreesh**tal**

cup chávena (f) **sha**vunah

cupboard armário (m) ahr**ma**reeoo

cure *(remedy)* cura (f) **koo**rah

to cure curar koo**rar**

curly encaracolado/a
ehnkahrahkoo**la**doo/ah

current currente (f) koor**rehnt**

curtain cortina (f) koor**tee**nah

curve curva (f) **koor**vah

cushion almofada (f) almoo**fa**dah

customs alfândega (f) al**fãhn**dugah

cut corte (m) kort

to cut cortar koor**tar**

to cut oneself cortar-se koor**tar**su

cutlery talheres (mpl) tah**lle**rush

cycling andar de bicicleta ahn**dar** du
beesee**ku**letah

cyclist ciclista (m/f) seeku**leesh**tah

cystitis cistite (f) seesh**teet**

D

daily diário/a dee**aree**oo

damaged estragado/a eeshtra**ga**doo/ah

damp húmido/a **oo**meedoo/ah

dance dança (f) **dahn**sah

to dance dançar dahn**sahr**

danger perigo (m) pu**ree**goo

dangerous perigoso puree**goh**zoo

dark escuro/a eesh**koo**roo/ah

data dados (mpl) **da**doosh

date *(day)* data (f) **dah**tah

daughter filha (f) **fee**llah

daughter-in-law nora (f) **no**rah

day dia (m) **dee**ah

» **day after tomorrow** depois de
amanhã du**poh**eesh du amahn**nyãh**

» **day before yesterday** anteontem
ahntu**ohn**taheem

dead morto/a **mohr**too/**mor**tah

deaf surdo/a **soor**doo/ah

dear *(loved)* querido/a ku**ree**doo/ah

death morte (f) mort

debt dívida (f) **dee**veedah

decaffeinated descafeinado/a
dushkahfahee**na**doo/ah

deck convés (m) kohn**vesh**

deckchair cadeira de lona (f)
kah**dahee**rah du **loh**nah

to decide decidir dusee**deer**

to declare declarar dukla**hrar**

deep profundo/a proo**foon**doo/ah

deer veado (m) vee**a**doo

defect defeito (m) du**fahee**too

definitely absolutamente
ahbsooloo**tah**mehnt

defrost descongelar dushkohnju**lar**

degree *(temperature)* grau (m)
graoo; *(university)* licenciatura (f)
leesehn**see**ah**too**rah

delay atraso (m) ah**tra**zoo

delicate delicado/a du**lee**kadoo/ah

delicious delicioso/a dulee**see**ohzoo

to deliver distribuir dushtree**booer**

delivery entrega (f) un**trêh**gah

demonstration demonstração (f) *dumohnshtrahsãhoo*

dentist dentista (m/f) *dehnteeshtah*

denture dentura (f) *dehntahdoorah*

deodorant desodorizante (f) *duzodooreezahnt*

department departamento (m) *dupahrtahmehntoo*

department store armazéns (mpl) *armahzahensh*

departure *(bus,car,train)* partida (f) *pahrteedah*; *(plane)* embarque (m) *aheembahrku*

departure lounge sala de embarque (f) *sala du aheembahrku*

deposit depósito (m) *dupozeetoo*

desert deserto (m) *duzertoo*

to **describe** descrever *dushkruvehr*

description descrição (f) *dushkreesãhoo*

design desenho (m) *duzehnnyoo*

to **design** desenhar *duzunnyar*

dessert sobremesa (f) *soobrumehzah*

destination destino (m) *dushteenoo*

detail pormenor (m) *poormunor*

detergent detergente (m) *duturjehnt*

to **develop** *(film)* revelar *ruvular*

diabetic diabético/a *deeahbeteekoo*

to **dial** marcar *mahrkar*

dialling code indicativo (m) *eendeekahteevoo*

dialling tone sinal de marcar (m) *seenal du mahrkar*

diamond diamante (m) *deeahmahnt*

diarrhoea diarreia (f) *deeahrraheeah*

diary agenda (f) *ahjehndah*

dice dado (m) *dadoo*

dictionary dicionário (m) *deeseeoonareeoo*

to **die** morrer *moorrehr*

diesel gasóleo (m) *gazoleeoo*

diet dieta (f) *deeetah*

different different *deefurehnt*

difficult difícil *deefeeseel*

digital digital *deegeetal*

dining room sala de jantar (f) *salah du jahntar*

dinner jantar *jahntar*

direct *(train)* directo/a *deeretoo*

direction direcção (f) *deeresãhoo*

directory lista telefónica (f) *leeshtah tulufoneekah*

dirty sujo/a *soojoo/ah*

disabled deficiente (m/f) *dufeeseeehnt*

disappointed desiludido/a *duzeeloodeedoo/ah*

disc *(computer)* disquete (f) *deeshket*

disco discoteca (f) *deeshkootekah*

discount disconto (m) *deeshkohntoo*

dish prato (m) *pratoo*

dishwasher máquina de lavar loiça *makeenah du lahvar loheesah*

disinfectant desinfectante *duzeenfetahnt*

dislocated deslocado/a *dushlookadoo/ah*

disposable descartáveis *dushkahrtavaheesh*

distance distância (f) *deeshtahnseeah*

distilled destilado/a *dushteeladoo/ah*

district zona (f) *zohnah*

to **dive** mergulhar *murgoollar*

diversion desvio (m) *dushveeo*

diving mergulho (m) *murgoollo*

divorced divorciado/a *deevoorseeadoo*

dizzy tonto/a *tohntoo/ah*

to **do** fazer *fahzehr*

doctor médico/a *medeekoo*

document documento (m) *dookoomehntoo*

dog cão (m) *kãhoo*

doll boneca (f) *boonekah*

dollar dolar (m) *dolahr*

dome cúpula (f) *koopoolah*

donkey burro (m) *boorroo*

door porta (f) *portah*

double duplo *dooploo*

double bed cama de casal (f) *kahmah du kahzal*

down *(movement)* abaixo *ahbaeeshoo*

to download fazer o download *fahzehr oo daoonlohd*
downstairs em baixo *aheeñ baeeshoo*
drain esgoto (m) *eeshgohtoo*
drama drama (m) *drahmah*
draught *(air)* corrente (f) *koorrehnt*
draught beer cerveja de barril (f) *survaheejah du bahrreel*
to draw desenhar *duzunnyar*
drawer gaveta (f) *gahvehtah*
drawing desenho *duzehnnyoo*
dress vestido (m) *vushteedoo*
to dress, get dressed vestir, vestir-se *vushteer, vushteersu*
dressing *(medical)* penso (m) *pehnsoo;* *(salad)* tempero (m) *tehmpehroo*
drink bebida (f) *bubeedah*
to drink beber *bubehr*
to drip pingar *peengar*
to drive conduzir *kohndoozeer*
driver motorista (m/f) *mootooreeshtah*
driving licence carta de condução (f) *kartah du kohndoosähoo*
to drown afogar-se *ahfoogarsu*
drug droga (f) *drogah*
drug addict viciado/a em drogas *veeseeadoo/ah aheeñ drogahsh*
drum tambor (m) *tahmbohr*
drunk bêbado/a *behbahdoo/ah*
dry seco/a *sehkoo/ah*
dry-cleaner's limpeza a seco (f) *leempehzah ah sehkoo*
duck pato (m) *patoo*
dull *(weather)* nublado *noobladoo*
dumb mudo/a *moodoo/ah*
dummy *(baby's)* chupeta (f) *shoopehtah*
during durante *doorahnt*
dust pó (m) *po*
dustbin caixote do lixo (m) *kaeeshot doo leeshoo*
duty *(tax)* imposto (m) *eempohshtoo*
duty-free livre de direitos *leevru du deeraheetoosh*
duvet edredão (m) *ehdrudähoo*
dyslexic dislexico/a *deeshlekseekoo/ah*

E

each cada *kahdah*
ear ouvido *ohveedoo*
earache dor de ouvidos (m) *dohr du ohveedoosh*
eardrops pingos dos ouvidos *peengoosh doosh ohveedoosh*
earlier mais cedo *maeesh sehdoo*
early cedo *sehdoo*
to earn ganhar *gaeennyar*
earring brinco (m) *breenkoo*
earth terra (f) *terrah*
earthquake terramoto (m) *turrahmotoo*
east este *ehsht*
eastern oriental *oreeehntal*
Easter Páscoa (f) *pashkooah*
easy fácil *faseel*
to eat comer *koomehr*
economical económico *ehkonomeekoo*
economy economia (f) *ehkonoomeeah*
edible comestível *koomushteevel*
either ou *oh*
either ... or .... ou ... ou ... *oh ... oh ...*
election eleição (f) *eelaheesähoo*
electric eléctrico/a *eeletreekoo*
electrician electricista (m) *eeletreeseeshtah*
electricity luz *loosh (wiring, etc.)* electricidade (f) *eeletreeseedad*
electronic electrónico *eeletroneekoo*
to email mandar um email *mahndar ooñ eemaheel*
to embark *(boat)* embarcar *ehmbahrkar*
embarrassing embaraçoso/a *ehmbahrahsohzoo*
embassy embaixada (f) *ehmbaeeeshadah*
emergency emergência (f) *eemurjehnseeah*
empty vazio/a *vahzio/ah*
to empty esvaziar *eeshvahzeear*
end fim (m) *feeñ*
to end acabarr *ahkahbar*
energy energia (f) *eenurjeeah*

engaged (to be married) comprometido/a *kohmproomutee*doo; (occupied) ocupado/a *ookoo*padoo

engine motor (m) *moo*tohr

engineer engenheiro *aheenjeennyahee*roo

England Inglaterra (f) *eenglah*terrah

English inglês/inglesa *eenglehsh/ eenglehzah*

to **enjoy** gozar *goozar*

enough bastante *bahsh*tahnt

to **enter** entrar *ehn*trar

entertainment diversão (f) *deevur*sãhoo

enthusiastic interessado/a *eenturusa*doo/ah

entrance entrada (f) *ehn*tradah

envelope envelope (m) *ehnvu*lop

environment ambiente (m) *ahmbee*ehnt

environmentally friendly não faz mal ao ambiente *nãhoo fash mal aoo ahmbee*ehnt

equal igual *ee*gooal

equipment equipamento (m) *ehkeepah*mehntoo

euro euro (m) *ee*roo

escalator escada rolante (f) *eeshkadah roolahnt*

especially especialmente *eeshpuseeal*mehnt

essential essencial *eesehn*seeal

even (including) até *ah*te; (not odd) par *par*

evening tarde (f) *tard*

every cada *kah*dah

everyone todos *toh*doosh

everything tudo *too*doo

everywhere em todo o lado *aheem toh*doo oo *la*doo

exact(ly) exacto/a, exactamente *ehza*too/ah, *ehzatah*mehnt

examination examinação (f) *ehzahmeenah*sãhoo

example exemplo (m) *eezehm*ploo

» **for example** por exemplo *poor eezehm*ploo

excellent excelente *aheeshsu*lehnt

except excepto *aheesh*setoo

excess baggage excesso de bagagem (m) *aheeshsesoo du bahgajaheem*

to **exchange** trocar *troo*kar; (money) cambiar *kahmbee*ar

exchange rate câmbio (m) *kahm*beeoo

excited excitado/a *aheeshsee*tadoo

exciting emocionante *ehmooseeoo*nahnt

excursion excursão (f) *aheeshkoor*sãhoo

excuse me desculpe *dush*koolp

exercise exercício (m) *ehzursee*seeoo

exhibition exposição (f) *aheeshpoozee*sãhoo

exit saída (f) *sa*eedah

to **expect** esperar *eeshpu*rar

expensive caro/a *ka*roo/ah

experience experiência *aheeshpuree*unseeyah

expert perito (m) *pu*reetoo

to **explain** explicar *aheeshplee*kar

explosion explosão (f) *aheeshploo*zãhoo

to **export** exportar *aheeshpoor*tar

express expresso (m) *aheesh*presoo

extension cable extensão (f) *aheeshtehn*sãhoo

external externo *aheesh*ternoo

extra extra *aheesh*trah

eye olho (m) *oh*lloo

eyebrow sobrancelha (f) *soobrahn*saheellah

eyelash pestana (f) *push*tahnah

F

fabric tecido (m) *tu*seedoo

face cara (f) *ka*rah

facilities instalações (fpl) *eenshtahlah*sõheesh

fact facto (m) *fa*too

» **in fact** de facto *du fa*too

factory fábrica (f) *fa*breekah

to fail *(exam/test)* chumbar *shoombar*

failure fracasso (m) *frahkasoo*

to faint desmaiar *dushmaheear*

fair *(haired)* louro/a *lohroo/ah*

fair feira (f) *faheerah*

fairly bastante *bahshtahnt*

faith fé (f) *fe*

fake falso/a *falsoo*

to fall *(down/over)* cair *kaheer*

false falso/a *falsoo/ah*

familiar familiar *fahmeeleear*

family família *fahmeeleeah*

famous famoso/a *fahmohzoo*

fan *(air)* leque (m) *lek;* *(supporter)* adepto (m) *ahdeputoo*

fantastic fantástico/a *fahntashteekoo*

far *(away)* longe *lohnj*

fare preço do bilhete (m) *prehsoo doo beelleht*

farm quinta (f) *keentah*

farmer agricultor/a *ahgreekooltohr/ah*

fashion moda (f) *modah*

fashionable/in fashion na moda *nah modah*

fast rápido/a *rrapeedoo*

fat *(adj/noun)* gordo/a *gohrdoo/ah*

fatal fatal *fahtal*

father pai (m) *paee*

father-in-law sogro (m) *sohgroo*

fault defeito (m) *dufaheetoo*

faulty defeituoso/a *dufaheetooohzoo*

favourite favorito/a *fahvooreetoo*

fax fax (m) *faks*

feather pena (f) *pehnah*

to be fed up farto *fartoo*

fee remuneração (f) *rumoonurahsãhoo*

to feed dar de comer *dar du koomehr*

to feel *(ill/well)* sentir-se *sehnteersu*

female fêmea *femêhah*

feminine feminino/a *fumuneenoo*

feminist feminista *fumuneeshtah*

fence vedação (f) *vudahsãhoo*

ferry ferry-boat (m) *feree-boht*

festival festival (m) *fushteeval*

to fetch ir buscar *eer booshkar*

fever febre (f) *febru*

(a) few poucos/as *pohkoosh/ahsh*

fiancé(e) noiva (f) *noheevah*

field campo (m) *kahmpoo*

to fight lutar *lootar*

to fill encher *ehnshehr*

filling *(dental)* chumbo (m) *shoomboo*

film filme (m) *feelm*

filter filtro (m) *feeltroo*

finance finanças (fpl) *feenahnsahsh*

to find encontrar *ehnkohntrar*

fine *(OK)* está bem *eeshta baheem;* *(penalty)* multa (f) *mooltah;* *(weather)* bom/boa bohm/*bohah*

finger dedo (m) *dehdoo*

to finish acabar *ahkahbar*

fire fogo (m) *fohgoo*

fire brigade bombeiros (mpl) *bohmbaheeroosh*

fire extinguisher extinto (m) *aheeshteentoo*

firework fogo de artifício (m) *fohgoo du ahrteefeeseeoo*

firm firme *feerm*

firm *(business)* empresa (f) *ehmprehzah*

first primeiro/a *preemaheeroo*

first aid primeiros socorros (mpl) *preemaheeroosh sohkorroosh*

fish peixe (m) *paheeshu*

to fish/go fishing pescar *pushkar*

fishing rod cana de pesca (f) *kahnah du peshkah*

fishmonger's peixaria (f) *paheeshahreeah*

fit *(healthy)* em forma *aheem formah*

to fit servir *surveer*

fitting room sala de provas (f) *salah du provahsh*

to fix *(mend)* consertar *kohnsurtar*

fizzy com gás *kohm gash*

flag bandeira (f) *bahndaheerah*

flash *(camera)* flash (m) *flash*

flat (apartment) apartamento (m) *ahpahrtah**mehn**too*

flat (level) plano/a *plahnoo*; (empty) em baixo *aheeñ baeeshoo*

flavour sabor (m) *sahbohr*

flaw defeito (m) *dufaheetoo*

flea market mercado (m) *murkadoo*

flight voo (m) *vohoo*

flippers barbatanas (fpl) *bahrbah**tah**nahsh*

flood inundação (f) *eenoondah**sã**hoo*

floor chão (m) *shãhoo*

» **on the first floor** no primeiro andar *noo preemaheeroo ahndar*

flour farinha (f) *fahreennyah*

flower flor (f) *flohr*

flu gripe (f) *greep*

fluent (language) fluente *flooehnt*

fluid líquido (m) *leekeedoo*

fly mosca (f) *mohshkah*

fly sheet duplo-tecto (m) *dooploo-teto*

to fly voar *vooar*

fog nevoeiro (m) *nuvooaheeroo*

foil folha de alumínio (f) *fohllah du ahloomeeneeoo*

folding (e.g. chair) dobradiço/a *doobrah**dee**soo/ah*

folk music música popular (f) *moozeekah poopoolar*

to follow seguir *sugeer*

following (next) seguinte *sugeent*

food comida (f) *koomeedah*

food poisoning intoxicação alimentar (f) *eentokseekahsãhoo ahleemehntar*

foot pé (m) *pe*

» **on foot** a pé *ah pe*

football futebol (m) *footubol*

footpath caminho (m) *kahmeennyoo*

for para, por *pahrah, poor*

forbidden proibido/a *prooeebeedoo/ah*

foreign, foreigner estrangeiro/a *eeshtranjaheeroo/ah*

forest floresta (f) *flooreshtah*

to forget esquecer *eeshkesehr*

to forgive perdoar *purdooar*

fork garfo (m) *garfoo*

form impresso (m) *eempresoo·*

fortnight quinze dias *keeñz deeahsh*

fortress forte (m) *fort*

forward adiante *ahdeeahnt*

fountain fonte (f) *fohnt*

fox raposa (f) *rahpozah*

foyer hall (m) *ol*

fracture fractura (f) *fratoorah*

fragile frágil *frajeel*

freckles sardas (fpl) *sardahsh*

free grátis *grateesh*; (available/ unoccupied) livre *leevru*

freedom liberdade (f) *leeburdad*

to freeze congelar *kohnjular*

freezer congelador (m) *kohnjuladohr*

frequent frequente *frukoowehnt*

fresh fresco/a *frehshkoo*

fridge frigorífico (m) *freegooreefeekoo*

fried frito/a *freetoo/ah*

friend amigo/a *ahmeegoo/ah*

frightened assustado/a *ahsooshtadoo/ah*

frog rã (f) *rãh*

from de *du*

front fronte (f) *frohnt*

» **in front of** em frente de *aheeñ frehnt du*

frontier fronteira (f) *frohntaheerah*

frost geada (f) *jeadah*

frozen congelado/a *kohnjuladoo/ah*

fruit fruta (f) *frootah*

to fry fritar *freetar*

frying pan frigideira (f) *freejeedaheerah*

fuel combustível (m) *kohmbooshteevel*

full cheio/a *shaheeoo*

full board pensão completa (f) *pehnsãhoo kohmpletah*

full up (booked up) cheio/a, completo/a *shaheeoo/ ah, kohmpletoo/ah*

fun: **to have fun** divertir-se *deevurteersu*

funeral funeral (m) *foonural*

funfair feira popular *faheerah poopoolar*

funny engraçado/a *aheengrahsadoo/ah*; (*strange*) esquisito/a *eeshkuzeetoo/ah*

fur pêlo *pehloo*

furniture mobília (f) *moobeeleeah*

further on mais adiante *maeesh ahdeeahnt*

fuse fusível (m) *foozeevel*

fusebox caixa dos fusíveis (f) *kaeeshah doosh foozeevaheesh*

G

gallery galeria (f) *gahlureeah*

gambling jogo (m) *johgoo*

game (*match*) jogo (m) *johgoo*

garage (*parking*) garagem (f) *gahrajaheem; (petrol)* garagem (f) *gahrajaheem*

garden jardim (m) *jahrdeem*

gardener jardineiro (m) *jahrdeenaheeroo*

garlic alho (m) *alloo*

gas gás *gash*

gas bottle/cylinder garrafa de gás *gahrrafah du gash*

gas refill carga de gás *kargah du gash*

gate portão (m) *poortãhoo* (*airport*) porta (f) *portah*

gay (*homosexual*) homosexual *omoseksooal*

gel (*hair*) gel (m) *jel*

general geral *jural*

» **in general** em geral *aheem jural*

generous generoso/a *junurohzoo/ah*

gentle gentil *jehnteel*

gentleman/men cavalheiro/os *kahvahllaheeroo/oosh;* (*gents*) homens (mpl) *omaheensh*

genuine autêntico/a *aootehnteekoo*

German alemão/alemã *ahlumãhoo/ãh*

Germany Alemanha (f) *ahlumahnnyah*

to **get** obter *obutehr*

» **to get off** (*bus*) sair *saheer*

» **to get on** (*bus*) entrar (em) *ehntrar*

» **to get through** (*phone*) conseguir falar *kohnsugeer fahlar*

gift presente (m) *pruzehnt*

gin gin *jeen*

girl rapariga (f) *rahpahreegah*

girlfriend namorada (f) *nahmooradah*

to **give** dar *dar*

to **give back** dar de volta *dar du voltah*

glass copo (m) *kopoo; (made of)* vidro (m) *veedroo*

glasses copos (mpl) *kopoosh*

gloves luvas (fpl) *loovahsh*

glue cola (f) *kolah*

to **go** ir *eer*

» **let's go!** Vamos! *vahmoosh*

to **go away** ir embora *eer aheemborah*

to **go down** descer *dussehr*

to **go in** entrar (em) *ehntrar*

to **go out** sair *saheer*

to **go round** (*visit*) visitar *veezeetar*

goal objectivo (m) *obujeteevoo;* (*football*) golo (m) *gohloo*

goat cabra (f) *kabrah*

God Deus (m) *dehoosh*

goggles óculos de mergulho (mpl) *okooloosh du murgoolloo*

gold ouro (m) *ohroo*

golf golfe (m) *golf*

golf clubs tacos de golfe (mpl) *takoosh du golf*

golf course campo de golfe (m) *kampoo du golf*

good bom, boa *bohm, bohah*

» **good day** bom dia (m) *bohm deeah*

» **good evening** boa tarde (f) *bohah tard*

» **good morning** bom dia (m) *bohm deeah*

» **good night** boa noite (f) *bohah noheet*

goodbye adeus *ahdehoosh*

Good Friday Sexta-feira Santa *saheeshtah-faheerah sahntah*

government governo (m) *goovehrnoo*

gramme grama (m) *grahmah*

grammar gramática (f) *grahmateekah*

grandchildren netos (mpl) *netoosh*

granddaughter neta (f) *netah*

grandfather avô (m) *ahvoh*

grandmother avó (f) *ahvo*

grandparents avós (mpl) *ahvosh*

grandson neto (m) *netoo*

grass relva (f) *relvah*

grateful agradecido/a *ahgrahduseedoo/ ahgrahduseedah*

great! óptimo *oteemoo*

green verde *vehrd*

greengrocer's frutaria (f) *frootahreeah*

to **greet** saudar *saoodar*

grey cinzento/a *seenzehntoo*

grilled grelhado/a *grulladoo*

grocer's mercearia (f) *murseeahreeah*

ground chão (m) *shãhoo*

groundsheet chão da tenda (m) *shãhoo dah tehndah*

ground floor rés-do-chão (m) *rrésh-doo-shãhoo*

group grupo (m) *groopoo*

guarantee garantia (f) *garahnteeah*

guest convidado/a *kohnveedadoo (hotel)* hóspede (m) *oshpudu*

guest house pensão (f) *pehnsãhoo*

guide guia (m/f) *geeah*

guided tour visita com guia (f) *veezeetah kohm̃ geeah*

guidebook guia turístico (m) *geeah tooreeshteekoo*

guilty culpado/a *kulpado*

guitar guitarra (f) *geetarrah*

gun arma (f) *armah*

H

habit costume (m) *kooshtoomu*

hail granizo (m) *grahneezoo*

hair cabelo (m) *kahbehloo*

hairbrush escova (f) *eeshkohvah*

haircut corte de cabelo (m) *kort du kahbehloo*

hairdresser cabeleireira/o *kahbulaheeraheerah*

hairdryer secador de cabelo (m) *sukahdohr du kahbehloo*

half metade *mutad*

half (adj) meio/a *maheeoo/ah*

  » **half an hour** meia hora (f) *maheeah orah*

  » **half past** e meia *ee maheeah*

half board meia pensão (f) *maheeah pehsãhoo*

half price metade do preço (a) *mutad doo prehsoo*

hall (in house) hall (m) *ol*

ham presunto (m) *pruzoontoo*

hamburger hamburguer (m) *amboorger*

hammer martelo (m) *mahrteloo*

hand mão (f) *mãhoo*

hand luggage bagagem de mão *bahgajaheem̃ du mãhoo*

hand made feito à mão *faheetoo a mãhoo*

handbag mala de mão *malah du mãhoo*

handkerchief lenço (m) *lehnsoo*

handle asa (f) *azah*

to **hang up (telephone)** desligar *dushleegar*

hangover ressaca (f) *rrusakah*

to **happen** acontecer *ahkohntusehr*

happy feliz *fuleesh*

harbour porto (m) *pohrtoo*

hard duro/a *doorool/ah (difficult)* difícil *deefeeseel*

hard shoulder berma (f) *behrmah*

hardware shop loja de hardware *lojah du ardwer*

to **hate** odiar *odeear*

to **have** ter *tehr*

hay feno (m) *fehnoo*

he ele *ehl*

head cabeça (f) *kahbehsah*

headache dores de cabeça (fpl) *dohrush du kahbehsah*

headphones auscultadores (mpl) *aooshkooltahdohrush*

to **heal** curar *koorar*

health saúde (f) *sahood*

healthy são/sã *sãhoo/sãh*

to **hear** ouvir *ohveer*

hearing

hearing aid aparelho de surdez (m) *ahpahrehllo*

heart coração (m) *koorahsãhoo*

heart attack ataque de coração (m) *ahtaku du koorahsãhoo*

heat calor (m) *kahlohr*

heater aquecedor (m) *ahkehsadohr*

heating aquecimento (m) *ahkeseemehntoo*

heavy pesado/a *puzadoo/ah*

heel (shoe) salto (m) *saltoo*

height altura (f) *altoorah*

helicopter helicóptero *ehleekoputuroo*

hello olá *ola*

helmet (motorbike) capacete (m) *kahpahsehtu*

help ajuda (f) *ahjoodah*

help! Socorro! *sohkohrroo*

to **help** ajudar *ahjoodar*

her (adj, pronoun) a, lhe, ela *ah, llu, elah*

herb erva (f) *ervah*

herbal tea chá de ervas (m) *sha du ervahsh*

here aqui *ahkee*

hers dela *delah*

hiccups: to have hiccups ter soluços *tehr sooloosoosh*

high alto/a *altoo/ah*

high chair cadeira de bébé (f) *kahdaheerah du bebe*

to **hijack** sequestrar *sukushtrar*

hill colina (f) *kooleenah*

him o, lhe, ele *oo, llu, ehl*

to **hire** alugar *ahloogar*

his (adj, pronoun) o/a...dele *oo/ah...dehle*

history história (f) *eeshtoreeah*

to **hit** bater *bahtehr*

to **hitchhike** andar à boleira *ahndar a boolaheeah*

HIV positive HIV positivo *aga ee veh poozeeteevoo*

hobby passatempo (m) *pasahtehmpoo*

to **hold** segurar *sugoorar*

hole buraco (m) *boorakoo*

holiday (public) feriado (m) *fureeadoo*

  » **on holiday** de férias *du fereeahsh*

holidays (school, etc.) férias (fpl) *fereeahsh*

holy santo/a *sahntoo/ah*

home casa (f) *kazah*

  » **at home** em casa *aheem kazah*

homeopathic homeopático/a *omeeopateekoo/ah*

homosexual homosexual (m) *omoseksooal*

honest honesto/a *ooneshtoo*

honeymoon lua de mel (f) *looah du mel*

to **hope** esperar *eeshpurar*

  » **I hope so** espero que sim *eeshperoo ku seem*

horrible horrível *orreevel*

horse cavalo (m) *kahvaloo*

hospital hospital (m) *oshpeetal*

host hospedeiro (m) *oshpudaheeroo*

hot quente *kehnt;* (spicy) picante *peekahnt*

hotel hotel (m) *otel*

hour hora (f) *orah*

house casa (f) *kazah*

hovercraft hovercraft (m) *ovurkraft*

how como *kohmo*

  » **how far?** é longe? *e lohnj*

  » **how long?** quanto tempo? *kwahñtoo tehmpoo*

  » **how many?** quantos/as? *kwahñtoosh/ahsh*

  » **how much?** quanto custa? *kwahñtoo kooshtah*

human humano (m) *oomahnoo*

human being ser humano (m) *sehr oomahnoo*

hungry fome *fom*

  » **to be hungry** estar com fome *eeshtar kohm fom*

to **hunt** caçar *kahsar*

hunting caça (f) *kasah*
hurry: to be in a hurry estar com pressa *eeshtar kohm presah*
to hurt doer *dooehr*
husband marido (m) *mahreedoo*
hut cabana (f) *kahbahnah*
hydrofoil folha metálica hidrólica (f) *fohllah mutaleekah eedroleekah*

I eu *ehoo*
ice gelo (m) *jehloo*
ice rink ringue de patinagem (m) *rreengu du pahteenajaheem*
icy gelado/a *juladoo/ah*
idea ideia *eedaheeah*
if se *su*
ill doente *dooehnt*
illness doença (f) *dooehnsah*
to imagine imaginar *eemahjeenar*
imagination imaginação (f) *eemahjeenahsãhoo*
immediately imediatamente *eemudeeatahmehnt*
immersion heater aquecedor de imersão (m) *ahkesudohr du eemursãhoo*
important importante *eempoortahnt*
impossible impossível *eempooseevel*
impressive impressionante *eempruseeooonahnt*
in em, no, na, dentro de *ahem, noo, nah, dehntroo du*
included incluído/a *eenklooeedoo/ah*
independent independente *eendupehndehnt*
indigestion indigestão (f) *eendeejushtãhoo*
indoors dentro *dehntroo*
industry indústria (f) *eendooshtreeah*
infected infectado/a *eenfetadoo/ah*
infection infecção (f) *eenfesãhoo*
infectious contagioso/a *kohntahjeeeohzoo/ah*
inflamed inflamado/a *eenflahmadoo/ah*

influenza gripe (f) *greep*
informal informal *eenfoormal*
information informação (f) *eenfoormahsãhoo*
information office posto de informação (m) *pohshtoo du eenfoormahsãhoo*
injection injecção (f) *eenjesãhoo*
to injure ferir *fureer*
injured ferido/a *fureedoo/ah*
injury ferida/a *fureedah/ah*
innocent inocente *eenoosehnt*
insect insecto (m) *eensetoo*
insect bite picada de insecto (f) *peekadah du eensetoosh*
insect repellent repelente de insectos (m) *rupulehnt du eensetoosh*
inside dentro *dehntroo*
to insist insistir *eenseeshteer*
instead of em vez de *ahem vehsh du*
instructor instrutor (m)/ora (f) *eenshtrootohr/ohrah*
insulin insulina (f) *eensooleenah*
insult insulto (m) *eensooltoo*
insurance seguro (m) *sugooroo*
to insure assegurar *ahsugoorar*
insured está no seguro *eeshta noo sugooroo*
intelligent inteligente *eentuleejehnt*
interest (money) juros (mpl) *jooroosh*
interested interessado/a *eenturusadoo/ah*
interesting interessante *eenturusahnt*
international internacional *eenturnahseeooonal*
Internet internet (f) *eenternet*
to interpret interpretar *eenturpretar*
interpreter intérprete (m) *eenterprutu*
interval (theatre, etc.) intervalo (m) *eenturvaloo*
interview entrevista (f) *ehntruveeshtah*
into em *aheem*
to introduce apresentar *ahpruzehntar*
invitation convite (m) *kohnveet*
to invite convidar *kohnveedar*

iodine iodo (m) *eeohdoo*
Ireland Irlanda (f) *eerlahndah*
Irish irlandês/esa *eerlahndehsh*
iron *(metal, for clothes)* ferro (m) *ferroo*
to **iron** passar a ferro *pahsar ah ferroo*
is é *e*
   » **is there... ?** há... ? *a...*
Islam islamismo (m) *eeshlahmeeshmoo*
Islamic islâmico/a *eeshlahmeekoo/ah*
island ilha (f) *eellah*
itch comichão (f) *koomeeshãhoo*

J

jacket casaco (m) *kahzakoo*
jam doce (m) *dohsu*
jar frasco (m) *frashkoo*
jaw queixo (m) *kaheeshoo*
jazz jazz (m) *jaz*
jeans jeans (mpl) *jeens*
jelly *(pudding)* gelatina (f) *julahteenah*
jellyfish medusa (f) *mudoozah*
jetty cais (m) *kaeesh*
jeweller's joalharia (f) *jooahllahreeah*
Jewish judeu/judia *joodehoo/joodeeah*
job emprego (m) *ehmprehgoo*
to **jog** jog *jog*
joke piada (f) *peeadah*
journey viagem (f) *veeajaheem*
jug jarro (m) *jarroo*
juice sumo (m) *soomoo*
to **jump** saltar *saltar*
jump leads cabos de emergência (mpl)
   kaboosh du eemurjehnseeah
jumper camisola (f) *kahmeezolah*
junction *(road)* cruzamento (m)
   kroozahmehntoo
just *(only)* só *so*

K

to **keep** guardar *gooahrdar*; *(to put by)*
   pôr de parte *pohr du part*
kettle chaleira (f) *shahlaheerah*
key chave (f) *shav*
key ring porta-chaves (m) *portah-*

shavush
kidney rim (m) *rreem*
to **kill** matar *mahtar*
kilo(gram) quilo (m) *keeloo*
kilometre quilómetro (m) *keelomutroo*
kind *(sort)* tipo (m) *teepoo*;
   (generous) amável *ahmavel*
king rei (m) *rrahee*
kiss beijo (m) *baheejoo*
to **kiss** beijar *baheejar*
kitchen cozinha (f) *koozeennyah*
knee joelho (m) *jooehlloo*
knickers cuecas (fpl) *kooekahsh*
knife faca (f) *fakah*
to **knock** bater *bahtehr*
knot nó *no*
to **know** *(someone)* conhecer *koonnyusehr;*
   (something) saber *sahbehr*
   » **I don't know** não sei *nãhoo sahee*

L

label etiqueta (f) *ehteekehtah*
ladder escada (f) *eeshkadah*
lady senhora (f) *sunnyohrah*
ladies senhoras (fpl) *sunnyohrahsh*
lager cerveja (f) *survaheejah*
lake lago (m) *lagoo*
lamb *(meat)* cordeiro (m) *koordaheeroo*
lamp candeeiro (m) *kahndeeaheeroo*
land terra (f) *terrah*
to **land** aterrar *ahturrar*
landlady senhoria *sunnyohreeah*
landlord senhorio *sunnyohreeoo*
language língua (f) *leengooah*
large grande *grahnd*
last último/a *oolteemoo/ah*
to **last** durar *doorar*
late tarde *tard*
later mais tarde *maeesh tard*
laugh riso (m) *rreezoo*
to **laugh** rir *rreer*
launderette lavandaria automática (f)
   lahvahndahreeah aootomateekah
laundry lavandaria (f) *lahvahndahreeah*
law lei (f) *lahee*

lawyer advogado/a *aduvoo**ga**doo/ah*
laxative laxativo (m) *lahshah**tee**voo*
lazy preguiçoso/a *prugee**soh**zoo*
lead chumbo (m) *shoomboo*
leaf folha (f) *fohllah*
leaflet folheto (m) *fohllehtoo*
to lean out debruçar-se *dubroo**sar**su*
to learn aprender *ahprehndehr*
least: at least pelo menos *pehloo mehnoosh*
leather pele (f) *pel*
to leave deixar *daheeshar (to go away)* partir *pahrteer*
left esquerda (f) *eeshkehrdah*
left luggage *(office)* depósito de bagagem (m) *dupozeetoo du bagajaheem*
leg perna (f) *pernah*
lemon limão (m) *leemãhoo*
lemonade limonada (f) *leemoonadah*
to lend emprestar *ehmprushtar*
length comprimento (m) *kohmpreemehntoo*
lens *(camera)* lente (fpl) *lehntu*
lesbian lésbica (f) *leshbeekah*
less menos *mehnoosh*
lesson lição (f) *leesãhoo*
to let *(allow)* deixar *daheeshar; (rent)* alugar *ahloogar*
letter carta (f) *kartah (of alphabet)* letra (f) *lehtrah*
letterbox marco do correio (m) *markoo doo koorraheeoo*
lettuce alface (f) *alfasu*
leukemia leuquemia (f) *lehookumeeah*
level *(height, standard)* nível (m) *neevel; (flat)* andar (m) *ahndar*
level crossing passagem de nível (f) *pahsajaheem du neevel*
library biblioteca (f) *beebleeootekah*
licence *(driving)* carta de condução (f) *kartah du kohndoosãhoo (fishing, etc.)* licença (f) *leesehnsah*
lid tampa (f) *tahmpah*

to lie down deitar-se *daheetarsu*
life vida (f) *veedah*
lifebelt cinto salva-vidas (m) *seentoo salvah-veedahsh*
lifeboat bote salva-vidas (m) *bot salvah-veedahsh*
lifeguard nadador-salvador (m) *nahdahdohr salvahdohr*
lifejacket colete salava-vidas (m) *kooleht salvah-veedahsh*
lift elevador (m) *eeluvahdohr*
light luz (f) *loosh*
light bulb lâmpada (f) *lahmpahdah*
light *(coloured)* claro/a *klaroo/ah; (weight)* ligeiro/a *leejaheeroo/ah*
to light *(fire)* acender *ahsehndehr*
lighter *(cigarette)* isqueiro (m) *eeshkaheeroo*
lighter fuel gás para o isqueiro (m) *gash pahrah oo eeshkaheeroo*
lightning relâmpago (m) *rulahmpahgoo*
like *(similar to)* como *kohmoo*
to like *(food, people)* gostar *gooshtar*
» **I like** gosto *goshtoo*
likely provável *proovavel*
limited limitado/a *leemeetadoo/ah*
line linha (f) *leennyah*
lip lábio (m) *labeeoo*
liqueur licor (m) *leekohr*
liquid líquido (m) *leekeedoo*
list lista (f) *leeshtah*
to listen ouvir *ohveer*
litre litro (m) *leetroo*
litter lixo (m) *leeshoo*
little pequeno/a *pukehnoo/ah*
» **a little** um pouco (de) *oom pohkoo*
to live viver *veevehr; (dwell)* morar *moorar*
liver fígado (m) *feegahdoo*
living-room sala de estar *salah du eeshtar*
loan empréstimo (m) *aheem preshteemoo*
local local *lookal*
lock fechadura (f) *fushahdoorah*
to lock fechar à chave *fushar a shav*

locker cadiado (m) *kahdeeadoo*

lonely só, sozinho/a *so, sozeennyoo/ah*

long comprido/a *kohmpreedoo/ah*

long-distance longe *lohnj*

long-distance call para fora *pahrah forah*

to look (at) olhar *ollar*

to look for procurar *prokoorar*

loose largo/a *largoo/ah*

lorry camião (m) *kameeaāhoo*

to lose perder *purdehr*

lost property office posto de perdidos e achados (m) *pohshtoo du purdeedoosh ee ahshadoosh*

a lot (of) muito/a *mooeentoo/ah*

lotion loção (f) *loosāhoo*

lottery lotaria (f) *lootahreeah*

loud alto/a *altoo/ah*

lounge sala de estar (f) *sala du eeshtar*

love amor (m) *ahmohr*

to love amar *ahmar*

low baixo/a *baeeshoo/ah*

low-fat com poucas gorduras *kohm̄ pohkahsh goordoorahsh*

lower inferior *eenfureeohr*

lucky: to be lucky ter sorte *tehr sort*

luggage bagagem (f) *bahgajaheem̄*

lump (swelling) inchaço (m) *eenshasoo*

lunch almoço (m) *almohsoo*

M

machine máquina (f) *makeenah*

mad louco/a *lohkoo/ah*

madam senhora (f) *sunnyohrah*

magazine revista (f) *ruveeshtah*

mail correio (m) *koorraheeoo*

main principal *preenseepal*

to make fazer *fahzehr*

make-up maquilhagem (f) *makeellajaheem̄*

male macho (m) *mashoo*

man homem (m) *omaheem̄*

to manage (cope) poder com *poodehr kohm̄*

manager gerente (m/f) *jurehnt*

many muitos/as *mooeentoosh/ahsh*

» **not many** poucos/as *pohkoosh/ahsh*

map mapa (m) *mapah*

marble mármore (m) *marmooru*

margarine margarina (f) *mahrgahreenah*

market mercado (m) *murkadoo*

married casado/a *kahzadoo/ah*

» **to get married** casar-se *kahzarsu*

mascara rimel (m) *reemel*

masculine masculino/a *mashkooleenoo/ah*

mask máscara (f) *mashkahrah*

mass (church) missa (f) *meesah*

match fósforo (m) *foshfuroo (game)* partida (f) *pahrteedah*

material (clothes) pano (m) *pahnoo*

matter: it doesn't matter não faz mal *nāhoo fash mal*

» **what's the matter?** Que se passa? *ku su pasah?*

mattress colchão (m) *kolshāhoo*

» **air mattress** colchão de ar (m) *kolshāhoo du ar*

mature (cheese) maduro/a *mahdooroo/ah*

me me, mim *mu, meem̄*

meal refeição (f) *rufaheesāhoo*

mean: what does this mean? Que quer dizer? *ku ker deezehr*

meanwhile entretanto *ehntrutahntoo*

measles sarampo *sahrahm̄poo*

» **German measles** rubéola (f) *rubeoolah*

to measure medir *mudeer*

measurement medida (f) *mudeedah*

meat carne (f) *karnu*

mechanic mecânico (m) *mukahneekoo*

medical médico/a *medeekoo/ah*

medicine (drug) medicamento (m) *mudeekahmehntoo*

medieval medieval *mudeeahval*

Mediterranean mediterrâneo *mudeeturrahneeoo*

medium (size) médio/a *medeeoo/ah*; **(steak)** média *medeeah*; **(wine)** meio *maheeoo*

meeting reunião (f) *rehooneeãhoo*

member membro (m) *mehmbroo*

memory memória (f) *mumoreeah*

memory stick *(for camera)* cartão de memória (m) *kahrtãhoo du mumoreeah*

men homens (mpl) *omaheeñsh*

to **mend** reparar *rupahrar*

menu *(a la carte)* ementa (f) *eemehntah*; *(set)* ementa turística (f) *eemehntah tooreeshteekah*

message mensagem (f) *mehnsajaheem̃*

metal metal (m) *mutal*

meter contador (m) *kohntahdohr*

metre metro (m) *metrooo*

microwave oven micro-ondas (m) *meekro-ohndahsh*

midday meio-dia (m) *maheeoo deeah*

middle centro (m) *sehntroo*

middle-aged de meia idade *du maheeah eedad*

midnight meia-noite (f) *maheeah-noheet*

migraine enxaqueca (f) *ehnshahkekah*

mild suave *sooav*

mile milha (f) *meellah*

milk leite (m) *laheet*

mill moinho (m) *mooeennyoo*

mind: do you mind if...? importa-se que...? *eemportahsu...*
» **I don't mind** não me importo *nãhoo mu eemportoo*

mine *(of me)* meu (m)/minha (f) *mehoo/meennyah*

minibus micro-ónibus (m) *meekro-oneeboosh*

minute minuto (m) *meenootoo*

mirror espelho (m) *eeshpehlloo*

to **miss** *(bus, etc.)* perder *purdehr*; *(nostalgia)* saudade (f) *sahoodad*

mist névoa (f) *nevooah*

mistake erro (m) *ehrroo*
» **to make a mistake** fazer um erro *fahzehr oom̃ ehrroo*

mixed misturado/a *meeshtooradoo/ah*

mixture mistura (f) *meeshtoorah*

mobile telemóvel (m) *telemovel*

model modelo (m) *moodehloo*

modem modem (m) *modem*

modern moderno/a *moodernoo*

moisturiser creme hidratante (m) *krem heedrahtahnt*

moment momento (m) *moomehntoo*

monastery mosteiro (m) *mooshtaheeroo*

money dinheiro (m) *deennyaheeroo*

month mês (m) *mehsh*

monthly mensal *mehnsal*

monument monumento (m) *moonoomehntoo*

moon lua (f) *looah*

moped bicicleta motorizada (f) *beeseekletah mootooreezadah*

more mais *maeesh*

morning manhã (f) *mahñnyãh*

mortgage empréstimo (m) *ehmpreshteemoo*

mosque mesquita (f) *mushkeetah*

mosquito mosquito (m) *mooshkeetoo*

mosquito net rede para mosquitos (f) *rehd pahrah mooshkeetoosh*

most (of) a maior parte (de) *ah maeeor part (du)*

mother mãe (f) *mãhee*

mother-in-law sogra (f) *sograh*

motor motor (m) *mootohr*

motorbike motorizada (f) *mootooreezadah*

motorboat barco a motor (m) *barkoo ah mootohr*

motor racing automobilismo (m) *aootoomoobeeleeshmoo*

motorway autoestrada (f) *aootooeeshtradah*

mountain montanha (f) *mohntahnnyah*

mountaineering alpinismo (m) *alpeeneeshmoo*

moustache bigode (m) *beegod*

mouth boca (f) *bohkah*

to move mover *moovehr*

to move house mudar de casa *moodar du kazah*

Mr Senhor (m) *sunnyohr*

Mrs Senhora (f) *sunnyohrah*

much muito/a *mooeentoo/ah*

mug *(cup)* caneca (f) *kahnekah*

to mug *(someone)* roubar *rrohbar*

mullah mullah *moolah*

to murder matar *mahtar*

museum museu (m) *moozehoo*

music música (f) *moozeekah*

musical musical *moozeekal*

musician músico (m) *moozeekoo*

Muslim muculmano/a *moosoolmahnoo/ moosoolmahnah*

must: you must tem (de) *taheeñ (de)*

my o meu... (m) /a minha... (f) *oo mehoo... /ah meennyah...*

mystery mistério (m) *meeshtereeoo*

N

nail *(carpentry)* prego (m) *pregoo; (finger, toe)* unha (f) *ooñnyah*

»» **nail clippers/scissors** tesoura de unhas (f) *tuzohrah du ooñnyahsh*

naked nú/nua *noo/nooah*

name nome (m) *nohm*

napkin guardanapo (m) *gooahrdahnapoo*

nappy fralda (f) *fraldah*

»» **disposable nappy** fralda descartável (f) *fraldah dushkahrtavel*

national nacional *nahseeoonal*

nationality nacionalidade (f) *nahseeoonahleedad*

natural(ly) natural(mente) *nahtooral(mehnt)*

naughty travesso/a *trahvehsoo/ah*

navy marinha (f) *mahreennyah*

navy blue azul marinho *ahzool mahreennyoo*

near perto (de) *pertoo (du)*

nearby próximo *proseemoo*

nearly quase *kwaz*

necessary necessário/a *nususareeoo/ah*

necklace colar (m) *koolar*

to need precisar *pruseezar*

needle agulha (f) *ahgoollah*

negative *(photo)* negativo (m) *nugahteevoo*

neighbour vizinho/a *veezeennyoo/ah*

neither ... nor ... nem ... nem *naheeñ ... naheeñ*

nephew sobrinho (m) *soobreennyoo*

nervous nervoso/a *nurvohzoo/nurvozah*

net rede (f) *rehdu*

never nunca *noonkah*

new novo/a *nohvoo/novah*

New Year's Day Dia de Ano Novo (m) *deeah du ahnoo nohvoo*

news notícias (fpl) *nooteeseeahsh*

newspaper jornal (m) *joornal*

newspaper kiosk quiosque (m) *keeoshku*

next próximo/a *proseemoo/ah*

next to ao lado (de) *aoo ladoo (du)*

nice *(person)* simpático/a *seempateekoo/ah; (place)* bonito/a *booneetoo/ah*

niece sobrinha (f) *soobreennyah*

night noite (f) *noheet*

nightclub boite (f) *booat*

no não *nãhoo*

nobody ninguém *neengaheeñ*

noise barulho *bahroolloo*

noisy barulhento/a *bahroollehntoo/ah*

non-alcoholic sem-álcool *saheeñ -alkoool*

none nenhum/nenhuma *nunnyooñ /nunnyoomah*

non-smoking não-fumadores *nãhoo foomahdohrush*

normal normal *normal*

normally normalmente *normalmehnt*

north norte (m) *nort*

nose nariz (m) *nahreesh*

nosebleed hemorragia nasal (f) *ehmoorrahjeeah nahzal*

not não *nãhoo*

note *(bank)* nota (f) *notah*

notepad bloco para notas (m) *blokoo pahrah notahsh*

nothing nada *nadah*

» **nothing else** mais nada *maeesh nadah*

now agora *ahgorah*

nowhere em lado nenhum *aheeÑ ladoo nunnyooÑ*

number número (m) *noomuroo*

nurse enfermeiro/a *ehnfurmaheeroo/ah*

nut nóz (f) *nosh*

O

object *(thing)* objecto (m) *obujetoo*

obvious óbvio/a *obuveeoo*

occasionally às vezes *ash vehzush*

occupied ocupado/a *okoopadoo/ah*

odd estranho/a *eeshtrahnyoo/ah (not even)* ímpar *eempar*

of de *du*

of course claro *klaroo*

off *(light)* desligado/a *dushleegadoo/ah; (milk)* estragado/a *eeshtrahgadoo/ah*

offended ofendido/a *ofehndeedoo/ah*

offer oferta (f) *ofertah*

» **special offer** oferta especial (f) *ofertah eeshpuseeal*

office escritório (m) *eeshkreetoreeo*

officer oficial (m) *ofeeseeal*

official oficial *ofeeseeal*

often muitas vezes *mooeentahs vehzush*

» **how often?** quantas vezes? *kwahÑtahsh vehzush*

oil óleo (m) *oleeoo*

OK está bem *eeshta baheeÑ*

old velho/a *velloo/ah*

old-fashioned antiquado/a *ahnteekooadoo/ah*

olive azeitona (f) *ahzaheetohnah*

olive oil azeite (m) *ahzaheet*

on em *aheeÑ*

once uma vez *oomah vehsh*

only só *so*

open aberto/a *ahbertoo*

to **open** abrir *ahbreer*

opera opera (f) *opurah*

operation operação (f) *opurahsãhoo*

opinion opinião (f) *opeeneeãhoo*

» **in my opinion** na minha opinião *nah meennyah opeeneeãhoo*

opposite contrário/a *kohntrareeoo*

optician oculista (m) *okooleeshtah*

or ou *oh*

orange *(fruit)* laranja (f) *lahrahnjah; (colour)* cor de laranja (f) *kohr du lahrahnjah*

order ordem (f) *ordaheeÑ*

to **order** pedir *pudeer*

ordinary vulgar *voolgar*

to **organise** organizar *orgahneezar*

original original *oreejeenal*

other outro/a *ohtroo/ah*

our nosso/nossa *nosoo/ah*

out (of) fora (de) *forah (du)*

outside ao ar livre *aoo ar leevru*

over sobre *sohbru*

to **overtake** ultrapassar *ooltrahpahsar*

to **owe** dever *duvehr*

ozone-friendly não faz mal ao ozónio *nãhoo fash mal ao ohzohneeoo*

P

package tour excursão organizada (f) *aheeshkoorsãhoo*

packet embrulho (m) *ehmbroolloo*

paddle *(canoeing)* remo (m) *rremoo*

padlock cadeado (m) *kahdeeadoo*

page página (f) *pajeenah*

pain dor (f) *dohr*

painful doloroso/a *dooloorohzoo/ah*

painkiller analgésico *ahnaljezeekoo*

to **paint** pintar *peentar*

painter pintor/ora *peentohr*

painting pintura (f) *peentoorah*

pair par *par*

palace palácio (m) *pahlaseeoo*

pale pálido/a *paleedoo*

pants cuecas (fpl) *kooekahsh*

paper papel (m) *pahpel*

paraffin parafina (f) *pahrahfeenah*

paralysed paralisado/a *pahrahleezadoo*

parcel embrulho (m) *ehmbroolloo*

pardon? desculpe? *dushkoolp*

parents pais (mpl) *paeesh*

park parque (m) *park*

to park estacionar *eeshtahseeoonar*

parking estacionamento (m) *eeshtahseeoonahmehntoo*

parking meter parquímetro (m) *parkeemutroo*

parliament parlamento (m) *pahrlahmehntoo*

part parte (f) *part*

particular: in particular em particular *aheeñ pahrteekoolar*

partly em parte *aheeñ part*

partner sócio/a *soseeoo/ah*

party festa (f) *feshtah*; (political) partido (m) *pahrteedoo*

to pass (on road) passar *pahsar*

passenger passageiro/a *pahsahjaheeroo/ah*

passion paixão (f) *paeeshãhoo*

passport passaporte (m) *pasahport*

passport control controle (m) *kohntrol*

past passado (m) *pahsadoo*

» in the past no passado *noo pahsadoo*

pasta massa (f) *masah*

pastry massa (f) *masah*

path caminho (m) *kahmeennyoo*

patient (hospital) doente (f) *dooehnt*

pattern padrão (m) *pahdrãhoo*

pavement passeio (m) *pahsaheeoo*

to pay pagar *pahgar*

» to pay cash pagar a dinheiro *pahgar ah deennyaheeroo*

peace paz (f) *pash*

peanut amendoim (m) *ahmehndooeeñ*

pedal pedal (m) *pudal*

pedal-boat barco a pedais (m) *barkoo ah pudaeesh*

pedestrian peão (m) *peeãhoo*

pedestrian crossing passagem de peões (f) *pahsajaheeñ du peeõheesh*

to peel pelar *pular*

peg mola (f) *molah*

pen caneta (f) *kahnehtah*

pencil lápis (m) *lapeesh*

penfriend correspondente (m/f) *koorrushpohndehnt*

penknife canivete (m) *kahneevet*

penicillin penicilina (f) *puneesooleenah*

pension pensão (f) *pensãhoo*

pensioner pensionista (m/f) *pehnseeooneeshtah*

people pessoas (fpl) *pusohahsh*

pepper pimenta (f) *peemehntah*

per pôr *pohr*

perfect perfeito/a *purfaheetoo*

performance representação (f) *repruzehntahsãhoo*

perfume perfume (m) *purfoom*

perhaps talvez *talvehsh*

period (menstrual) período (m) *pureeoodoo*

» period pains dores do período (fpl) *dohrush doo pureeoodoo*

perm permanente (f) *purmahnehnt*

permit licença (f) *leesehnsah*

to permit permitir *purmeeteer*

personal pessoal *pusooal*

petrol gasolina (f) *gahzooleenah*

petrol can lata de gasolina (f) *latah du gahzooleenah*

petrol station estação de serviço (f) *eeshtahsãhoo du surveesoo*

photocopy fotocópia (f) *fotokopeeah*

to photocopy fotocopiar *fotokoopeear*

photo fotografia (f) *footoograhfeeah*

photographer fotógrafo (m) *footografoo*

phrase book guia de conversação (m) *geeah du kohnvursahsãhoo*

piano piano (m) *peeahnoo*

to pick (choose) escolher *eeshkoollehr*

picnic piquenique (m) *peekuneek*

picture quadro (m) *kwadroo*

piece pedaço (m) *pudasoo*

pier cais (m) *kaeesh*

pig porco (m) *pohrkoo*

pill comprimido (m) *kohmpreemeedoo*

» **the pill** pílula (f) *peeloolah*

pillow almofada (f) *almoofadah*

pilot piloto (m) *peelohtoo*

pilot light piloto (m) *peelohtoo*

pin alfinete (m) *alfeeneht*

pink cor-de-rosa *kohr du rrozah*

pipe *(smoking)* cachimbo (m) *kahsheemboo* *(drain)* cano (m) *kahnoo*

place lugar (m) *loogar*

plain simples *seemplush*

plan mapa (m) *mapah*

plane avião (m) *ahveeãhoo*

plant planta (f) *plahntah*

plaster *(sticking)* penso adesivo (m) *pehnsoo aduzeevoo*

plastic plástico (m) *plashteekoo*

plastic bag saco de plástico (m) *sakoo du plashteekoo*

plate prato (m) *pratoo*

platform plataforma (f) *plahtahformah*

play *(theatre)* obra (f) *obrah*

to **play** brincar *breeñkar*

pleasant agradável *ahgrahdavel*

please por favor *poor fahvohr*

plenty (of) bastante *bahshtahnt*

plug *(bath)* tampa (f) *tahmpah;* *(electrical)* tomada (f) *toomadah*

plumber canalizador (m) *kahnahleezahdohr*

pocket bolso (m) *bohlsoo*

point ponto (m) *pohntoo*

poison veneno (m) *vunehnoo*

poisonous venenoso/a *vununohzoo*

police polícia (m) a mulher polícia (f) *pooleeseeah, ah mooler pooleeseeah*

police station esquadra da polícia (f) *eeshkwadrah dah pooleeseeah*

polish graixa (f) *graeeshah*

polite bem educado/a *baheeñ ehdookadoo/ah*

politician político (m) *pooleeteekoo*

politics política (f) *pooleeteekah*

polluted poluído *poolooeedoo*

pollution poluição (f) *poolooeesãhoo*

pool *(swimming)* piscina (f) *peeshseenah*

poor pobre *pobru*

Pope Papa (m) *papah*

popular popular *poopoolar*

pork porco (m) *pohrkoo*

port *(harbour)* porto (m) *pohrtoo; (wine)* vinho do porto (m) *veennyoo doo pohrtoo*

portable portável *poortavel*

porter porteiro (m) *poortaheeroo*

portion porção (f) *poorsãhoo*

portrait retrato (m) *rrutratoo*

positive *(sure)* positivo/a *poozeeteevoo/poozeeteevah*

possible possível *pooseevel*

possibly possivelmente *pooseevelmenht*

post *(mail)* correio (m) *koorraheeoo*

to **post** pôr no correio *pohr noo koorraheeoo*

postbox marco do correio (m) *markoo doo koorraheeoo*

postcard postal (m) *pooshtal*

postcode código postal (m) *kodeegoo pooshtal*

post office correios (mpl) *koorraheeoosh*

to **postpone** adiar *ahdeear*

pot frasco (m) *frashkoo*

potato batata (f) *bahtatah*

» **crisps** batata frita (f) *bahtatah freetah*

pottery cerâmica (f) *surãhmeekah*

potty *(child's)* penico (m) *puneekoo*

pound *(sterling)* libra (f) *leebrah*

to **pour** deitar *daheetar*

powder pó (m) *po*

powdered milk leite em pó (m) *laheet aheeñ po*

power poder (m) *poodehr* *(physical strength)* força (f) *fohrsah*

power cut falta de luz (f) *faltah du loosh*

pram carrinho de bébé (m) *kahrreennyoo du bebe*

to **prefer** preferir *prufureer*

pregnant grávida *graveedah*

to **prepare** preparar *prupahrar*

prescription receita (f) *rrusaheetah*

present *(gift)* presente (m) *prezehnt*

press *(newspapers)* prensa (f) *prehnsah*

to **press** fazer pressão *fahzehr prusãhoo*

pretty bonito/a *booneetou/ah*

price preço (m) *prehsoo*

priest padre (m) *padru*

prime minister primeiro ministro (m/f) *preemaheeroo meeneeshtroo*

prince príncipe (m) *preensupu*

princess princesa (f) *preensehzah*

print *(photo)* fotografia (f) *footoograhfeeah*

to **print** imprimir *ehmpreemeer*

prison prisão (f) *preezãhoo*

private privado *preevadoo*

prize prémio (m) *premeeoo*

probably provavelmente *proovavelmehnt*

problem problema (m) *prooblehmah*

profession profissão (f) *proofeesãhoo*

programme programa (m) *proograhmah*

prohibited proibido *prooeebeedoo*

to **promise** prometer *proomutehr*

to **pronounce** pronunciar *proonoonseear*

properly correctamente *korretahmehnt*

property propriedade (f) *proopreeudad*

public público (m) *poobleekoo*

public holiday feriado (m) *furreeadoo*

to **pull** puxar *pooshar*

to **pump up** encher *ehnshehr*

puncture furo (m) *fooroo*

pure puro/a *pooroo/ah*

purple purpúreo/a *poorpoeõhoo/ah*

purse carteira (f) *kahrtaheerah*

to **push** empurrar *empoorrar*

push-chair carrinho de criança (m) *kahrreennyoo du kreeahnsah*

to **put down** pôr *pohr*

to **put on** *(clothes)* vestir *vushteer*

pyjamas pijama (m) *peejahmah*

quality qualidade (f) *kwahleedad*

quarter quarto *kwartoo*

quay cais (m) *kaeesh*

queen rainha (f) *rraheennyah*

question pergunta (f) *purgoontah*

queue fila (f), bicha (f) *feelah, beeshah*

quick(ly) depressa *dupresah*

quiet calado/a *kahladoo/ah*

quite bastante *bahshtahnt*

rabbi rabino (m) *rrahbeenoo*

rabbit coelho (m) *kooehlloo*

rabies raiva (f) *rraeevah*

racing corridas (fpl) *koorreedahsh*

racket *(tennis)* raqueta (f) *rraketah*

radiator radiador (m) *rradeeoodahdohr*

radio rádio (m) *rradeeoo*

raft jangada (f) *jahngadah*

railway caminho de ferro (m) *kahmeennyoo du ferroo*

railway station estação de ferro (f) *eeshtahsãhoo du ferroo*

rain chuva (f) *shoovah*

raincoat gabardine (f) *gabardeenu*

rare raro/a *rraroo/ah* *(steak)* mal passada *mal pahsadah*

rash *(spots)* erupção cutânea (f) *ehroopusãhoo kootahneeah*

rate *(speed)* velocidade (f) *vulooseedad*; *(tariff)* tarifa (f) *tahreefah*

rather *(quite)* bastante *bahshtahnt*

raw cru/a *kroo/krooah*

razor gilete (f) *jeelet*

razor blade lâmina de barbear (f) *lahmeenah du bahrbeear*

to reach chegar a *shugar ah*
to read ler *lehr*
reading leitura (f) *laheetoorah*
ready pronto/a **prohntoo/ah**
real *(authentic)* autêntico/a *aootehnteekoo/ah*
really mesmo *mehshmoo*
rear traseiras (fpl) *trahzaheerahs*
reason razão (f) *rrahzãhoo*
receipt recibo (m) *ruseeboo*
receiver *(telephone)* auscultador (m) *aooshkooltahdohr*
reception recepção (f) *rrusesãhoo*
receptionist recepcionista (m/f) *rrusepuseeooneeshtah*
recipe receita (f) *rrusaheetah*
to recognise reconhecer *rrukoonnyusehr*
to recommend recomendar *rrukoomehndar*
to recover *(from an illness)* recuperar (de) *rrukoopurar (duh)*
red vermelho/a *vurmehlloo/ah*
reduction redução (f) *rrudoosãhoo*
to refill reencher *ruenshehr*
refrigerator frigorífico (m) *freegooreefeekoo*
refund reembolso (m) *rreeehmbohlsoo*
to refund reembolsar *rreeehmbohlsar*
region região (f) *rrujeeãhoo*
to register registar *rrujeeshtar*
registered registada/o *rujeeshtadah/oo*
registration number número da placa (m) *noomuroo dah plakah*
registration document *(car)* documentos de registo do carro *dookoomehntoosh de rejeeshtoo do karroo*
relation familiar (m) *fahmeeleear*
religion religião (f) *rrulujeãhoo*
to remain ficar *feekar*
to remember lembrar-se *lehmbrarsu*
to remove tirar *teerar*
rent aluguer (m) *ahlooger*
to rent alugar *ahloogar*
to repair reparar *rrupahrar*

to repeat repetir *rruputeer*
reply resposta (f) *rrushposhtah*
to reply responder (a) *rrushpohndehr (ah)*
report relatório (m) *rrulahtoreeoo*
to report dar parte (de) *dar part*
to rescue salvar *salvar*
reservation reserva (f) *ruzervah*
to reserve reservar *ruzurvar*
reserved reservado/a *rruzurvadoo/ah*
responsible responsável *rrushpohnsavel*
to rest descansar *dushkahnsar*
restaurant restaurante (m) *rrushtaurahnt*
result resultado (m) *rruzooltadoo*
retired reformado/a *rrufoormadoo*
return volta (f **voltah** (ticket) ida e volta **eedah ee voltah**
to return voltar *voltar*
to reverse *(car)* fazer marcha atrás *fazehr marshah ah trash*
reverse-charge call chamada a pagar pelo destinatário (f) *shahmadah ah pahgar pehloo dushteenahtareeoo*
rheumatism reumatismo (m) *rehoomahteeshmoo*
rice arroz (m) *ahrrohsh*
rich rico/a *reekoo*
to ride *(a horse/bike)* andar (a cavalo/de bicicleta) *ahndar (ah kahvaloo/du beeseekletah)*
right direita (f) *deeraheetah (correct)* correcto/a *koorretoo/ah*
  » **to be right** ter razão *tehr rahzãhoo*
right-hand direito/a *deeraheetoo/ah*
ring *(jewellery)* anel (m) *ahnel*
ripe maduro/a *mahdooroo/ah*
river rio (m) *rreeoo*
road rua (f) *rrooah*
roadworks obras (f) *obrahsh*
roast assado/a *ahsadoo/ah*
to rob roubar *rrohbar*
robbery roubo (m) *rrohboo*
roof tecto (m) *tetoo*
room quarto (f) *kwartoo (space)* espaço (m) *eeshpasoo*

rope corda (f) **kordah**

rose rosa (f) **rrozah**

rotten podre **pohdru**

rough (surface) áspero/a **ashpuroo/ah;** (sea) bravo/a **bravoo/ah**

round redondo/a **rrudohndoo/ah**

roundabout rotunda (f) **rrootoondah**

row (theatre, etc.) fila (f) **feelah**

to row remar **rrumar**

rowing boat barco a remos (m) **barkoo ah rremoosh**

royal real **rreeal**

rubber borracha (f) **boorrashah**

rubbish lixo (m) **leeshoo**

rucksack mochila (f) **moosheelah**

rude mal educado/a **mal ehdookadoo/ah**

ruins ruínas (fpl) **rrooeenahsh**

ruler (for measuring) régua (f) **rregooah**

rum rum (m) **rroom**

to run correr **koorrehr**

rush hour hora de ponta (f) **orah du pohntah**

rusty ferrugento/a **furroojehntoo/ah**

S

sad triste **treeshtu**

safe (strongbox) cofre (m) **kofru**

safe seguro/a **sugooroo/ah**

safety pin alfinete de segurança (m) **alfeenehtu du sugoorahnsah**

sailing vela (f) **velah**

sailing boat barco a vela (m) **barkoo a velah**

saint santo/a **sahntoo/ah**

salad salada (f) **sahladah**

sale (bargains) saldos (mpl) **saldoosh**

salmon salmão (m) **salmãhoo**

salt sal (m) **sal**

salty salgado/a **salgadoo/ah**

same mesmo/a **mehshmoo/ah**

sample amostra (f) **ahmoshtrah**

sand areia (f) **ahraheeah**

sandals sandálias (fpl) **sahndaleeahsh**

sandwich sanduíche (m) **sahndweesh**

sandy arenoso **ahrunohzoo**

sanitary towel penso higiénico (m) **pehnsoo eejeeeneekoo**

sauce molho (m) **mohlloo**

saucepan panela (f) **pahnelah**

saucer pires (m) **peerush**

sauna sauna (f) **saoonah**

to save (money) poupar **pohpar**

to say dizer **deezehr**

to scald queimar **kaheemar**

scales balança (f) **bahlahnsah**

scarf cachecol (m) **kashkol** (head) lenço de cabeça (m) **lehnsoo du kahbehsah**

scene cena (f) **sehnah**

scenery paisagem (f) **paeezajaheem**

scent perfume (m) **purfoomu**

school escola (f) **eeshkolah**

scissors tesoura (f) **tuzohrah**

scooter lambreta (f) **lahmbrehtah**

score: what's the score? a quantos estão? **ah kwahñtoosh eeshtãhoo**

Scotland Escócia (f) **eeshkoseeah**

Scottish escocês/escocesa **eeshkoseshh/eeshkosehzah**

scratch risco (m) **rreeshkoo**

to scratch riscar **rreeshkar**

screen ecrã (m) **ekrahñ**

screw parafuso (m) **pahrahfoozoo**

screwdriver chave de parafusos (f) **shav du pahrahfoozoosh**

sculpture escultura (f) **eeshkooltoorah**

sea mar (m) **mar**

seafood marisco (m) **mahreeshkoo**

seasick enjoado/a **ehnjooadoo/ah**

season estação (f) **eeshtahsãhoo**

season ticket entrada de assinatura (f) **ehntradah du ahseenahtoorah**

seat assento (m) **ahsehntoo**

seatbelt cinto de segurança (m) **seentoo du sugoorahnsah**

second segundo (m) **sugoondoo** (adj) segundo/a **sugoondoo/ah**

second (time period) segundo (m) **sugoondoo**

secret segredo (m) *sugrehdoo*

section secção (f) *sekusãhoo*

sedative sedativo (m) *sudahteevoo*

to **see** ver *vehr*

to **seem** parecer *pahrusehr*

self-catering sem pensão *saheeñ pehnsãhoo*

self-service self-service (m) *self-serveesu*

to **sell** vender *vehndehr*

to **send** mandar *mahndar*

senior citizen pensionista (m/f) *pehnseeooneeshtah*

sensible sensato/a *sehnsatoo/ah*

sentence frase (f) *frazu*

to **separate** separar *supahrar*

separated separado/a *supahradoo/ah*

serious sério/a *sereeoo/ah* (grave) grave *grav*

to **serve** servir *surveer*

service (charge) serviço (m) *surveesoo;* (church) cerimónia religiosa (f) *sureemoonneeah ruleejeeoozah*

several vários/as *vareeoosh/ah*

to **sew** cozer *koozehr*

sex (gender) sexo (m) *seksoo;* (intercourse) relações sexuais (fpl) *rulahsõheesh seksooaeesh*

shade (not sunny) sombra (f) *sohmbrah*

shadow sombra (f) *sohmbrah*

shampoo champô (m) *shampoh*

sharp aguçado *ahgoosadoo*

shave fazer a barba *fahzehr ah barbah*

shaving cream/foam creme de barbear (m) *krem du barbeear*

she ela *elah*

sheep ovelha (f) *ohvehllah*

sheet lençol (m) *lehnsol*

shelf prateleira (f) *prahtulaheerah*

shell (egg, nut) casca (f) *kashkah*

shelter abrigo (m) *ahbreegoo*

shiny brilhante *breellahnt*

ship navio (m) *nahveeoo*

shirt camisa (f) *kahmeezah*

shock (electrical) choque (m) *shok;* (emotional) susto (m) *sooshtoo*

shocked chocado/a *shookadoo/ah*

shoe(s) sapato (m) *sahpatoo*

shoe polish graxa (f) *grashah*

shoe repairer's sapateiro (m) *sahpahtaheeroo*

shoe shop sapataria (f) *sahpahtahreeah*

shop loja (f) *lojah*

shop assistant empregado/a de balcão *ehmprugadoo/ah du balkãhoo*

shopping: to go shopping ir às compras *eer ash kohmprahsh*

shopping centre centro comercial (m) *sehntroo koomurseeal*

short curto/a *koortoo/ah*

shorts calções (mpl) *kalsõheesh*

shout grito (m) *greetoo*

show espectáculo (m) *eeshpetakoolooo*

to **show** mostrar *mooshtrar*

shower chuveiro (m) *shoovaheeroo*

to **shrink** encolher *ehnkoollehr*

shut fechado/a *fushadoo/ah*

to **shut** fechar *fushar*

shutter persiana (f) *purseeahnah*

sick doente *dooehnt*

» **to be sick** vomitar *voomeetar*

» **to feel sick** sentir-se mal *sehnteersu mal*

side lado (m) *ladoo*

sieve peneira (f) *punaheerah*

sight visão (f) *veezãhoo* (tourist) local de interesse (m) *lookal du eenterehsu*

sightseeing turismo (m) *tooreeshmoo*

sign sinal (m) *seenal*

to **sign** assinar *ahseenar*

signal sinal (m) *seenal*

signature assinatura (f) *ahseenahtoorah*

silent silencioso/a *seelehnseeohzoo/ah*

silk seda (f) *sehdah*

silver prata (f) *pratah*

similar semelhante *sumullahnt*

simple simples *seemplush*

since desde *dehshd*

to **sing** cantar *kahntar*

single (room, ticket) simples *seemplush;* (unmarried) solteiro/a *soltaheeroo/ah*

sink lava-loiça (m) *lavah-loheesah*

sir senhor (m) *sunnyohr*

sister irmã (f) *eermãh*

sister-in-law cunhada (f) *koonnyadah*

to **sit (down)** sentar-se *sehntarsu*

size tamanho (m) *tahmahnnyoo*

skates (ice) patins de gelo (mpl) *pahteensh du gehloo*; (roller) patins de rodas (mpl) *pahteensh du rrodahsh*

to **skate** patinar *pahteenar*

ski esqui (m) *eeshkee*

to **ski** fazer esqui *fahzehr eeshkee*

skimmed milk leite desnatado (m) *laheet dushnahtadoo*

skin pele (f) *pel*

skirt saia (f) *saeeah*

sky céu (m) *seoo*

to **sleep** dormir *doormeer*

sleeper/sleeping-car carruagem-cama (f) *kahrrooajaheeñ-kahmah*

sleeping bag saco de dormir (m) *sakoo du doormeer*

sleeve manga (f) *mahngah*

slice fatia (f) *fahteeah*

sliced às fatias *ash fahteeahsh*

slim esbelto/a *eeshbeltoo/ah*

slippery escorregadio/a *eeshkoorrugahdeeoo/ah*

slow vagaroso/a *vahgahrohzoo/ozah*

slowly devagar *duvahgar*

small pequeno/a *pukehnoo/ah*

smell cheiro (m) *shaeeroo*

to **smell** cheirar *shaeerar (of) a ah*

smile sorriso (m) *soorrezoo*

to **smile** sorrir *soorreer*

smoke fumo (m) *foomoo*

to **smoke** fumar *foomar*

smooth macio/a *mahseeoo/ah*

to **sneeze** espirrar *eeshpeerrar*

snorkel tubo de ar (m) *tooboo du ar*

snow neve (f) *nev*

to **snow** nevar *nuvar*

so tão *tãhoo*; (therefore) por isso *poor eesoo*

soap sabonete (m) *sahbooneht*

sober sóbrio/a *sobreeoo/ah*

sock meia (f) *maheeah*

socket tomada (f) *toomadah*

soft macio/a *mahseeoo/ah*

soft drink bebida não alcoólica (f) *bubeedah nãhoo alkoooleekah*

sold out vendido *vehndeedoo*

solicitor advogado (m) *aduvoogadoo*

solid solido *soleedoo*

some alguns/algumas *algoonsh/algoomahsh*

somehow de alguma maneira *du algoomah mahnaheerah*

someone alguém *algaheeñ*

something alguma coisa *algoomah koheezah*

sometimes às vezes *ash vehzush*

somewhere algures *algoorush*

son filho (m) *feelloo*

song canção (f) *kahnsãhoo*

son-in-law genro (m) *jehnrroo*

soon em breve *aheeñ brev*

» **as soon as possible** quanto antes *kwahñtoo ahntush*

sore doloroso *dooloorohzoo*

sorry: I'm sorry peço desculpa *pesoo dushkoolpah*

sort tipo (m) *teepoo*

sound som (m) *sohñ*

soup sopa (f) *sohpah*

sour amargo/a *ahmargoo/ah*

south sul (m) *sool*

souvenir lembrança (f) *lehmbrahnsah*

space espaço (m) *eeshpasoo*

spade espada (f) *eeshpadah*

spare disponível *deeshpooneevel*

sparkling (wine) espumante *eeshpoomahnt*

to **speak** falar *fahlar*

special especial *eeshpuseeal*

special offer oferta especial (f) *ofertah eeshpuseeal*

specialist especialista (m) *eeshpuseeahleeshtah*

speciality especialidade (f) *eeshpuseeahleedad*

spectacles óculos (mpl) *okooloosh*

speed velocidade (f) *vulooseedad*

speed limit limite de velocidade (m) *leemeet du vulooseedad*

to spend *(money)* gastar *gahshtar*; *(time)* passar *pahsar*

spice especiaria (f) *eeshpuseeahreeah*

spicy picante *peekahnt*

spirits licores (mpl) *leekohrush*

splinter lasca (f) *lashkah*

to spoil estragar *eeshtrahgar*

sponge *(bath)* esponja (f) *eeshpohnjah*

spoon colher (f) *kooller*

sport desporto (m) *dushpohrtoo*

spot borbulha (f) *boorboollah*; *(place)* sítio (m) *seeteeoo*

to sprain torcer *toorsehr*

sprained torcido/a *toorseedoo/ah*

spray spray (m) *suprahee*

spring *(season)* Primavera (f) *preemahverah*

square *(town)* praça (f) *prasah*; *(shape)* quadrado (m) *kwahdradoo*

stadium estádio (m) *eeshtadeeoo*

stain nódoa (f) *nodooah*

stairs escadas (fpl) *eeshkadahsh*

stalls *(theatre)* plateia (f) *plahtaheeah*

stamp *(postage)* selo (m) *sehloo*

stand *(stadium)* bancadas (fpl) *bahnkadahsh*

to stand estar de pé *eeshtar du pe*

to stand up levantar-se *luvahntarsu*

star estrela (f) *eeshtrelah*

start começo (m) *koomehsoo*

to start começar *koomusar*

starter *(food)* entradas (fpl) *ehntradahsh*

state estado (m) *eeshtadoo*

station estação (f) *eeshtahsãhoo*

stationer's papelaria (f) *pahpulahreeah*

statue estátua (f) *eeshtatooah*

to stay *(live)* morar *moorar* *(remain)* ficar *feekar*

to steal roubar *rrohbar*

steam vapor (m) *vahpohr*

steep íngreme *eengrumu*

step *(footstep)* passo (m) *pasoo*; *(stairs)* degraus (mpl) *dugraoosh*

step-brother meio-irmão (m) *maheeoo-eermãhoo*

step-children enteados *ehnteeadoosh*

step-father padrasto (m) *pahdrashtoo*

step-mother madrasta (f) *mahdrashtah*

step-sister meia-irmã (f) *maheeah-eermãh*

stereo stéreo (m) *sutereeoo*

stick pau (m) *paoo*

sticky pegajoso/a *pugahjohzoo/ pugahjozah*

stiff rígido/a *rreejeedoo/ah*

still *(yet)* ainda *aeendah*

still *(non-fizzy)* sem gás *saheeḿ gash*

sting picada (f) *peekadah*

to sting picar *peekar*

stockings meias (fpl) *maheeahsh*

stolen roubado/a *rrohbadoo/ah*

stomach estômago (m) *eeshtohmahgoo*

stomach ache dor de estômago *dohr du eeshtohmahgoo*

stomach upset perturbação gástrica (f) *purtoorbahsãhoo gashtreekah*

stone pedra (f) *pedrah*

stop *(bus)* paragem (f) *pahrajaheeḿ*

to stop parar *pahrar*

stop! pare! *paru*

stopcock torneira de segurança (f) *toornaheerah du sugoorahnsah*

story história (f) *eeshtoreeah*

stove forno (m) *fohrnoo*

straight direito/a *deeraheetoo/ah*

straight on em frente *aheeḿ frehnt*

strange estranho/a *eeshtrahnnyoo/ah*

stranger estranho (m) *eeshtrahnnyoo*

strap correia (f) *koorraheeah*

straw *(drinking)* palha (f) *pallah*

stream ribeiro (m) *rreebaheeroo*

street rua (f) *rrooah*

stretcher maca (f) *makah*
strike greve (f) *grev*
string corda (f) *kordah*
stripe risca (f) *rreeshkah*
strong forte *fort*
to **stick: it's stuck** está entalado/ah *eeshta ehntahladoo/ah*
student estudante (m/f) *eeshtoodahntu*
to **study** estudar *eeshtoodar*
style estilo (m) *eeshteeloo*
subtitles legendas (fpl) *lujehndahsh*
suburb arredores (mpl) *ahrrudorush*
succeed ter sucesso *tehr soosesoo*
success sucesso (m) *soosesoo*
such tal *tal*
suddenly de repente *du rrupehnt*
sugar açucar (m) *ahsookar*
suit fato (m) *fatoo*
suitcase mala (f) *malah*
summer Verão (m) *vurãhoo*
sun sol (m) *sol*
to **sunbathe** tomar banhos de sol *toomar bahnnyoosh du sol*
sunburn queimadura solar (f) *kaheemahdoorah soolar*
sunglasses óculos de sol (mpl) *okooloosh du sol*
sunstroke insolação (f) *eendoolahsãhoo*
suntan lotion creme bronzeador (m) *creme brohnzeeahdohr*
supermarket supermercado (m) *soopermurkadoo*
supper ceia (f) *saheeah*
supplement suplemento (m) *sooplumehntoo*
suppose: I suppose so suponho que sim *soopohnnyoo ku seeñ*
suppository supositório (m) *soopoozeetoreeoo*
sure seguro/a *sugooroo/ah*
surface superfície (f) *soopurfeeseeu*
surname apelido (m) *ahpuleedoo*
surprise surpresa (f) *soorprehzah*
surrounded by rodeado de *rroodeeadoo du*

to **sweat** transpirar *trahnshpeerar*
to **sweep** barrer *bahrrehr*
sweet doce (m) *dohsu*
sweetener adoçante (m) *ahdoosahnt*
sweets rebuçados (mpl) *rruboosadoosh*
swelling inchaço (m) *eenshasoo*
to **swim** nadar *nahdar*
swimming natação (f) *nahtahsãhoo*
swimming pool piscina (f) *peeshseenah*
swimsuit, swimming trunks fato de banho (m) *fatoo du bahnnyoo*
switch interruptor (m) *eenturrooputohr*
to **switch off** desligar *dushleegar*
to **switch on** ligar *leegar*
swollen inchado/a *eenshadoo/ah*
symptom sintoma (m) *seentohmah*
synagogue sinagoga (f) *seenagogu*
system sistema (m) *seeshtehmah*

T

table mesa (f) *mehzah*
tablet comprimido (m) *kohmpreemeedoo*
tailor alfaiate (m) *alfaheeat*
to **take** tomar *toomar;* (photo) tirar *teerar;* (time) levar *luvar*
taken (seat) estar ocupado/a *eeshtar okoopadoo/ah*
to **take off** (clothes) tirar *teerar;* (plane) levantar voo *luvahntar vohoo*
talcum powder pó talco (m) *po talkoo*
to **talk** falar *fahlar*
tall alto/a *altoo/ah*
tampon tampão (m) *tahmpãhoo*
tap torneira (f) *toornaheerah*
tape measure fita métrica (f) *feetah metreekah*
taste sabor (m) *sahbohr*
to **taste** saborear *sahbooreear*
tax imposto (m) *eempohshtoo*
taxi táxi (m) *taksee*
taxi rank praça de táxis (f) *prasah du takseesh*
tea chá (m) *sha*
teabag saqueta de chá (f) *sahketah du sha*

to teach ensinar *ehnseenar*

teacher professor/ora *proofusohr/ohrah*

team equipa (f) *ehkeepah*

tear *(rip)* rasgão (m) *rrahshgãhoo;*
(*cry*) lágrima (f) *lagreemah*

teaspoon colher de chá (f) *kooller du sha*

teat *(for baby's bottle)* chupeta (f)
shoopehtah

teenager adolescente (m/f)
ahdoolushsehnt

telegram telegrama (m) *tulugrahmah*

telephone telefone (m) *tulufon*

telephone card credifone (m) *kredeefon*

telephone directory lista telefónica (f)
leeshtah tulufoneekah

to telephone telefonar *tulufoonar*

television televisão (f) *tuluveezãhoo*

to tell dizer *deezehr*

temperature febre (f) *febru*

» **to have a temperature** ter febre
tehr febru

temporarily temporariamente
tehmpoorareeahmehnt

tender tenro/a *tehnrroo/ah*

tennis ténis (m) *teneesh*

tennis court campo de ténis (m)
kahmpoo du teneesh

tent tenda (f) *tehndah*

tent peg cavilha (f) *kahveellah*

tent pole ferro (m) *ferroo*

terminal *(airport)* terminal (m)
turmeenal

terrace terraço (m) *turrasoo*

terrible terrível *turreevel*

terrorist terrorista (m) *turrooreeshtah*

to text mandar uma mensagem de texto
*mandar oomah mehnsajaheem du
tehshtoo*

than que *ku*

thank you obrigado/a *obreegadoo/ah*

that (one) esse/a, aquele/a *ehs/esah,
ahkehl/ahkelah*

the o/a *oo/ah*

theatre teatro (m) *teeatroo*

their seu/sua *sehoo/sooah*

theirs seus/suas *sehoosh/sooahs*

them os/as, lhes *oosh/ahsh, llush*

then então *ehntãhoo*

there ali *ahlee*

there is/are há *a*

therefore por isso *poor eesoo*

thermometer termómetro (m)
turmomutroo

these estes/estas *ehshtush/eshtahsh*

they eles/elas *ehlush/elahsh*

thick espesso/a *eeshpehsoo/ah*

thief ladrão/ladra *lahdrãhoo/ladrah*

thin delgado/a *delgadoo/ah*

thing coisa (f) *koheezah*

to think pensar *pehnsar; (believe)* acreditar
ahkrudeetar

third terceiro/a *tursaheeroo/ah*

thirsty com sede *kohm sehdu*

this (one) este/a *ehsht/eshtah*

those aqueles/as *ahkehlush/ahkelahsh*

thread linha (f) *leennyah*

throat lozenges/pastilles pastilhas (fpl)
pahshteellahsh

through entre *ehntru*

to throw amandar *ahmandar*

to throw away deitar fora *daheetar forah*

thumb polgar *pohlgar*

thunder trovão (m) *troovãhoo*

ticket bilhete (m) *beellehtu*

ticket office bilheteira (f) *beellutaheerah*

tide *(high/low)* maré (f) *mahre*

tidy arrumado/a *ahrroomadoo/ah*

tie gravata (f) *grahvatah*

to tie atar *ahtar*

tight *(clothes)* apertado/a *ahpurtadoo/ah*

tights meias(fpl) *maheeahsh*

till *(until)* até *ahte*

time tempo (m) *tehmpoo (on clock)*
hora (f) *orah*

timetable *(train)* horário (m) *orareeoo*

tin lata (f) *latah*

tinned enlatado *ehnlahtadoo*

tin opener abre-latas *abru-latahsh*

tip (in restaurant) gorjeta (f) goor**jeh**tah

tired cansado/a kahn**sa**doo/ah

tissues lenços de papel (mpl) **lehn**soosh du pah**pel**

to (with places) a ah, para pah**rah**

toast torrada (f) toor**ra**dah

tobacco tabaco (m) tah**ba**koo

tobacconist's tabacaria (f) tahbahkah**ree**ah

toboggan tobogã (m) tooboo**gã**

today hoje ohj

toiletries artigos de toilete (mpl) ahr**tee**goosh du tooa**let**

toilets casas de banho (fpl) **ka**zahsh du **bah**nnyoo

toilet paper papel higiénico (m) pah**pel** eejee**ee**neekoo

toll portagem (f) poor**ta**jaheeñ

tomato tomate (m) too**ma**tu

tomorrow amanhã amahnn**yã**

tongue língua (f) **leen**gooah

tonight esta noite **esh**tah noheet

too muito moo**een**too; (as well) também tahm**ba**heeñ

tool ferramenta (f) furrah**mehn**tah

tooth dente (m) dehnt

toothache dor de dentes (f) dohr du **dehn**tush

toothbrush escova de dentes (f) eesh**koh**vah du **dehn**tush

toothpaste pasta de dentes (f) **pash**tah du **dehn**tush

toothpick palito (m) pah**lee**too

top (mountain) cimo (m) **see**moo

» **on top of** em cima de aheeñ **see**mah du

torch lanterna (f) lahn**ter**nah

torn rasgado/a rrahsh**ga**doo/ah

total total (m) too**tal**

totally totalmente too**tal**mehnt

to touch tocar too**kar**

tough (meat) duro/a **doo**roo/ah

tour excursão (f) aheeshkoor**sã**oo

to tour fazer turismo fah**zehr** too**reesh**moo

tourism turismo (m) too**reesh**moo

tourist turista (m/f) too**reesh**tah

tourist office agência de turismo (f) ah**jehn**seeah du too**reesh**moo

to tow rebocar rruboo**kar**

towards para pah**rah**

towel toalha (f) too**a**llah

tower torre (f) **toh**rru

town vila (f) **vee**lah

town centre centro (m) **sehn**troo

town hall câmara municipal (f) **kah**mahrah mooneesee**pal**

toy brinquedo (m) breen**keh**doo

track linha (f) **leen**nyah

traditional tradicional trahdeesee**oo**nal

traffic tráfico (m) tra**fee**koo

traffic jam engarrafamento (m) ehngahrrahfah**mehn**too

traffic lights semáforos (mpl) su**ma**furoosh

trailer atrelado (m) ahtru**la**doo

train comboio (m) kohm**boo**eeoo

trainers sapatos de treino (mpl) sah**pa**toosh du tra**hee**noo

tram eléctrico (m) ee**le**treekoo

tranquilliser tranquilizante (m) trahnkoo**ee**lee**zahnt**

to translate traduzir trahdoo**zeer**

translation tradução (f) trahdoo**sã**hoo

to travel viajar veea**hjar**

travel agency agência de viagens (f) ah**jehn**seeah du veea**ja**heensh

travellers' cheques travellers cheques (mpl) **tra**vulursh **she**kush

travel sickness enjoo (m) ehn**jo**hoo

tray tabuleiro (m) tahboo**la**heeroo

treatment tratamento (m) trahtah**mehn**too

tree árvore (f) **ar**vooroo

trip viagem (f) veea**ja**heeñ

trousers calças (fpl) **kal**sahsh

trout truta (f) **troo**tah

true verdadeiro/a vurdah**da**heeroo/ah

to try experimentar aheeshpureemehn**tar**

to try on experimentar
   aheeshpureemehntar

T-shirt t-shirt (f) *teeshurt*

tube *(pipe)* tubo (m) *tooboo;*
   (underground) metro (m) *metroo*

tuna atum (m) *ahtoom*

tunnel túnel (m) *toonel*

turn: it's my turn é a minha vez *e ah*
   meennyah vehsh

to turn voltar *voltar*

to turn off desligar *dushleegar*

turning *(side road)* transversal (f)
   trahnshvursal

twice duas vezes *dooahs vehzush*

twin beds duas camas *dooahs kahmahsh*

twins gémios/as *jemeeoosh/ah*

twisted *(ankle)* torcido/a *toorseedoo/ah*

type *(sort)* tipo (m) *teepoo*

typical típico/a *teepeekoo/ah*

U

ugly feio/a *faheeoo/ah*

ulcer úlcera (f) *oolsurah*

umbrella sombrinha (f)
   sohmbreennyah

uncle tio (m) *teeoo*

uncomfortable descomfortável
   duskohmfoortavel

under debaixo *dubaeeshoo*

underground *(tube)* metro (m) *metroo*

underpants cuecas (fpl) *kooekahsh*

to understand compreender
   kohmpreeehndehr

underwater debaixo de água
   dubaeeshoo dJ agooah

underwear roupa de baixo (f) *rrohpah*
   du dubaeeshoo

to undress despir *dushpeer*

unemployed desempregado/a
   duzehmprugadoo/ah

unfortunately infelizmente
   eenfuleeshmehnt

unhappy infeliz *eenfuleesh*

uniform uniforme (m) *ooneeformu*

university universidade (f)
   ooneevurseedad

unleaded petrol gasolina sem chumbo
   (f) *gahzooleenah saheem shoomboo*

unless a não ser que *ah nãhoo sehr ku*

to unpack desfazer as malas *dushfahzehr*
   ash malahsh

to unscrew desaparafusar
   duzahpahrahfoozar

until até *ahte*

unusual invulgar *eenvoolgar*

unwell indisposto/a *eendeeshpohshtoo/*
   eendeeshposhtah

up em/para cima *aheem/pahrah seemah*

upper de cima *du seemah*

upstairs lá em cima *la aheem seemah*

urgent urgente *oorjehntu*

urine urina (f) *ooreenah*

us nós *nosh*

to use usar *oozar*

useful útil *ooteel*

useless inútil *eenooteel*

usually normalmente *normalmehnt*

V

vacant livre *leevru*

vacuum cleaner aspirador (m)
   ahshpeerahdohr

valid válido/a *valeedoo/ah*

valley vale (m) *val*

valuable de valor *du vahlohr*

van camioneta (f) *kameeoonetah*

vanilla baunilha (f) *baooneellah*

vase vaso (m) *vazoo*

VAT IVA *eevah*

vegan naturalista (m/f)
   nahtoorahleeshtah

vegetables legumes (mpl) *lugoomush*

vegetarian vegetariano/a
   vujutahreeahnoo/ah

vehicle veículo *vaheekooloo*

very muito *mooeentoo*

vet veterinário (m) *vutureenareeoo*

via via (f) *veeah*

video video (m) *veedeeoo*

view vista (f) *veeshtah*

villa vila (f) *veelah*

village aldeia (f) *aldaheeah*

vinegar vinagre (m) *veenagru*

vineyard vinha (f) *veennyah*

virgin virgem (f) *veerjaheem̃*

visa visa (m) *veezah*

to **visit** visitar *veezeetar*

visitor visitante (m/f) *veezeetahnt*

vitamin vitamina (f) *veetahmeenah*

voice voz (f) *vosh*

volleyball voleibol (m) *volaheebol*

voltage voltagem (f) *voltajaheem̃*

to **vote** votar *vootar*

W

wage ordenado (m) *ordunadoo*

waist cintura (f) *seentoorah*

to **wait (for)** esperar *eeshpurar*

waiter empregado (m) *ehmprugadoo*

waiting room sala de espera (f) *salah du eeshperah*

waitress empregada (f) *ehmprugadah*

Wales País de Gales (m) *paheesh du galush*

to **walk** andar *ahndar*

walking stick bengala (f) *behngalah*

wall (inside) parede (f) *pahrehd*; (outside/garden) muro (m) *mooroo*

wallet carteira (f) *kahrtaheerah*

to **want** querer *kurehr*

war guerra (f) *gerrah*

warm morno/a *mohrnoo/mornah*

to **wash** lavar *lahvar*

wash-basin lavatório (m) *lahvahtoreeoo*

washing lavagem (f) *lahvajaheem̃*

washing machine máquina de lavar a roupa (f) *makeenah du lahvar ah rrohpah*

washing powder detergente em pó (m) *duturjehnt aheem̃ po*

wastepaper basket cesto do lixo (m) *sehshtoo doo leeshoo*

watch (clock) relógio (m) *rrulojeeoo*

to **watch** ver *vehr*

water água (f) *agooah*

water heater aquecedor (m) *ahkehsadohr*

waterfall queda de água *kedah du agooah*

waterproof impermeável (m) *eempurmeeavel*

water-skiing esqui aquático (m) *eeshkee ahkooateekoo*

water-skis esquis aquáticos (mpl) *eeshkeesh ahkooateekoosh*

wave onda (f) *ohndah*

way (path) caminho (m) *kahmeennyoo*

wax cera (f) *sehrah*

we nós *nosh*

weather tempo (m) *tehm̃poo*

weather forecast previsão (f) *pruveezãhoo*

wedding casamento (m) *kahzahmehntoo*

week semana (f) *sumahnah*

weekend fim de semana (m) *feem̃ du sumahnah*

weekly semanal *sumahnal*

to **weigh** pesar *puzar*

weight peso (m) *pehzoo*

well bem *baheem̃*

well done (steak) bem passado *baheem̃ pahsadoo*

Welsh galês/galesa *galehsh/galehshah*

west oeste (m) *oesht*

western do oeste *doo oesht*

wet molhado/a *moolladoo/ah*

wetsuit fato de mergulho (m) *fatoo du murgoolloo*

what? que? *keh*

wheel roda (f) *rrodah*

wheelchair cadeira de rodas (f) *kahdaheerah du rrodahsh*

when quando *kwahñdoo*

where onde *ohnd*

which qual *kwal*

while enquanto *ehnkwahñtoo*

white branco/a *brahnkoo/ah*

who? quem *kaheeñ*

whole todo *tohdoo*

why? porquê *poorkeh*

wide largo/a *largoo/ah*

widow/er viúvo/a *veeoovoo/ah*

wife mulher (f), esposa (f) *mooller, eeshpohzah*

wild bravo/a *bravoo/ah*

wind vento (m) *vehntoo*

windmill moinho (m) *mooeennyoo*

window janela (f) *jahnelah*; *(shop)* montra (f) *mohntrah*

to **windsurf** fazer windsurf *fahzehr weendsurf*

windy está vento *eeshta vehntoo*

wine vinho *veennyoo*

wine merchant/shop casa de vinhos (f) *kasah du veennyoosh*

wing asa (f) *azah*

winter Inverno (m) *eenvernoo*

with com *kohm*

without sem *saheeñ*

woman mulher (f) *mooller*

wonderful maravilhoso/a *mahrahveellohzoo/llozah*

wood madeira (f) *madaheerah*

wool lã (f) *läh*

word palavra (f) *pahlavrah*

work trabalho (m) *trahballoo*

to **work** *(job)* trabalhar *trahbahllar*; *(function)* funcionar *foonseeoonar*

world *(noun)* mundo (m) *moondoo*; *(adj)* mundial *moondeeal*

worried preocupado/a *preeokoopadoo/ preeokoopadah*

worse pior *peeor*

worth: it's worth vale a pena *val ah pehnah*

» **it's not worth it** não vale a pena *nähoo val ah pehnah*

wound ferida (f) *fureedah*

to **wrap (up)** embrulhar *embroollar*

wrong errado/a *eerradoo/ah*

to **write** escrever *eeshkruvehr*

X

X-ray raio-X (m) *raeeoosheesh*

Y

yacht iate (m) *eeat*

to **yawn** bucejar *boosujar*

year ano (m) *ahnoo*

yellow amarelo/a *ahmahreloo*

yes sim *seeñ*

yesterday ontem *ohntaheeñ*

yet ainda *aeendah*

yoghurt iogurte (m) *eeogoort*

you *(formal)* o senhor/a senhora *oo sunnyohr, ah sunnyohrah*; *(informal singular)* você, tu *voseh, too*; *(informal plural)* vocês *vosehsh*

young jovem (m/f) *jovaheeñ*

your o seu/a sua *oo sehoo/ah sooah*

yours os seus/as suas *oosh sehoosh/ ahsh sooahsh*

youth juventude (f) *joovehntood*

Z

zip fecho (m) *fehshoo*

zoo jardim zoológico (m) *jahrdeeñ zoolojeekoo*

Portuguese – English dictionary

A

a at, of, to
a (f) the
a ... (quilómetros) ... (kilometres) away
a maior parte (de) most (of)
a não ser que unless
a pé on foot
abadia (f) abbey
abaixo down *(movement)*
abcesso (m) abscess
abelha (f) bee
aberto/a open
aborrecido/a boring
abregarrafas (m) bottle opener
abre-latas tin opener
abrigo (m) shelter
abrir to open
absolutamente definitely
acabado (m) complete *(finished)*
acabar to finish
acabar to end
acampar to camp
aceitar to accept *(take)*
acender to light *(fire)*
acento (m) seat
acidente (m) accident
ácido/a acid *(adj)*
acima above
acontecer to happen
acreditar to believe
açúcar (m) sugar
adaptador (m) adaptor
adepto (m) supporter (football)
adeus goodbye
adiante forward
adiar to postpone
adoçante (m) sweetener
adolescente (m/f) teenager
adoptado/a adopted
adulto/a adult
advogado/a lawyer; solicitor

aeroporto (m) airport
afogar-se to drown
agência (f) agency
agência de turismo (f) tourist office
agência de viagens (f) travel agency
agenda (f) diary
agora now
agradável pleasant
agradecido/a grateful
água (f) water
água destilada (f) distilled water
aguçado sharp
agulha (f) needle
ainda still; yet
ajuda (f) help
ajudar to help
alarme (m) alarm
alcatifa (f) carpet
álcool (m) alcohol
alcoólico/a alcoholic
aldeia (f) village
além disso besides
Alemanha (f) Germany
alemão/alemã German
alérgico/a a allergic to
alface (f) lettuce
alfaiate (m) tailor
alfândega (f) customs
alfinete (m) pin
algodão (m) cotton; cotton wool
alguém anyone; someone
algum/alguma (sing) any; some
alguma coisa something
alguns/algumas (pl) any; some
algures somewhere
alho (m) garlic
ali there
almoço (m) lunch
almofada (f) cushion
alojamento (m) accommodation
alpinismo (m) mountaineering

alpinista (m/f) climber
alto/a high; loud; tall
altura (f) height
alugar to hire; rent
aluguer (m) rent
aluguer de carros (m) car hire
ama (f) babysitter
amaciador (m) conditioner
amandar to throw
amanhã tomorrow
amar to love
amarelo/a yellow
amargo/a bitter; sour
amável generous
ambição (f) ambition
ambiente (m) environment
ambulância (f) ambulance
amendoim (m) peanut
amigo/a friend
amor (m) love
amostra (f) sample
analgésico painkiller
andar to walk
andar (a cavalo) to ride (a horse)
andar à boleira to hitchhike
anel (m) ring (jewellery)
anestésico geral (m) general anaesthetic
anestésico local (m) local anaesthetic
animal (m) animal
aniversário (m) anniversary; birthday
ano (m) year
ansioso/a anxious
antena (f) aerial
anteontem day before yesterday
antes before
antibiótico (m) antibiotic
antiguidade (f) antique
antiquado/a old-fashioned
anti-séptico (m) antiseptic
ao ar livre outdoors; outside
ao lado (de) next to
ao redor de around
apanhar to catch (train/bus)
aparelho de surdez (m) hearing aid

apartamento (m) apartment
apelido (m) surname
apendicite (f) appendicitis
apertado/a tight (clothes)
aprender to learn
apresentar to introduce
aproximadamente approximately
aquecimento (m) (central) heating
aqueles/as those
aqui here
ar (m) air
ar condicionado (m) air conditioning
arbusto (m) bush
arco (m) arch
área (f) area
areia (f) sand
arenoso sandy
argumento (m) argument
arma (f) gun
armário (m) cupboard
armazéns (mpl) department store
arredores (mpl) suburb
arroz (m) rice
arrumado/a tidy
art art
artigo (m) article
artigos de toilete (mpl) toiletries
artista artist
artrite (f) arthritis
árvore (f) tree
às fatias sliced
às vezes occasionally; sometimes
asa (f) handle; wing
asma (f) asthma
áspero/a rough (surface)
aspirador (m) vacuum cleaner
aspirina (f) aspirin
assado/a roast
assegurar to insure
assinar to sign
assinatura (f) signature
assistente assistant
assoalhada (f) room
assustado/a frightened

atacadores (mpl) shoelace
atacar to attack
ataque de coração (m) heart attack
atar to tie
até even (including); till
aterrar to land
atletismo (m) athletics
atmosfera (f) atmosphere
atraente attractive
atrás at the back; behind
atravessar to cross (border)
atrazo (m) delay
atrelado (m) trailer
atum (m) tuna
auscultador (m) receiver (telephone)
auscultadores (mpl) headphones
autêntico/a genuine; real
autocarro (m) coach; bus
autoestrada (f) motorway
automático/a automatic
automobilismo (m) motor racing
avalanche (f) avalanche
avariar to break down
avião (m) aeroplane
avó (f) grandmother
avô (m) grandfather
avós (mpl) grandparents
azeite (m) olive oil
azeitona (f) olive
azul blue
azul marinho navy blue

B

babete (m) bib
bacia (f) bowl; basin (sink)
baga (f) berry
bagagem (f) luggage
bagagem de mão hand luggage
baía (f) bay
baixo/a low
balança (f) scales
balcão (m) balcony; counter (shop)
balde (m) bucket
banana (f) banana

banco (m) bank
banda (f) band (music)
bandeira (f) flag
banho (m) bath
bar (m) bar
barato/a cheap
barba (f) beard
barbatanas (fpl) flippers
barbeiro (m) barber's
barco (m) boat
» barco a motor (m) motorboat
» barco a pedais (m) pedal-boat
» barco a remos (m) rowing boat
» barco à vela (m) sailing boat
barrer to sweep
barulhento/a noisy
barulho noise
bastante fairly; plenty (of); quite
batata (f) potato
batata frita (f) potato crisps; chips
bater to hit; to knock
baton (m) lipstick
baunilha (f) vanilla
bêbado/a drunk
bebé (m/f) baby
beber to drink
bebida (f) drink
bebida não alcoólica (f) soft drink
beco (m) alley
bege beige
beijar to kiss
beijo (m) kiss
belas artes (fpl) fine arts
beliche (m) berth
bem well
bem educado/a polite
bengala (f) walking stick
berço (m) cot
berma (f) hard shoulder
biberão (m) baby's bottle
Bíblia (f) Bible
biblioteca (f) library
bica (f) strong, dark coffee
bicha (f) queue

bicicleta (f) bicycle

bigode (m) moustache

bilhete (m) ticket *(travel, theatre, etc.)*

bilheteira (f) booking office; box office

binóculos (mpl) binoculars

bloco (m) writing pad

bloqueado/a blocked

blusa (f) blouse

boa good

boa noite (f) good night

boa tarde (f) good evening

bob (m) curler *(hair)*

boca (f) mouth

bochecha (f) cheek

boi (m) bull

boite (f) nightclub

bola (f) ball

bolacha (f) biscuit

bolha (f) blister

bolinha (f) bread roll

bolo (m) cake

bolso (m) pocket

bom good

bom dia (m) good day; good morning

bomba (f) bomb

bombeiros (mpl) fire brigade

boneca (f) doll

bonito/a beautiful, pretty

borboleta (f) butterfly

borbulha (f) spot

borda (f) border *(edge)*

borracha (f) rubber

bota (f) boot *(shoe)*

botão (m) button

botas de esqui (fpl) ski boots

bote salva-vidas (m) lifeboat

braçadeiras (fpl) armbands *(swimming)*

bracelete (f) bracelet

braço (m) arm

branco/a white

bravo/a rough *(sea)*; wild

brilhante shiny

brincar to play

brinco (m) earring

brinquedo (m) toy

britânico/a British

broche (m) brooch

brochure (f) brochure

bronquite (f) bronchitis

bronze (m) bronze

bronzeado (m) suntan

bucejar to yawn

buffet (m) buffet

buraco (m) hole

burro (m) donkey

bússola (f) compass

C

cabana (f) hut

cabeça (f) head

cabedal (m) leather

cabeleireira/o hairdresser

cabelo (m) hair

cabide (m) coat-hanger

cabine (f) cabin

cabos de emergência (mpl) jump leads

cabra (f) goat

caçar to hunt

cachecol (m) scarf

cachimbo (m) pipe *(smoking)*

cada each; every

cadeado (m) padlock

cadeia (f) chain; jail

cadeira (f) chair

» cadeira de bebé (f) high chair

» cadeira de lona (f) deckchair

» cadeira de rodas (f) wheelchair

caderneta (f) booklet *(bus tickets)*

cadiado (m) locker

café (m) black coffee; cafe

cãibra (f) cramp

cair to fall (down/over)

cais (m) jetty; pier

caixa (f) cash desk; cashier; box

caixa de primeiros socorros (f) first aid kit

caixa dos fusíveis (f) fusebox

caixote (m) bin

caixote do lixo (m) dustbin
calado/a quiet
calcanhar (m) heel
calças (fpl) trousers
calções (mpl) shorts
calções de banho (mpl) swimming trunks
caldeira (f) boiler
calmo/a calm
calor (m) heat
cama (f) bed
» cama de campismo (f) camp bed
» cama de casal (f) double bed
camada de ozônio ozone layer
câmara municipal (f) town hall
camarote (m) cabin (ship); box (theatre)
cambiar change money
câmbio (m) exchange rate
camião (m) lorry
caminho (m) footpath; path; way
caminho de ferro (m) railway
camioneta (f) van
camisa (f) shirt
camisola (f) jumper
camisola interior (f) vest
campainha (f) bell
campismo (m) camping
campo (m) country(side); field
canalizador (m) plumber
canção (f) song
cancelar to cancel
cancro (m) cancer
caneca (f) mug (cup)
caneta (f) pen
canivete (m) penknife
cano (m) drain
canoa (f) canoe
cansado/a tired
cantar to sing
cão (m) dog
capacete (m) helmet (motorbike)
capela (f) chapel
capital (f) capital (city)
capitão (m) captain (boat)
cara (f) face

caranguejo (m) crab
careca bald
carga de gás gas refill
carne (f) meat
carne de vaca (f) beef
caro/a expensive
carreira (f) career
carrinho de bébé (m) pram
carrinho de criança (m) push-chair
carro (m) car
carro da policia (m) police car
carruagem (m) carriage (rail)
carruagem-cama (f) sleeping-car
carta (f) letter
carta de condução (f) driving licence
cartão de crédito (m) credit card
cartão de embarque (m) boarding card
cartaz (m) poster
carteira (f) purse; wallet
carteiro (m) postman, postwoman
casa (f) home; house
casa de banho (f) bathroom
casa de campo (f) cottage
casa de vinhos (f) wine merchant/shop
casaco (m) coat; jacket
casaco de malha (m) cardigan
casado/a married
casamento (m) wedding
casar-se to get married
casas de banho (fpl) toilets
casca (f) shell (egg, nut)
castanho/a brown
castelo (m) castle (palace)
cathedral (f) cathedral
católico/a Catholic
causar to cause
cavalheiro/os gentleman/men
cavalo (m) horse
cave (f) basement; cellar
cavilha (f) tent peg
cedo early; blind
ceia (f) supper
cemitério (m) cemetery
cena (f) scene

centímetro (m) centimetre
central central
centro (m) centre; middle; town centre
centro comercial (m) shopping centre
cera (f) wax
cerâmica (f) pottery
cérebro (m) brain
cerimónia religiosa (f) ceremony *(church)*
certificado (m) certificate
certo/a right
cerveja (f) beer; lager
cerveja de barril (f) draught beer
cesto (m) basket
céu (m) sky
chá (m) tea
chá de ervas (m) herbal tea
chalé (m) chalet
chaleira (f) kettle
chamada a pagar pelo destinatário (f)
    reverse-charge call
chamar-se to be called
champanhe (m) champagne
champô (m) shampoo
chão (m) floor; ground
chão da tenda (m) groundsheet
chapéu de sol (m) sunshade
charuto (m) cigar
chave (f) key
chávena (f) cup
chefe (m) chef
chega enough
chegada (f) arrival
chegar to arrive
chegar a to reach
cheio/a crowded; full; booked up
cheirar to smell
cheque (m) cheque
chocado/a shocked
chocolate (m) chocolate
choque (m) shock *(electric)*
chorar to cry
chumbo (m) lead
chupeta (f) dummy *(baby's)*
chuva (f) rain

chuveiro (m) shower
ciclista (m/f) cyclist
cidade (f) city
ciência (f) science
cigarro (m) cigarette
cimo (m) top *(mountain)*
cinto (m) belt
cinto de segurança (m) seatbelt
cinto salva-vidas (m) lifebelt
cintura (f) waist
cinzas (fpl) ash
cinzeiro (m) ashtray
cinzento/a grey
círculo (m) circle
cistite (f) cystitis
claro of course
claro/a light *(coloured)*; clear
classe (f) class
clima (m) climate
clínica (f) clinic
clube (m) club
cobertor (m) blanket
cobrar to cash
cobre (m) copper
código postal (m) postcode
coelho (m) rabbit
cofre (m) safe *(strongbox)*
coisa (f) thing
cola (f) glue
colar (m) necklace
colarinho (m) collar
colchão (m) mattress
colecção collection *(e.g. stamps)*
colega (m/f) colleague
colégio (m) college
colete (m) waistcoat
colete salava-vidas (m) lifejacket
colher (f) spoon
colher de chá (f) teaspoon
colina (f) hill
com with
com antecedência in advance
com certeza certainly
com gás fizzy

com poucas gorduras low-fat
com sede thirsty
comboio (m) train
combustível (m) fuel
começar to begin; to start
começo (m) beginning; start
comédia (f) comedy
comer to eat
comercial commercial
comestível edible
comfortável comfortable
comichão (f) itch
comida (f) food
comidas saudáveis health foods
como as; how; like *(similar to)*
companhia (f) company
comparado/a com compared with
compartimento (m) compartment
completo (m) whole
complicado/a complicated
compositor (m) /ora (f) composer
comprar to buy
compreender to understand
comprido/a long
comprimento (m) length
comprimido (m) pill, tablet
comprometido/a engaged *(to be married)*
computador (m) computer
comum shared
concerto (m) concert
concordar to agree
concussão (f) concussion
condição (f) condition *(state)*
conduzir to drive
conferência (f) conference
confirmar to confirm
congelado/a frozen
congelador (m) freezer
congelar to freeze
conhaque (m) brandy
conhecer to know *(someone)*
conjuntivite (m) conjunctivitis
consciente conscious
conseguir falar to get through *(phone)*

consertar to fix *(mend)*
conservação (f) conservation
construir to build
consulado (m) consulate
consulta (f) appointment *(doctor)*
consultor (m) consultant
conta (f) account *(bank)*; bill
contador (m) meter
contagioso/a infectious
contar to count
contente pleased
continente (m) continent
continuar to carry on *(walking/driving)*
contra against
contraceptivo (m) contraceptive
contracto (m) contract
contrário/a opposite
controlar to check
controle (m) control *(passport)*
conveniente convenient
convento (m) convent
convés (m) deck
convidado/a guest
convidar to invite
convite (m) invitation
cópia (f) copy
copo (fm) glass
cor (f) colour
cor de laranja (f) orange *(colour)*
coração (m) heart
corda (f) rope; string
cordeiro (m) lamb *(meat)*
cor-de-rosa pink
coroa (f) crown
corpo (m) body
correctamente properly
correcto/a correct
correia (f) strap
correio (m) post *(mail)*
correios (mpl) post office
corrente (f) draught *(air)*
correr to run
corridas (fpl) racing
cortar to cut

cortar-se to cut oneself

corte (m) cut

corte de cabelo (m) haircut

cortina (f) curtain

costa (f) coast

costume (m) habit

cozer to boil; to sew

cozinha (f) kitchen

cozinhado cooked

cozinhar to cook

cozinheiro (m) cook

credifone (m) telephone card

creme (m) cream *(colour; lotion)*

» creme bronzeador (m) suntan lotion

» creme de barbear (m) shaving cream

» creme de cara (m) face cream

» creme de limpeza (m) cleansing lotion

» creme de mão (m) hand cream

» creme hidratante (m) moisturiser

criança (f) child

cristal (m) crystal

Cristão/Cristã Christian

cru/a raw

cruz (f) cross

cruzamento (m) crossroads; junction

cruzeiro (m) cruise

cubo de açúcar (m) sugar lump

cuecas (fpl) knickers, pants

cuidado (m) caution

cuidadoso/a careful

culpado/a guilty

cunhada (f) sister-in-law

cunhado (m) brother-in-law

cúpola (f) dome

cura (f) cure *(remedy)*

curar to cure; to heal

curso (m) course *(lessons)*

curto/a short

curva (f) bend

custar to cost

D

dado (m) dice

dados (mpl) data

daltónico/a colour-blind

dançar to dance

dar to give

» dar de comer to feed *(inc. baby)*

» dar de volta to give back

» dar parte (de) to report

data (f) date *(day)*

de from, of

» de alguma maneira somehow

» de autocarro by bus

» de carro by car

» de cima upper

» de comboio by train

» de facto in fact

» de férias on holiday

» de meia idade middle-aged

» de qualquer maneira anyway

» de repente suddenly

» de valor valuable

debaixo under

debaixo de água underwater

debruçar-se to lean out

decidir to decide

declarar to declare

dedo (m) finger

defeito (m) defect; fault; flaw

defeituoso/a defective; faulty

deficiente (m/f) disabled

degraus (mpl) stairs

deitar to pour

deitar fora to throw away

deitar-se to lie down

deixar to leave; to let *(allow)*

dela hers

delgado/a thin

delicado/a delicate

delicioso/a delicious

demonstração (f) demonstration

denim denim

dente (m) tooth

dentista (m/f) dentist

dentro indoors; inside

dentura (f) denture

departamento (m) department

depois afterwards

depois de after

» depois de amanhã day after tomorrow

depósito (m) deposit

depósito de bagagem (m) left luggage

depressa quick(ly)

desagradável unpleasant

desaparafusar to unscrew

descafeinado/a decaffeinated

descansar to rest

descarado/a cheeky

descartáveis disposable

descer to go down

descomfortável uncomfortable

descongelar defrost

descrever to describe

descrição (f) description

descuidadoso/a careless

desculpe excuse me

desculpe? pardon?

desde since

desempregado/a unemployed

desenhar to design; to draw

desenho drawing

desenhista (m/f) designer

deserto (m) desert

desfazer as malas unpack

desiludido/a disappointed

desinfectante disinfectant

desligado/a off (TV, light)

desligar to hang up (telephone); to switch off

deslocado/a dislocated

desmaiar to faint

desodorizante (f) deodorant

despertador (m) alarm clock

despir to undress

desporto (m) sport

destino (m) destination

destruição (f) delivery

desvio (m) diversion

detergente (m) detergent

Deus (m) God

devagar slowly

dever to owe

dia (m) day

Dia de Ano Novo (m) New Year's Day

Dia de Natal (m) Christmas Day

dia útil (m) weekday

diabetes (mpl) diabetes

diabético/a diabetic

diamante (m) diamond

diário/a daily

diarreia (f) diarrhoea

dicionário (m) dictionary

dieta (f) diet

diferent(emente) different(ly)

difícil difficult

digital digital

dinheiro (m) cash; money

direcção (f) direction

directo/a direct (train)

direita (f) right

direita/a right-hand; straight

desconto (m) discount

discoteca (f) disco

dislexico/a dyslexic

disponível spare

disquete (f) floppy disc

distância (f) distance

diversão (f) entertainment

divertir-se to have fun

dívida (f) debt

divorciado/a divorced

dizer to say; tell

do oeste western

do outro lado de across

dobradiço/a folding (e.g. chair)

doce (m) jam; sweet

documento (m) document

» documentos de registo do carro registration document (car)

doença (f) illness

doente ill

doente (m/f) patient (hospital)

doer to hurt

» dói it hurts

dolar (m) dollar
doloroso/a painful, sore
dor (f) pain
» dor de dentes (f) toothache
» dor de estômago (f) stomach ache
» dor de ouvidos (f) earache
» dores de cabeça (fpl) headache
» dores do período (fpl) period pains
dormir to sleep
droga (f) drug
duas camas twin beds
duas vezes twice
duplo double
duplo-tecto (m) fly sheet
durante during
durar to last
duro/a hard; tough (meat)

E

e and
é is
e meia half past
ecrã (m) screen
edredão (m) duvet
ela she
ele he
electricista (m) electrician
electricidade (f) electricity
eléctrico (m) tram; cable car
eleição (f) election
eles/elas they
elevador (m) lift
elevador cadeira (m) chair lift
em into; on
» em baixo downstairs; empty
» em breve soon
» em cima up
» em cima de on top of
» em frente straight on
» em frente de opposite; in front of
» em greve on strike
» em lado nenhum nowhere
» em negócios on business
» em parte partly

» em qualquer parte anywhere
» em todo o lado everywhere
» em vez de instead of
embaixada (f) embassy
embaixador (m) ambassador
embaraçoso/a embarrassing
embarcar to board
embarque (m) boarding (plane)
embora although
embrulhar to wrap (up)
embrulho (m) packet
ementa (f) menu (à la carte)
ementa turística (f) (set) menu
emergência (f) emergency
emocionante exciting
empregado/a (m/f) waiter/waitress
empregado/a de balcão shop assistant
emprego (m) job
empresa (f) firm (company)
emprestar to lend
empréstimo (m) loan
empurrar to push
encaracolado/a curly
encher to fill; to pump up
encolher to shrink
encontrar to find
energia (f) energy
enfarte (m) heart attack
enfermeiro/a nurse
engarrafamento (m) traffic jam
engenheiro engineer
engraçado/a funny (amazing)
enjoado/a seasick
enjoo (m) travel sickness
enlatado tinned
enquanto while
ensinar to teach
então then
entiados step-children
entrada (f) admission; entrance
entrada de assinatura (f) season ticket
entradas (fpl) starter (food)
entrar to come in
entrar (em) to get on (bus)

entre among; between; through
entregar to deliver
entretanto meanwhile
entrevista (f) interview
envelope (m) envelope
enxaqueca (f) migraine
equipa (f) team
equipamento (m) equipment
errado/a wrong
erro (m) mistake
erupção cutânea (f) rash *(spots)*
erva (f) herb
esbelto/a slim
escada (f) ladder
escada rolante (f) escalator
escadas (fpl) stairs
escocês/escocesa Scottish
Escócia (f) Scotland
escola (f) school
escolher to choose
escorregadio/a slippery
escova (f) brush
escova do cabelo (f) hairbrush
escova de dentes (f) toothbrush
escrever to write
escritor/ora writer
escritório (m) office
escultura (f) sculpture
escuro/a dark
escutar listen
esgoto (m) drain
esmalte (m) enamel
espaço (m) space
espada (f) spade
especial special
especialidade (f) speciality
especialmente especially
especiaria (f) spice
espectáculo (m) show
espelho (m) mirror
esperar to expect; to wait (for)
esperar que to hope
» espero que sim I hope so
espesso/a thick

espirrar to sneeze
esponja (f) sponge *(bath)*
esposa (f) wife
espumante sparkling (wine)
esquadra da polícia (f) police station
esquecer to forget
esquentador da água (m) water heater
esquerda (f) left
esqui (m) ski; skiing
esqui aquático (m) water-skiing
esquina (f) corner *(outside)*
esse/a, aquele/a that (one)
essencial essential
está bem all right *(OK); fine
está no seguro insured
esta noite tonight
estação (f) season; station
estação de autocarros (f) bus station
estação de ferro (f) railway station
estação de serviço (f) petrol station
estacionamento (m) parking
estacionar to park
estádio (m) stadium
estado (m) state
estar to be
» estar com fome to be hungry
» estar com pressa to be in a hurry
» estar constipado/a to have a cold
» estar de pé to stand
» estar ocupado/a to be taken *(seat)*
estátua (f) statue
este (m) east
este/a this (one)
estes/estas these
estilo (m) style
estômago (m) stomach
estragado/a damaged
estrangeiro (m) abroad
estrangeiro/a foreign; foreigner
estranho (m) stranger
estranho/a odd; strange
estrela (f) star
estudante (m/f) student
estudar to study

estúpido/a stupid
esvaziar to empty
etiqueta (f) label
Eu I
euro (m) euro
evitar to avoid
exacto/a exact(ly)
examinação (f) examination
excelente excellent
excepto except
excesso de bagagem (m) excess baggage
excitado/a excited
excursão (f) excursion; tour
excursão organizada (f) package tour
exemplo (m) example
exercício (m) exercise
exército (m) army
experiência (f) experience
experimentar to try
explicar to explain
explosão (f) explosion
exportação (f) export
exportar to export
exposição (f) exhibition
expresso (m) express
extensão (f) extension cable
externo external
extinto (m) fire extinguisher
extra extra

F

fábrica (f) factory
faca (f) knife
fácil easy
facto (m) fact
falar to speak
falso/a fake; false
falta de luz (f) power cut
família family
familiar common *(usual)*; familiar
familiar (m) relation
famoso/a famous
fantástico/a fantastic
farinha (f) flour

farmácia (f) chemist
farto to be fed up
fatia (f) slice
fato (m) suit *(man's)*
fato de banho (m) bathing costume
fato de mergulho (m) wetsuit
fato de senhora (m) suit *(woman's)*
favorito/a favourite
fazer to do; make
» fazer esqui to ski
» fazer jogging jogging
» fazer marcha atrás to reverse *(car)*
» fazer pressão to press
» fazer turismo to tour
» fazer um erro to make a mistake
fé (f) faith
febre (f) fever
febre dos fenos (f) hayfever
fechado/a shut; closed
fechadura (f) lock
fechar to close; shut
fechar à chave to lock
fecho (m) zip
feijões (mpl) beans
feio/a ugly
feira (f) fair
» feira de indústrias (f) trade fair
» feira popular funfair
feito à mão hand made
feliz happy
feminino/a feminine
feminista feminist
feno (m) hay
feriado (m) public holiday
férias (fpl) holidays *(school, etc.)*
ferida (f) wound; injury
ferido/a injured
ferir to injure
ferramenta (f) tool
ferro (m) iron *(metal)*; tent pole
ferrugento/a rusty
ferry-boat (m) ferry
festa (f) party
festival (m) festival

ficar to remain
fígado (m) liver
fila (f) row *(theatre, etc.)*; queue
filha (f) daughter
filho (m) son
filme (m) film
fim (m) end
fim de semana (m) weekend
finanças (fpl) finance
firme firm
fita tape
flor (f) flower
floresta (f) forest
fluente fluent *(language)*
fogão (m) cooker
fogo (m) fire
fogo de artifício (m) firework
folha (f) leaf
folha metálica hidrólica (f) hydrofoil
folheto (m) leaflet
fome hungry
fonte (f) fountain
fora (de) out (of)
força (f) physical strength
força aérea (f) air force
forno (m) stove
forte strong
forte (m) fortress
fósforo (m) match
fotocópia (f) photocopy
fotografia (f) photo
fotógrafo (m) photographer
fracasso (m) failure
fractura (f) fracture
frágil fragile
fralda (f) nappy
fraldas descartáveis disposable nappies
frasco (m) jar; pot
frase (f) sentence
frequente frequent
fresco/a fresh; cool
frigideira (f) frying pan
frigorífico (m) fridge
frio/a cold

fritar to fry
frito/a fried
fronha (f) pillowcase
fronte (f) front
fronteira (f) frontier
fruta (f) fruit
frutaria (f) greengrocer's
fumar to smoke
fumo (m) smoke
funcionar to function
funcionário/a clerk
fundo (m) bottom
funeral (m) funeral
furo (m) puncture
fusível (m) fuse
futebol (m) football

G

gabardine (f) raincoat
galão (m) coffee with milk in a glass
galês/esa Welsh
galeria (f) gallery
galinha (f) chicken
ganhar to earn; win
garagem (f) garage
garantia (f) guarantee
garfo (m) fork
garrafa (f) bottle
garrafa de gás gas bottle/cylinder
gás gas
gás butano (m) butane gas
gás para o isqueiro (m) lighter fuel
gasóleo (m) diesel
gasolina (f) petrol
gasolina sem chumbo (f) unleaded
   petrol
gastar to spend *(money)*
gato (m) cat
gaveta (f) drawer
geada (f) frost
gelado/a icy
geleia (f) jelly
geleria (f) cool box
gelo (m) ice

dictionary

gémios/as twins
generoso/a generous
genro (m) son-in-law
gentil gentle
geral general
gerente (m/f) manager
gilete (f) razor
gin (m) gin
golfe (m) golf
golo (m) goal *(football)*
gordo/a fat *(adj/noun)*
gordura (f) fat
gorduroso/a greasy
gorjeta (f) tip *(in restaurant, etc.)*
gostar to like *(food, people)*
gosto I like
governo (m) government
gozar to enjoy
grama (m) gramme
gramática (f) grammar
grande big; large
granizo (m) hail
grátis free
grau (m) degree *(temperature)*
gravar to record
gravata (f) tie
grave serious
grávida pregnant
graxa (f) shoe polish
grelhado/a grilled
greve (f) strike
gripe (f) flu
grito (m) shout
groselha preta (f) blackcurrant
grupo (m) group
gruta (f) cave
guardanapo (m) napkin
guardar to keep
guarda-chuva (m) umbrella
guerra (f) war
guia (m/f) guide
guia de conversação (m) phrase book
guia turístico (m) guidebook
guitarra (f) guitar

H

há there is/are
» há ... anos ... years ago
» há...? is/are there... ?
hemorragia nasal (f) nosebleed
hipódromo (m) racecourse
história (f) history; story
hoje today
homem (m) man
homens (mpl) men
honesto (m) honest
hora (f) hour
hora de ponta (f) rush hour
horário (m) timetable *(train)*
horrível dreadful; horrible
hóspede (m) guest *(hotel)*
hospedeiro (m) host
hospital (m) hospital
humano (m) human
húmido/a damp

I

iate (m) yacht
ida e volta return *(ticket)*
idade (f) age
ideia idea
igreja (f) church
igual equal
ilha (f) island
imaginação (f) imagination
imaginar to imagine
imediatamente immediately
impedido/a blocked *(road)*
impedir to block *(road)*
impermeável (m) waterproof
importante important
impossível impossible
imposto (m) duty *(tax)*
impresso (m) form
impressionante impressive
imprimir to print
inchaço (m) lump *(swelling)*
inchado/a swollen
incluído/a included

independente independent
indicativo (m) dialling code
indigestão (f) indigestion
indisposto/a unwell
indústria (f) industry
infecção (f) infection
infectado/a infected
infeliz unhappy
infelizmente unfortunately
inferior lower
inflamado/a inflamed
informação (f) information
informal informal
Inglaterra (f) England
inglês/inglesa English
íngreme steep
injecção (f) injection
inocente innocent
insecto (m) insect
insistir to insist
insolação (f) sunstroke
instalações (fpl) facilities
instrutor (m) /ora (f) instructor
insulina (f) insulin
insulto (m) insult
inteligente clever
interessado/a interested
interessante interesting
internacional international
internet (f) Internet
interpretar to interpret
intérprete (m) interpreter
interruptor (m) switch
intervalo (m) interval *(theatre, etc.)*
intoxicação alimentar (f) food poisoning
inundação (f) flood
inútil useless
Inverno (m) winter
invulgar unusual
iodo (m) iodine
iogurte (m) yoghurt
ir to go
» ir às compras to go shopping
» ir buscar to fetch
» ir embora to go away
» ir para fora to leave the country
Irlanda (f) Ireland
irlandês/esa Irish
irmã (f) sister
irmão (m) brother
irritado/a annoyed
islâmico/a Islamic
islamismo (m) Islam
isqueiro (m) lighter *(cigarette)*
IVA VAT

J

já already
janela (f) window
jangada (f) raft
jantar dinner; supper
jardim (m) garden
jardim zoológico (m) zoo
jardineiro (m) gardener
jarra (f) carafe
jarro (m) jug
joalharia (f) jeweller's
joelho (m) knee
jogo (m) gambling
jogo (m) game *(match)*
jornal (m) newspaper
jovem (m/f) young
judeu/judia Jewish
juiz (m/f) judge
juros (mpl) interest *(money)*
juventude (f) youth

L

lã (f) wool
lá em cima upstairs
lábio (m) lip
lado (m) side
ladrão/ladra thief
lago (m) lake
lágrima (f) tear *(cry)*
lambreta (f) scooter
lâmina de barbear (f) razor blade
lâmpada (f) light bulb

lanterna (f) torch
lápis (m) pencil
laranja (f) orange *(fruit)*
largo/a broad; loose
lasca (f) splinter
lata (f) can *(tin)*
latão (m) brass
lavagem (f) washing
lava-loiça (f) sink
lavandaria (f) laundry
lavandaria automática (f) launderette
lavar to wash
lavar a loiça washing-up
lavatório (m) wash-basin
lavável washable
laxativo (m) laxative
legendas (fpl) subtitles
legumes (mpl) vegetables
lei (f) law
leite (m) milk
» leite desnatado (m) skimmed milk
» leite em pó (m) powdered milk
leitura (f) reading
lembrança (f) souvenir
lembrar-se to remember
lenço (m) handkerchief
lenço de cabeça (m) head scarf
lençol (m) sheet
lenços de papel (mpl) tissues
lentes (fpl) lens *(camera)*
lentes de contacto (fpl) contact lens
leque (m) fan *(air)*
ler to read
lésbica (f) lesbian
letra (f) letter *(of alphabet)*
leuquemia (f) leukemia
levantar voo take off *(plane)*
levantar-se to stand up
levar to carry; take *(time)*
lhe to him/her/you *(singular)*
lhes to them/you *(plural)*
liberdade (f) freedom
libra (f) pound *(sterling)*
lição (f) lesson

licença (f) licence *(fishing, etc.)*; permit
licenciatura (f) graduation *(university)*
licor (m) liqueur
licores (mpl) spirits
ligação (f) connection
ligar to switch on
ligeiro/a light *(weight)*
limão (m) lemon
limitado/a limited
limite de velocidade (m) speed limit
limonada (f) lemonade
limpar to clean
limpeza a seco (f) dry-cleaner's
limpo/a clean
língua (f) language; tongue
linha (f) cotton *(thread)*; line; track
linha aérea (f) airline
líquido (m) liquid; fluid
lista (f) list; menu
lista telefónica (f) telephone directory
litro (m) litre
livraria (f) bookshop
livre free
livre de direitos duty-free
livro (m) book
lixo (m) rubbish
local local
local de interesse (m) place of interest
loção (f) lotion
loja (f) shop
loja de ferramentas (f) hardware shop
Londres London
longe far *(away)*; long-distance
lotaria (f) lottery
louco/a mad
louro/a fair *(haired)*
lua (f) moon
lua de mel (f) honeymoon
lucro (m) profit
lugar (m) place
lutar to fight
luvas (fpl) gloves
luz (f) light

M

maca (f) stretcher
maçã (f) apple
macho (m) male
macio/a smooth; soft
maço (m) packet
madeira (f) wood
madrasta (f) step-mother
maduro/a ripe; mature *(cheese)*
mãe (f) mother
magoado/a hurt
magro/a thin
maior bigger
mais more
» mais adiante further on
» mais alguma coisa anything else
» mais cedo earlier
» mais nada nothing else
» mais ou menos approximately
» mais tarde later
mal educado/a rude
mal passada rare *(steak)*
mala (f) briefcase; suitcase
mala de mão handbag
mandar to send
manga (f) sleeve
manhã (f) morning
manteiga (f) butter
mão (f) hand
mapa (m) map; plan
maquilhagem (f) make-up
máquina (f) machine
máquina digital (f) digital camera
máquina fotográfica (f) camera
mar (m) sea
marca (f) brand
marcar to dial
marco do correio (m) letterbox, postbox
maré (f) tide *(high/low)*
margarina (f) margarine
marido (m) husband
marinha (f) navy
marisco (m) seafood
mármore (m) marble

martelo (m) hammer
mas but
máscara (f) mask
masculino/a masculine
massa (f) pasta; pastry; dough
matar to kill
matrícula (f) number plate
mau bad
maravilhoso/a wonderful
me me
mecânico (m) mechanic
média medium *(steak)*
medicamento (m) medicine
médico/a doctor; medical
medida (f) measurement
medieval medieval
médio/a medium *(size)*
medir to measure
mediterrâneo mediterranean
medusa (f) jellyfish
meia (f) sock
meia de leite (f) milky coffee
meia hora (f) half an hour
meia pensão (f) half board
meia-irmã (f) step-sister
meia-noite (f) midnight
meias (fpl) stockings, tights
meio (seco) half dry *(wine)*
meio/a half *(adj)*
meio-dia (m) midday
meio-irmão (m) step-brother
melhor better
membro (m) member
memória (f) memory
menina (f) young girl
menos less
mensagem (f) message
mensal monthly
mercado (m) market
mercearia (f) grocer's
mergulho (m) diving
mês (m) month
mesa (f) table
mesmo really

mesquita (f) mosque

metade half

metade do preço (a) half price

metro (m) underground *(tube)*

meu (m) mine *(of me)*

micro-disco (m) mini-disc

micro-ondas (m) microwave oven

micro-ónibus (m) minibus

milha (f) mile

mim me

ministro (m) minister

minuto (m) minute

missa (f) mass *(church)*

mistério (m) mystery

mistura (f) mixture

misturado/a mixed

mobília (f) furniture

mochila (f) rucksack

moda (f) fashion

modelo (m) model

moderno/a modern

moeda (f) coin

moinho (m) mill; windmill

mola (f) peg

molhado/a wet

molho (m) sauce

momento (m) moment

montanha (f) mountain

montra (f) window *(shop)*

monumento (m) monument

morada (f) address

morar live *(dwell);* to stay *(live)*

morder to bite

morno/a warm

morrer to die

morte (f) death

morto/a dead

mosca (f) fly

mosquito (m) mosquito

mosteiro (m) monastery

mostrar to show

motor (m) engine; motor

motorista (m/f) bus-driver; driver

motorizada (f) motorbike

mover to move

muculmano/a muslim

mudar de changing *(room; train)*

mudar de casa to move house

mudo/a dumb

muitas vezes often

muito too; very

muito/a a lot (of); much

muito bem well done *(steak)*

muitos/as many

muleta (f) crutch

mulher (f) woman; wife

multa (f) ticket *(penalty)*

multidão (f) crowd

mundial world *(adj)*

mundo (m) world

muro (m) wall *(outside; garden)*

museu (m) museum

música (f) music

» música popular (f) folk music

músico (m) musician

N

na in

na moda fashionable/in fashion

nacional national

nacionalidade (f) nationality

nada nothing

nadador-salvador (m) lifeguard

nadar to swim

namorado/a (m/f) boyfriend/girlfriend

não no; not

» não faz mal it doesn't matter

» não faz mal ao ambiente

   environmentally friendly

» não me importa I don't care/mind

» não sei I don't know

» não vale a pena it's not worth it

não-fumadores non-smoking

nariz (m) nose

natação (f) swimming

Natal (m) Christmas

naturalista (m/f) vegan

natural(mente) natural(ly)

navio (m) ship
necessário/a necessary
negativo (m) negative *(photo)*
negócios (mpl) business
negra (f) bruise
nem... nem... neither... nor...
nenhum/nenhuma none
nervoso/a nervous
neta (f) granddaughter
neto (m) grandson
nevar to snow
neve (f) snow
névoa (f) mist
nevoeiro (m) fog
ninguém nobody
nível (m) level *(height; standard)*
no in
 » no campo (m) in the country
 » no caso de case: in case
 » no passado in the past
 » no primeiro andar on the first floor
nó (m) knot
nódoa (f) stain
noite (f) night
noivo/a (m/f) fiancé/fiancée
nome (m) Christian name
nora (f) daughter-in-law
normalmente normally; usually
norte (m) north
nós us; we
nota (f) note *(bank)*
notícias (fpl) news
novo/a new
novo endereço (m) forwarding address
nóz (f) nut
nú/nua naked
nublado cloudy
número (m) number
nunca never
núvem (f) cloud

O

o (m) the
objectivo (m) goal

objecto (m) object *(thing)*
objectos de valor (mpl) valuables
obra (f) play *(theatre)*
obras (f) roadworks
obrigado/a thank you
obrigatório/a compulsory
obter to get
óbvio/a obvious
oculista (f) optician
óculos (mpl) spectacles
 » óculos de mergulho (mpl) goggles
 » óculos de sol (mpl) sunglasses
ocupado/a busy; occupied
odiar to hate
oeste (m) west
ofendido/a offended
oferta (f) offer
oferta especial (f) special offer
oficial official
oficial (m) officer
olá hello
óleo (m) oil
óleo de bronzear suntan oil
olhar to look (at)
olhar (m) look
olho (m) eye
onda (f) wave
onde where
ontem yesterday
opera (f) opera
operação (f) operation
opinião (f) opinion
óptimo great!
ordem (f) order
ordenado (m) wage
organizar to organise
oriental eastern
original original
os them
osso (m) bone
ou either; or
ou... ou... either... or...
ouro (m) gold
Outono (m) autumn

outra vez again
outro/a another; other
ouvido ear
ouvir to hear
ouvir to listen
ovelha (f) sheep
ovo cozido (m) boiled egg

P

padaria (f) baker's
padrão (m) pattern
padrasto (m) step-father
padre (m) priest
pagar to pay
página (f) page
pai (m) father
país (m) country
pais (mpl) parents
País de Gales (m) Wales
paisagem (f) scenery
paixão (f) passion
palácio (m) palace
palavra (f) word
palha (f) straw *(drinking)*
pálido/a pale
palito (m) toothpick
panela (f) saucepan
panela a vapor (f) steamer *(cooking)*
pano (m) cloth
pão (m) bread
pão de trigo (m) wholemeal bread
Papa (m) Pope
papel (m) paper
» papel de cigarro (m) cigarette paper
» papel de escrever (m) writing paper
» papel higiénico (m) toilet paper
papelaria (f) stationer's
par (m) couple *(pair)*
para towards; for
» para além de apart (from); beyond
» para atrás backwards
» para fora long-distance call
parafina (f) paraffin
parafuso (m) screw

paragem (f) stop *(bus)*
paragem de autocarros (f) bus stop
paralisado/a paralysed
parar to stop
Pare! stop!
parecer to seem
parede (f) wall *(inside)*
parlamento (m) parliament
parque (m) park
parque de campismo (m) campsite
parque de estacionamento (m) car park
parquímetro (m) parking meter
parte (f) part
partida (f) departure *(bus, car, train)*
partido (m) party *(political)*
partido/a broken
partir to break; to depart *(bus, car, etc.)*;
    to go away
Páscoa (f) Easter
passado (m) past
passageiro/a passenger
passagem de nível (f) level crossing
passagem de peões (f) pedestrian
    crossing
passagem inferior (f) underpass
passaporte (m) passport
passar to pass *(on road)*; pass *(time)*
passar a ferro to iron
pássaro (m) bird
passatempo (m) hobby
passeio (m) pavement
passo (m) step *(footstep)*
pasta de dentes (f) toothpaste
pastelaria (f) cake shop
pastilha elástica (f) chewing gum
pastilhas (fpl) throat lozenges/pastilles
patinar to skate
patins de gelo (mpl) skates *(ice)*
patins de rodas (mpl) roller blades
pato (m) duck
patrão (m) boss
pau (m) stick
paz (f) peace
pé (m) foot

peão (m) pedestrian
pechincha (f) bargain
pedaço (m) piece
pedal (m) pedal
pedir to ask; to order
pedra (f) stone
pegajoso/a sticky
pegas (fpl) clothes pegs
peixaria (f) fishmonger's
peixe (m) fish
pelar to peel
pele (f) skin; leather
pêlo fur
pelo menos at least
pena (f) feather
peneira (f) sieve
penico (m) potty *(child's)*
penicilina (f) penicillin
pensão (f) guest house; pension
pensão completa (f) full board
pensar to think
pensionista (m/f) pensioner
penso (m) bandage
penso adesivo (m) plaster *(sticking)*
penso higiénico (m) sanitary towel
pente (m) comb
pequeno/a little; small
pequeno almoço breakfast
perder to lose; to miss *(bus, etc.)*
perdoar to forgive
perfeito/a perfect
perfume (m) perfume; scent
pergunta (f) question
perigo (m) danger
perigoso dangerous
período (m) period *(menstrual)*
perito (m) expert
permanente (f) perm
permitido/a allowed
permitir to allow
perna (f) leg
persiana (f) shutter
pertencer to belong to
perto close (by); near

perto (de) near (to)
perturbação gástrica (f) stomach upset
pesado/a heavy
pesar to weigh
pescar to fish/go fishing
peso (m) weight
pessoal personal
pessoas (fpl) people
pestana (f) eyelash
petróleo (m) petrol
piada (f) joke
piano (m) piano
picada (f) sting
picada de insecto (f) insect bite
picante spicy
picar to sting
pijama (m) pyjamas
pilha (f) battery
piloto (m) pilot *(plane)*; pilot light
pílula (f) the pill
pimenta (f) pepper
pingar to drip
pingos dos ouvidos eardrops
pintar to paint
pintor/ora painter
pintura (f) painting
pior worse
piquenique (m) picnic
pires (m) saucer
piscina (f) swimming pool
plano/a flat *(level)*
planta (f) plant
plástico (m) plastic
plataforma (f) platform
plateia (f) stalls *(theatre)*
pneumonia (f) pneumonia
pó (m) dust; powder
pó talco (m) talcum powder
pobre poor
pó-de-arroz (m) face powder
poder can *(to be able)*
poder (m) power
poder com to manage *(cope)*
podre rotten

polgar thumb
polícia (m) policeman
política (f) politics
poluição (f) pollution
poluído polluted
ponte (f) bridge
ponto (m) point *(needle, pin)*
popular popular
por along; by *(author, etc.)*; per
» por avião by air
» por baixo below
» por exemplo for example
pôr to put down
pôr de parte to put by
por favor please
por isso therefore
pôr no correio to post
porção (f) portion
porco (m) pig
pormenor (m) detail
porque because
porquê why?
porta (f) door; gate *(airport)*
porta-chaves (m) key ring
portagem (f) toll
portão (m) gate
portável portable
porteiro (m) porter
porto (m) harbour
positivo/a positive *(sure)*
possível possible
possivelmente possibly
postal (m) postcard
posto de informação (m)
    information desk/office
posto de perdidos e achados (m)
    lost property office
poucos/as (a) few; not many
poupar to save *(money)*
pousada de juventude (f) youth hostel
praça (f) square
» praça de táxis (f) taxi rank
prado (m) meadow
praia (f) beach
prata (f) silver

prateleira (f) shelf
prato (m) dish; plate
precisar to need
preço (m) charge *(money)*; price
» preço de entrada (m) admission
    charge
» preço do bilhete (m) fare
prédio (m) building
preferir to prefer
preguiçoso/a lazy
prémio (m) prize
prensa (f) press *(newspapers)*
preocupado/a worried
preparar to prepare
presente (m) gift
preservativo (m) condom
preso/a under arrest
presunto (m) ham
preto/a black
previsão (f) weather forecast
Primavera (f) spring *(season)*
primeiro first
primeiro ministro (m/f) prime minister
primeiros socorros (mpl) first aid
primo/a cousin
princesa (f) princess
principal main
príncipe (m) prince
principiante (m/f) beginner
prisão (f) prison
prisão de ventre (f) constipation
privado private
proa (f) bow *(ship)*
problema (m) problem
procurar to look for
profissão (f) profession
profundo/a deep
programa (m) programme
proibido/a prohibited; forbidden
prometer to promise
pronto/a ready
pronunciar to pronounce
propriedade (f) property
proprietário/a owner
provável likely

provavelmente probably
próximo nearby
próximo/a next
publicidade (f) advertising
público (m) audience
público/a public (adj)
puro/a pure
purpúreo/a purple
puxar to pull

Q

quadrado (m) square (shape)
quadro (m) picture
qual which
qualidade (f) quality
qualquer coisa anything
quando when (with past tense)
quantas vezes? how often?
quantia (f) amount (money)
quanto antes as soon as possible
quanto custa how much?
quanto tempo how long?
quantos/as how many?
quarto quarter; room
quarto (m) bedroom
quase nearly
que than
que? what?
» que quer dizer? what does this mean?
» que se passa? what's the matter?
queda de água waterfall
queijo (m) cheese
queimado/a burnt (food)
queimadura (f) burn (on skin)
queimadura solar (f) sunburn
queimar to scald
queixo (m) chin; jaw
quem who?
quente hot
querer to want
querido/a dear
quilo (m) kilo(gram)
quilómetro (m) kilometre
quinta (f) farm

quinze dias fortnight
quiosque (m) newspaper kiosk

R

rã (f) frog
rabino (m) rabbi
radioactivo/a radioactive
radiodador (m) radiator
rainha (f) queen
raio-X (m) X-ray
raiva (f) rabies
ramo (m) branch (bank, etc.)
rapariga (f) girl
rapaz (m) boy
rápido/a fast
raposa (f) fox
raqueta (f) racket (tennis)
raro/a rare
rasgado/a torn
rasgão (m) tear (rip)
razão (f) reason
real royal
rebocar to tow
reboque (m) breakdown truck
rebuçados (mpl) sweets
receita (f) prescription
receita (f) recipe
recepção (f) reception
recepcionista (m/f) receptionist
recibo (m) receipt
reclamação (f) complaint
reclamar to complain
recolha (f) collection (postal/rubbish)
recolher to collect
recomendar to recommend
reconhecer to recognise
recuperar (de) to recover
rede (f) net
rede para mosquitos (f) mosquito net
redondo/a round
redução (f) reduction
reembolso (m) refund
reencher to refill
refeição (f) meal
reformado/a retired

refugiado/a refugee
região (f) region
registada/o registered *(letter)*
registar to register *(luggage, etc.)*
régua (f) ruler *(for measuring)*
rei (m) king
relações sexuais (fpl) sexual
   intercourse
relâmpago (m) lightning
relativamente relatively
relatório (m) report
religião (f) religion
relógio (m) clock; watch
relva (f) grass
remar to row
remo (m) paddle *(canoeing)*
remuneração (f) fee
reparar to mend; to repair
repelente de insectos (m) insect
   repellent
repetir to repeat
representação (f) performance
rés-do-chão (m) ground floor
reserva (f) booking; reservation *(hotel etc)*
reservado/a reserved
reservar to book; to reserve
respirar to breathe
responder to answer
responder to reply
responsável responsible
resposta (f) answer, reply
ressaca (f) hangover
restaurante (m) restaurant
resultado (m) result
retrato (m) portrait
reumatismo (m) rheumatism
reunião (f) meeting
revelar to develop (film)
revista (f) magazine
ribeiro (m) stream
rico/a rich
rígido/a stiff
rim (m) kidney
ringue de patinagem (m) ice rink
rio (m) river

rir to laugh
riscar to scratch
riso (m) laugh
rochedo (m) cliff
roda (f) wheel
roda sobresselente (f) spare tyre
rodeado de surrounded by
rosa (f) rose
rotunda (f) roundabout
roubado/a stolen
roubar to mug *(someone)*; to steal
roubo (m) robbery
roupa (f) clothes
roupa de baixo (f) underwear
rua (f) road, street
rubéola (f) German measles
ruínas (fpl) ruins
rum (m) rum

S

saber to know *(something)*
sabonete (m) soap
sabor (m) flavour; taste
saborear to taste
saca-rolhas (m) corkscrew
saco (m) bag
» saco de dormir (m) sleeping bag
» saco de enjoo (m) sick bag
» saco de plástico (m) plastic bag
» sacos do lixo (mpl) bin liners
saia (f) skirt
saída (f) exit
sair to come off *(e.g. button)*;
   to get off *(bus)*; to go out
sal (m) salt
sala de embarque (f) departure lounge
sala de espera (f) waiting room
sala de estar (f) lounge
sala de jantar (f) dining room
sala de provas (f) fitting room
salada (f) salad
saldos (mpl) sale *(bargains)*
salgado/a salty
salmão (m) salmon
saltar to jump

salto (m) heel *(shoe)*
salva vidas attendant *(bathing)*
salvar to rescue
sandálias (fpl) sandals
sande (f) sandwich
sandwiche (m) sandwich
sangrar to bleed
sangue (m) blood
santo/a holy; saint
são/sã healthy
sapataria (f) shoe shop
sapateiro (m) shoe repairer's
sapato (m) shoe(s)
sapatos de treino (mpl) trainers
saqueta de chá (f) teabag
sarampo measles
sardas (fpl) freckles
saudar to greet
Saúde! Cheers!
saúde (f) health
sauna (f) sauna
se if
sebe (f) hedge
secador de cabelo (m) hairdryer
secar to dry
secção (f) section
seco/a dry
século (m) century
seda (f) silk
sedativo (m) sedative
segredo (m) secret
seguinte following *(next)*
seguir to follow
segundo (m) second
segundo/a second *(adj.)*
segurar to hold
seguro (m) insurance
seguro/a certain; safe; sure
seio (m) breast
selo (m) stamp *(postage)*
sem without
  » sem chumbo lead-free
  » sem gás still *(non-fizzy)*
  » sem pensão self-catering
semáforos (mpl) traffic lights

sem-alcoól non-alcoholic
semana (f) week
semanal weekly
semelhante similar
sempre always
sempre que when *(whenever)*
Senhor Mr
senhor sir
senhora lady
senhora Madam; Mrs
senhoras ladies
senhorio/a landlord/landlady
sensato/a sensible
sentar-se to sit *(down)*
sentir-se to feel
sentir-se mal to feel sick
separado/a separated
separar to separate
sequestrar to hijack
ser to be
ser humano (m) human being
sério/a serious
serviço (m) service (charge)
servir to fit; to serve
seu(s) their(s)
sexo (m) sex *(gender)*
SIDA (f) AIDS
silencioso/a silent
sim yes
simpático/a nice *(person)*
simples plain; simple
simples single *(room; ticket)*
sinagogue (f) synagogue
sinal (m) sign; signal
sinal de marcar (m) dialling tone
sintético/a synthetic
sintoma (m) symptom
sistema (m) system
sítio (m) place
só just; only
só alone
sobrancelha (f) eyebrow
sobre over; about *(relating to)*
sobremesa (f) dessert
sobrinha (f) niece

sobrinho (m) nephew

sóbrio/a sober

sócio/a partner (business)

socorro! help!

sogra (f) mother-in-law

sogro (m) father-in-law

sol (m) sun

soldado (m) soldier

solido solid

solteiro/a unmarried

som (m) sound

sombra (f) shadow

sombrinha (f) umbrella

sopa (f) soup

soprar to blow

sorrir to smile

sorriso (m) smile

soutien (m) bra

sozinho/a lonely; alone

spray (m) spray

spray para moscas (m) fly spray

sua(s) their(s)

suave mild

subir to climb

subir a montanha up the hill

subir a rua up the road

sucesso (m) success

sujo/a dirty

sul (m) south

sumo (m) juice

superfície (f) surface

supermercado (m) supermarket

suplemento (m) supplement

supor to suppose

» suponho que sim I suppose so

supositório (m) suppository

surdo/a deaf

surpresa (f) surprise

surpreso/a surprised

susto (m) fright (emotional)

T

tabacaria (f) tobacconist's

tabaco (m) tobacco

tabuleiro (m) tray

tacos de golfe (mpl) golf clubs

tal such

talheres (mpl) cutlery

talho (m) butcher's

talvez perhaps

tamanho (m) size (clothes; shoes)

também also

também as well

tambor (m) drum

tampa (f) lid; plug (bath)

tampão (m) tampon

tanque séptico (m) septic tank

tão so

tarde late; afternoon; evening

tarifa (f) tariff

táxi (m) taxi

tchau 'bye (casual)

teatro (m) theatre

tecido (m) fabric

tecto (m) roof; ceiling

telefonar to call; to telephone

telefone (m) telephone

» telefone de emergência (m) emergency telephone

telefonema (m) call (phone)

telemóvel (m) mobile

televisão (f) television

tem (de) must: you must

tem/têm razão (pl) you're right

tempero (m) dressing (salad)

tempo (m) weather

tempo livre (m) spare time

temporariamente temporarily

tenda (f) tent

tenho medo afraid: I'm afraid (fear)

ténis (m) tennis

tenro/a tender

ter to have

» ter febre to have a temperature

» ter razão to be right

» ter soluços to have hiccups

» ter sorte to be lucky

terceiro/a third

terminal (m) terminal (airport)

termómetro (m) thermometer

terra (f) earth; land
terraço (m) terrace
terramoto (m) earthquake
terrível awful; terrible
terrorista (m) terrorist
tesoura (f) scissors
tesoura de unhas (f) nail clippers
teto (m) ceiling
tia (f) aunt
tinta (f) paint
tio (m) uncle
típico/a typical
tipo (m) kind; sort
tirar to remove; to take *(photo)*; to
  take off *(clothes)*
toalha (f) towel
toalhetes de bébé (mpl) baby wipes
tobogã (m) toboggan
tocar to touch
todo whole
todo (m)/toda (f) all
todos everyone
tomada (f) socket
tomada USB UBS lead
tomar to take
» tomar banho to have a bath
» tomar banhos de sol to sunbathe
tomate (m) tomato
tonto/a dizzy
torcer to sprain
torneira (f) tap
torneira de segurança (f) stopcock
tornozelo (m) ankle
torrada (f) toast
torre (f) tower
tosse (f) cough
tossir to cough
total (m) total
totalmente totally
toucinho fumado (m) bacon
trabalhar to work *(job)*
trabalho (m) work
tradicional traditional
tradução (f) translation
traduzir to translate

tráfico (m) traffic
tranquilo/a calm
tranquilizante (m) tranquilliser
transpirar to sweat
transversal (f) turning *(side road)*
traseiras (fpl) rear
tratamento (m) treatment
travessia (f) crossing *(sea)*
travesso/a naughty
trazeira (m) back *(reverse side)*
trazer to bring
tribunal (m) court *(law)*
triste sad
trocar to change *(clothes)*; to exchange
troco (m) change *(small coins)*
trovão (m) thunder
truta (f) trout
tu you *(informal singular)*
tubo (m) tube *(pipe)*
tubo de ar (m) snorkel
tudo everything
túnel (m) tunnel
turismo (m) sightseeing; tourism
turista (m/f) tourist

U

úlcera (f) ulcer
último/a last
ultrapassar to overtake
um/uma a, an
um pouco bit
um pouco de a little of
unha (f) nail *(finger, toe)*
uniforme (m) uniform
universidade (f) university
urgente urgent
urina (f) urine
usar to use
útil useful

V

vaca (f) cow
vagaroso/a slow
vale (m) valley
valer to be worth

» vale a pena it's worth it
valente brave
válido/a valid
vamos! let's go!
vapor (m) steam
varanda (f) balcony *(theatre, etc.)*
varicela (f) chickenpox
vários/as several
vaso (m) vase
vassoura (f) broom
vazio/a empty
veado (m) deer
vedação (f) fence
vegetariano/a vegetarian
veículo vehicle
vela (f) candle; sail; sailing
velejar to sail
velho/a old
velocidade (f) speed
vender to sell
vendido sold out
veneno (m) poison
venenoso/a poisonous
vento (m) wind
ver to see; to watch
Verão (m) summer
verdadeiro/a true
verde green
vermelho/a red
véspera de Natal (f) Christmas Eve
vestido (m) dress
vestido de noite (m) nightdress
vestir to put on *(clothes)*
vestir, vestir-se to dress, get dressed
veterinário (m) vet
vez (f) time *(occasion)*
» uma vez once *(number of times)*
via (f) via
viagem (f) journey, trip
» viagem de barco (f) boat trip
viajar to travel
vida (f) life
video (m) video
vidro (m) glass *(made of)*
vila (f) town

vila (f) villa
vinagre (m) vinegar
vinha (f) vineyard
vinho wine
vinho do porto (m) Port wine
violar to rape
vir to come
visa (m) visa
visão (f) sight *(vision)*
visita (f) visit
» visita com guia (f) guided tour
visitante (m/f) visitor
visitar to go round *(visit)*
vista (f) view
vitamina (f) vitamin
viúvo/a widower/widow
viver to live
vivo/a alive; bright *(colour)*
vizinho/a neighbour
voar to fly
você you *(informal singular)*
vocês you *(informal plural)*
voleibol (m) volleyball
volta (f) return
voltagem (f) voltage
voltar to turn; to come back; to return
vomitar to be sick
voo (m) flight
» voo charter (m) charter flight
votar to vote
voz (f) voice
vulgar ordinary

W
web (m) web *(Internet)*

X
xadrez (m) chess

Z
zangado/a angry
zona (f) district

index

index

223

Now you're talking!

If you're keen to progress to a higher level, BBC Active offers a wide range of innovative products, from short courses and grammars to build up your vocabulary and confidence to more in-depth courses for beginners or intermediates. Designed by language-teaching experts, our courses make the best use of today's technology, with book and audio, audio-only and multi-media products on offer. Many of these courses are accompanied by free online activities and television series, which are regularly repeated on the BBC TWO Learning Zone.

Independent, interactive study course
2 x PC CD-ROM; 144pp course book;
60-min audio CD; free online activities
and resources www.getinto.com

Short independent study course
128pp course book; 2 x 60-min
CDs; free online resources;
6-part television series on BBC TWO